Lecture Notes in Business Information Processing 152

Christian Huemer
Pasquale Lops (Eds.)

E-Commerce and Web Technologies

14th International Conference, EC-Web 2013
Prague, Czech Republic, August 27-28, 2013
Proceedings

Springer

Volume Editors

Christian Huemer
Vienna University of Technology
Institute of Software Technology and Interactive Systems
Business Informatics Group (BIG)
Vienna, Austria
E-mail: huemer@big.tuwien.ac.at

Pasquale Lops
Università di Bari
Dipartimento di Informatica
Bari, Italy
E-mail: pasquale.lops@uniba.it

ISSN 1865-1348 e-ISSN 1865-1356
ISBN 978-3-642-39877-3 e-ISBN 978-3-642-39878-0
DOI 10.1007/978-3-642-39878-0
Springer Heidelberg New York Dordrecht London

Library of Congress Control Number: 2013946092

Typesetting: Camera-ready by author, data conversion by Scientific Publishing Services, Chennai, India

Printed on acid-free paper

Springer is part of Springer Science+Business Media (www.springer.com)

Preface

We welcome you to the proceedings of the 14th International Conference on Electronic Commerce and Web Technologies—EC-Web 2013—which took place in Prague, Czech Republic, during August 27–28, 2013.

The series of EC-Web conferences provides a platform for researchers and practitioners interested in the theory and practice of e-commerce and Web technologies. In 2013, EC-Web focused on the following topics:

Recommender systems. Recommender and business intelligence systems supporting both the customer and the provider in making better business decisions is still a challenging issue.

Semantic e-business. Managing knowledge for the coordination of e-business processes through the systematic application of Semantic Web technologies is the focus of semantic e-business. It builds on Semantic Web technologies, knowledge management and e-business processes. Challenges address the conceptualization of how e-business related knowledge is captured, represented, shared, and processed by humans and intelligent software.

Business services and process management. Business services focus on the alignment of business and IT allowing smoother business operations and business processes. This also allows for more effective business process management approaches concerning the design, modeling, execution, monitoring, and optimization of business process life cycles.

Agent-based e-commerce. Agents are computer systems situated in an environment and capable of autonomous action to meet their design objectives.

We were happy to see that our community was still active in contributing to the body of knowledge on future trends in e-commerce and Web technologies. Accordingly, we received 43 submissions from authors of 24 countries addressing the EC-Web topics mentioned above. Each submission received at least three review reports from Program Committee members, whereby the reviews were based on four criteria—originality, quality, relevance, and presentation—which resulted in a recommendation of each reviewer. Based on these recommendations, we selected 13 full papers for publication and presentation at EC-Web 2013. Accordingly, the acceptance rate of EC-Web 2013 for full papers was about 30%. In addition, these proceedings include seven short papers that were also presented at EC-Web 2013.

These accepted papers were organized in six sessions:

- EC-Web Opening Session
- Semantic Services and Agents
- Business Processes
- Recommender Systems I, II and III (three sessions)

When organizing a scientific conference, one always has to count on the e?orts of many volunteers. We are grateful to the members of the Program Committee who devoted a considerable amount of their time in reviewing the submissions to EC-Web 2013.

We were privileged to work together with highly motivated people to arrange the conference and to publish these proceedings. We appreciate all the tireless support by the Publicity Chairs Cataldo Musto from University of Bari Aldo Moro and Christian Pichler from TU Vienna for announcing our conference on various lists. Special thanks go to Amin Anjomshoaa, who was always of great help in managing the conference submission system. Last, but not least, we want to express our thanks to Gabriela Wagner, who dedicated countless hours in making EC-Web 2013 a success. Not only was she always of great help in solving organizational matters, but she also maintained the EC-Web 2013 website and was responsible for the compilation of all the papers in the proceedings.

We hope that you find these proceedings a valuable source of information on e-commerce and Web technologies.

August 2013

Christian Huemer
Pasquale Lops
Fernando Lopes

Organization

Program Committee Chairs

Christian Huemer	Vienna University of Technology, Austria
Pasquale Lops	University of Bari "Aldo Moro", Italy

Steering Chair

Fernando Lopes	National Research Institute, Portugal

Publicity Chair

Cataldo Musto	University of Bari Aldo Moro, Italy

Program Committee

Liliana Ardissono	University of Turin, Italy
Pierpaolo Basile	University of Bari Aldo Moro, Italy
Alejandro Bellogín	Universidad Autonoma de Madrid, Spain
Shlomo Berkovsky	NICTA, Australia
Marko Boskovic	Research Studios Austria
Francesco Buccafurri	Università degli Studi Mediterranea di Reggio Calabria, Italy
Robin Burke	De Paul University, USA
Maria Laura Caliusco	Universidad Tecnológica Nacional, Argentina
Iván Cantador	Universidad Autonoma de Madrid, Spain
Cinzia Cappiello	Politecnico di Milano, Italy
Sven Casteleyn	Universidad Politécnica de Valencia, Spain
Federica Cena	University of Turin, Italy
Kuo-Ming Chao	University of Coventry, UK
Jen-Yao Chung	IBM Thomas J. Watson Research Center, USA
Marco Comuzzi	Eindhoven University of Technology, The Netherlands
Alfredo Cuzzocrea	ICAR-CNR and University of Calabria, Italy
Florian Daniel	University of Trento – DISI, Italy
Antonina Dattolo	University of Udine, Italy
Marco de Gemmis	University of Bari, Aldo Moro, Italy
Ernesto William De Luca	FH Potsdam, Germany
Tommaso Di Noia	Polytechnic University of Bari, Italy
Alexander Felfernig	Graz University of Technology, Austria

Alberto Fernández	University Rey Juan Carlos, Spain
Agata Filipowska	Poznan University of Economics, Poland
Fabio Gasparetti	Roma Tre University, Italy
Michele Gorgoglione	Polytechnic of Bari, Italy
Jingzhi Guo	University of Macau, P.R. China
Chang Heng	Huawei Technologies, Shenzhen, P.R. China
Birgit Hofreiter	TU Vienna, Austria
Leo Iaquinta	University of Milano-Bicocca, Italy
Dietmar Jannach	TU Dortmund, Germany
Alípio Mário Jorge	University of Porto, Portugal
Bart Knijnenburg	University of California, Irvine, USA
Joerg Leukel	University of Hohenheim, Germany
Philipp Liegl	TU Vienna, Austria
Fernando Lopes	LNEG - National Research Institute, Portugal
Heiko Ludwig	IBM Almaden Research Center, USA
Andrea Maurino	Università di Milano Bicocca, Italy
Stuart E. Middleton	University of Southampton, UK
Cataldo Musto	University of Bari Aldo Moro, Italy
Fedelucio Narducci	University of Milano Bicocca, Italy
Alex Norta	Independent, Finland
Umberto Panniello	Polytechnic of Bari, Italy
Christian Pichler	TU Vienna, Austria
Francesco Ricci	Free University of Bozen-Bolzano, Italy
Juan A. Rodriguez-Aguilar	IIA, CSIC, Spain
Szabolcs Rozsnyai	IBM T.J. Watson Research Center, USA
Andreas Schönberger	University of Bamberg, Germany
Giovanni Semeraro	Univeristy of Bari "Aldo Moro", Italy
Jun Shen	University of Wollongong, Australia
Yan Tang Demey	Vrije Universiteit Brussel, Belgium
Jiao Tao	Oracle, USA
Eloisa Vargiu	Barcelona Digital, Spain
Andreas Wombacher	University Twente, The Netherlands
Jih-Shyr Yih	IBM T.J. Watson Research Center, USA
Markus Zanker	University of Klagenfurt, Austria
Marco Zapletal	TU Vienna, Austria
Uwe Zdun	University of Vienna, Austria
Yong Zheng	DePaul University, Chicago, USA

External Reviewers

Geoffray Bonnin	TU Dortmund, Germany
Martina Deplano	University of Turin, Italy
Marcos Aurélio Domingues	Universidade de São Paulo, Brazil
Patrick Gaubatz	University of Vienna, Austria
Fatih Gedikli	TU Dortmund, Germany
Simon Tragatschnig	University of Vienna, Austria
João Vinagre	Universidade do Porto, Portugal
Floriano Zini	Free University of Bozen-Bolzano, Italy

Table of Contents

Session 4: Recommender I

Session 5: Recommender II

Session 6: Recommender III

BRF: A Framework of Retrieving Brand Names of Products in Auction Sites

Ivy Hong-Ieng Hoi, Mars Liwen Liao, Chih-Chieh Hung, and Evans Tseng

EC-Central Engineering Team, Yahoo! Taiwan
{crazygirl8170,smalloshin}@gmail.com,
{lliwen,tobala}@yahoo-inc.com

Abstract. Online auction sites give sellers extreme high degree of freedom to fill in the product information so that they can promote their products to attract bidders in many ways. One of the most popular ways to promote is to add brand names and model names in their product titles. However, the side effect of this promotion way is that the search results are seriously irrelevant to what users expect, especially when brand names are used as query terms. In this paper, we target at the problem of retrieving the brand name of a product from its title. First, the root causes could be categorized into three types by observing the real data on the online auction site of Yahoo! Taiwan. Then, a brand-retrieving framework BRF is proposed. Specifically, BRF first eliminates those brand and model names, which may not be the actual brand name of this product, in a product title; then BRF represents a product title by selecting representative keywords with their importance; finally, BRF models the problem as a classification problem which identify what the brand name (class) of a product title is. Extensive experiments are then conducted by using real datasets, and the experimental results showed the effectiveness of BRF. To best of our knowledge, this is the first paper to design a mechanism of retrieving the brand names of products in auction sites.

Keywords: e-commerce, brand name, auction, information retrieval.

1 Introduction

Without taking valuable time to search for an item from store to store, e-commerce provides users with a more convenient way in which to shop. Among several models in e-commerce, online auction is one of the most popular and effective ways of trading by participants bidding for products and services over the Internet. Online auction sites[1], such as Ebay in US, Taobao in China, and Yahoo! Auction in Taiwan, are perfect examples of this business model. One of the main characteristics why auction sites are so popular is the freedom. That is, an auction site provides a platform which allows users to fill out any information of their products, including the title, description, price, and so on. With such freedom, sellers on an auction site can promote their products to attract bidders in many ways.

[1] Online auction site is abbreviated as auction sites in the following sections of this paper.

C. Huemer and P. Lops (Eds.): EC-Web 2013, LNBIP 152, pp. 1–13, 2013.

Table 1. Statistics of how users find out products (2013/3/11~2013/3/17)

E-commerce properties in Taiwan	Category Navigation	Search by Queries
Shopping Center(B2C)	47.04%	5.54%
Shopping Mall(B2B2C)	12%	6.37%
Auction (C2C)	1.90%	17.40%

One of the most popular ways to promote is to add brand names and model names in their product titles. This approach can help sellers promote their products effectively since the proportion of the queries including brand names always exceeds 10% in top-1000 queries, according to the report of Yahoo! Auction Taiwan. However, you have got to take the good with the bad. The side effect of using this promotion way causes the search results irrelevant to what users expect when brand names are used as query terms. Such irrelevancy is seriously harmful to user experience in search since searching plays a much more important role in auction sites than other business models. Table 1 shows the statistics how users find out the products they want. It can be seen that users highly depends on search in auction sites. To improve the relevancy of the search results, it is a crucial issue to retrieve the actual brand names of products. Once the actual brand names of products can be retrieved, search engines in auction sites could extract the products with the given brand names precisely.

In this paper, we target at the problem of retrieving brand names of products in auction sites. A naïve method to find the actual brand names is to use a dictionary which contains a set of brand names and the mapping from model names to brand names. If there is any matched brand or model names in the product title, this match brand name can be identified as the actual brand name of this product. However, this naïve approach may fail since the brand names and model names are usually abused to promote products, the product titles may contain noisy and irrelevant information. Therefore, this paper proposed a framework, called BRF (standing for Brand-Retrieving Framework) to find the actual brand names of the products in auction sites. To best of our knowledge, this is the first paper to design a mechanism to solve this problem. Several issues remain to be addressed to effectively retrieve the actual brand names from product titles:

1. False-Use Problem

To improve the exposure rates of their products, sellers may add famous brand names or model names in their product titles. Buyers may obtain irrelevant results with respect to their queries. For example, Fig. 1 shows two products of the search results for query Acer in the auction site in Yahoo! Taiwan. The first one is relevant to the query Acer since the product is Acer 4820TG whereas the second one is irrelevant to the query Acer since this seller is going to sell his lab-top HP/COMPAQ NX7000. The reason is that the title contains the other famous brand names (i.e., sony, acer, and asus) which are underlined in the product title[2]. To address this issue, BRF uses the

[2]非 in Chinese means “non”.

brand-model map to eliminate those keywords in the product title which may interfere the identification of the actual brand names of products.

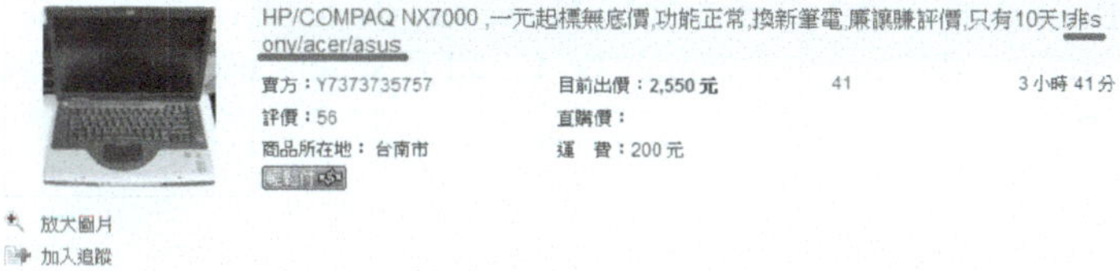

Fig. 1. An example for False-Use Problem

2. Accessory/Repair-Related Problem

Some accessories and maintenance service providers add the brand names into the titles of their products as well. The reason is that they intend to specify the brand names that their accessories can fit or their maintenance services can support. However, when users submit brand names as queries, they are likely to find the products instead of accessories [3]. For example, Fig. 2 shows the search results of query "apple". It can be seen that the product on the top is a protective shell for iPhone, which title contains "apple". The search results of accessories and maintenance services may disrupt users to find the products with the specific brand names due to the fact that the amount of the accessories and maintenance services are usually much larger than that of the products which specific brand names, especially for the famous brand names[3]. To address this issue, BRF uses the feature generation mechanism, which is based on Chi-Square and TF-IDF, to detect the features that represents for accessory and maintenance. Thus, these accessories and maintenance services can be distinguished from the actual products with the specific brand names.

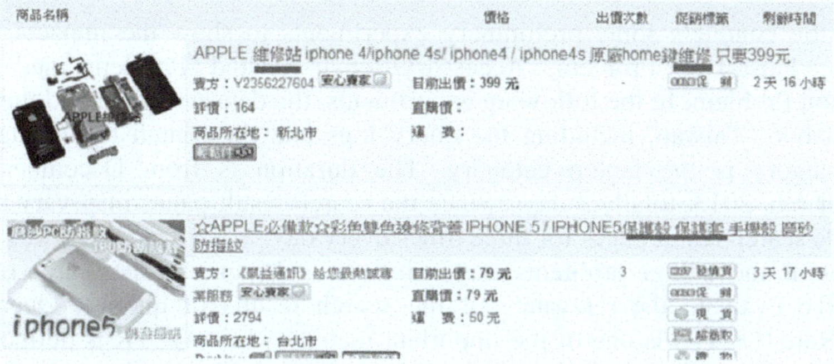

Fig. 2. An example for Accessory/Repair-Related Problem

3. Brand-Name-Omission Problem

Brand-Name-Omission Problem indicates that sellers may use model names to describe their products without mentioning the brand names. This problem usually

---

[3] 維修 in Chinese means "maintenance". 保護殼, 保護套 in Chinese means "protective shell".

happens in those products with the famous brand names. The reason is that people usually call these popular products by their model names instead of mentioning their brand names in their daily life. Fig. 3 shows an example that there is only the model name "MacBook Air" in the product title. However, the actual brand name "Apple" is missing. Therefore, this product cannot be found if sellers use "apple" as the query term to search.

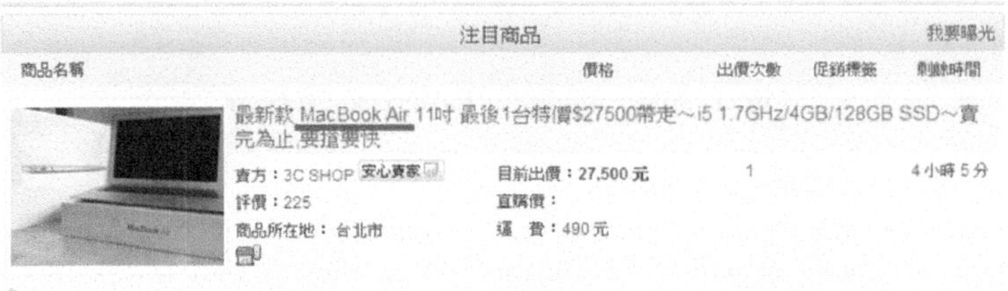

Fig. 3. An example for Brand-Name-Omission Problem

To address this problem, BRF proposed the feature generation mechanism so that the model names can be extracted, and the classifier can use the labels from training data to map the specific model names to their brand names.

The rest of this paper is organized as follows. Section 2 presents some statistics to show the impact of the three issues. Section 3 then describes the brand-retrieving mechanism BRF for finding brand names from product titles. Section 4 presents experimental results. Finally, Section 5 draws conclusions

2 Preliminary

This section conducts some preliminary experiments to show the impacts of three problems: False-Use Problem, Accessory/Repair-Related Problem, and Model-Convention Problem. In the following experiments, the dataset is obtained the auction site of Yahoo! Taiwan, including the query logs and the search result pages. The target category is the laptop category. The duration is from December 3rd to December 6th, 2013, totally 3 days. Since the search result pages may vary anytime, we sample search result pages for three times every day.

In general, these three problems may reduce the relevancy of the search results of queries. To evaluate the relevancy of the search results of queries, Query Click through Rate (QCTR) is one of the important metrics where QCTR is defined as the number that the query search results clicked divided by the number of queries reported. For example, if there are 200 search results clicked out of 1000 queries, the QCTR would be 20%. Obviously, the higher the QCTR is, the more relevant the search results of queries are.

2.1 False-Use Problem

The False-Use Problem leads to the decrease of QCTR. To show the impact of this problem, a preliminary experiment is conducted. The queries are the brand names.

For each query, we compute the QCTR of top-100 results extracted from two sources: (a) the original search results and (b) the refined search results which are exactly the products with brand names. Then, the relative error of QCTR of different brand names is computed. Obviously, the larger the relative error of QCTR is, the larger impact of False-Use Problem is. Fig. 4(a) shows the experimental results. It can be seen that "apple" has the largest QCTR difference, showing that many products in top-100 results are not clicked by users although their titles contain the brand name apple. This experiment shows that the False-Use Problem significantly reduces QCTR.

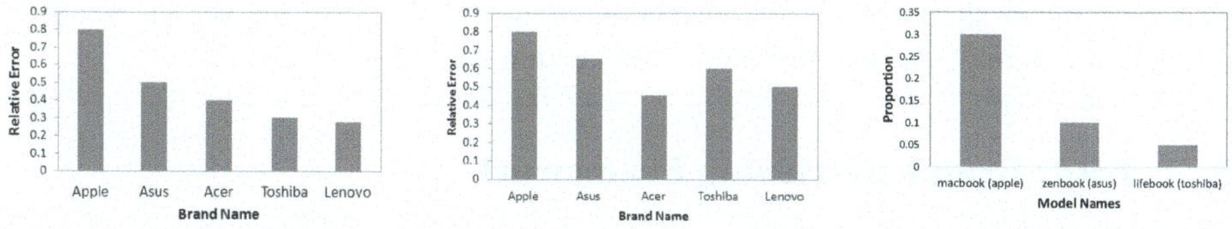

(a) (b) (c)

Fig. 4. Impact of (a) False-Use Problem, (b) Accessory/Repair-Related Problem, and (c) Brand-Name-Omission Problem

2.2 Accessory/Repair-Related Problem

Accessory/Repair-Related Problem indicates that the search results contain not only the products but also a list of accessories and maintenance services containing brand names when queries are brand names. To show the impact of this problem, a preliminary experiment is conducted. Following the same setting and dataset as the previous experiment, Fig. 4(b) shows the relative error of QCTR. It can be seen that the relative error of QCTR of each query term is larger than 0.5. Specifically, the relative error of QCTR of "Apple" is almost 0.8 while there are around 85% accessories and maintenance services in the top-100 search results in average. This result supports the claim that customers tends to find the products, instead of accessories and maintenance services, when they submit brand names as queries.

2.3 Brand-Name-Omission Problem

The Brand-Name-Omission problem indicates that sellers may use model names to describe their products without mentioning the brand names. Consequently, their listings will not be viewed by potential buyers who use brand names as their query terms. This problem usually happens in those products with the famous brand names. The impact of this problem is the potential revenue loss for both sellers and auction sites: since users may not use the convention terms to find the desired products, sellers are hard to sell their products and auction sites cannot get the commission charges from sellers. For example, users interested in iPhone 5 all know that it is a cell phone by Apple, and therefore might expect to see all listings of iPhone 5 for sale when a query term 'apple' is used. However, a listing of this model without the actual word 'Apple' in the title will not appear in the search results. To investigate the impact of this problem, a preliminary experiment is designed. We submit each selected model name as a query, and two types of the products can be obtained: a) listing titles with model names only and b) listing titles with both model and brand names. Let the numbers of the former and the latter types be Na and Nb. Then the proportion value is computed. Obviously, the larger the proportion is, the more products are likely to be found hardly if the queries are brand names. Fig. 4(c) shows the results. It can be seen that the query “macbook” has the largest proportion, which means many sellers usually use “macbook” only in the listing titles without specifying the brand “apple”. This case shows that around 30% macbook cannot be found in the search results of “apple”, which may cause both sellers’ and auction sites’ loss of revenue.

3 BRF: Brand-Retrieving Framework

3.1 System Architecture

To retrieve the brand names of products in auction sites, BRF models this problem as a classification problem which identify the brand name by given the product title. BRF is composed of two stages: training stage and classifying stage. In the training stage, the training dataset is given to train the classifier to generate the model for classification, where each entry in the training dataset is a pair of the product title and its brand name. The training stage is composed of three phases: 1. preprocessing, 2. feature generation, and 3. classifier training. In the preprocessing phase, notations and terms which are not helpful for classification will be eliminated. In the feature generation phase, terms with highly related to brand names will be extracted, say representative keywords, and each product title will be represented as a vector of representative keywords. In the classifier training stage, every pairs of (vector, brand) is used to train the classifier to generate the model. After generating the model, in the classifying stage, the product title will be presented into a vector of representative keywords generating in the training stage. Given the vector, the brand name of the product title can be predicted by the model. The technical details will be described in the later sections.

3.2 Preprocessing

Given the product title as the input, the main goal of this phase is to filter out the words that may decrease the accuracy of classification.

First of all, the conventional preprocessing approaches should be adopted, such as tokenization, punctuation elimination, stop word elimination, and so on. Besides these, we should also handle the False-Use Problem in this phase. As mentioned above, the False-Use Problem is that there are the other brand names in the product title. Thus, it is necessary to eliminate these irrelevant brand names in the product title so that our system can extract the actual brand name of this product more accurately. To eliminate the irrelevant brand and model names, the brand-model map is defined as follows:

Definition. Brand-Model Map

Let the product title be a sequence of tokenized words $<s_1,s_2,s_3,...,s_n>$. The brand-model map is a sequence $<b_1,b_2,...,b_n>$. Each entry b_i is the number of brand or model names in $<si-\delta,...,si+\delta>$ where δ is a specified parameter if s_i is a brand or model name. Otherwise, the value of b_i is 0.

For example, let δ be 2. Given a product title <Apple MacBook 13.3" Laptop, non Samsung, HP, Asus, Acer, Lenovo>, the brand-model map can be derived as <2, 2, 0, 0, 0, 3, 4, 5, 5, 4>.

Obviously, each entry in the brand-model map represents how dense the brand and model names appear surrounding a brand or a model name. According to the brand-model map, the product title $<s_1,s_2,...,s_n>$ can be partitioned into subsequences $<\sigma_1, \sigma_2, ..., \sigma_m>$ such that the total variance of these subsequences, i.e., $\sum_{i=1}^{m} \mathrm{Var}(\sigma_i)$, is minimized. The variance of a subsequence is $\mathrm{Var}(\sigma_i) = \sum_{b_j \in \sigma_i} |b_j - \mu| / |\sigma_i|$, where μ is the mean of all values in σ_i. To achieve this goal, we can borrow algorithm TC in [1]. The average of each subsequence is then computed. Given a parameter ε, those subsequences with average values larger than ε will be eliminated.

Following the example above, since the brand-model map is <2, 2, 0, 0, 0, 3, 4, 5, 5, 4>, we can partition the product title as $<\sigma_1$:(Apple MacBook), σ_2: (13.3" Laptop, non), σ_3: (Samsung, HP, Asus, Acer, Lenovo)>. Let ε be 4. Since the average value of σ_3 is (3+4+5+5+4)/5 = 4, the subsequence σ_3 is then eliminated from the product title.

The value of δ and ε are determined by the behavior how users add irrelevant brand and model names into the product title. In our current cases, the value of δ and ε can be set as 2 and 4 to achieve the acceptable results (specifically, the precision of classification is around 70%). The setting of δ and ε could be also trained by machine learning approaches. This issue is beyond our scope here and left as the future work.

3.3 Feature Generation

This section describes how to represent a product title into a vector. This phase consists of two steps: 1. Selecting the representative keywords, and 2. Determining the importance of representative keywords.

3.3.1 Selecting the Representative Keywords

Given the candidate keywords obtained from the previous phase, say $\{k_1,k_2,...,k_m\}$, in this phase, we are going to select the most representative keywords by Chi-Square attribute evaluation (χ^2). Note that the format of training data will be a pair of a product title (represented by a set of candidate keywords) and its brand name c_j.

Generally speaking, Chi-Square attribute evaluation evaluates the worth of a feature by computing the value of the chi-squared statistic with respect to the class [2]. To compute the value of χ^2 for multiple classes (i.e., brand names), we start from the definition of the Chi-Square value of a term k_i with respect to a class c_j: $\chi^2(k_i, c_j)$. Let A be the number of the term k_i belonging to the class c_j, B be the number of the term k_i not belonging to the class c_j, C be the number of the terms which are not k_i but belong to class c_j, and D be the number of the terms which are not k_i and not belonging to the class c_j. Supposing N=A+B+C+D, $\chi^2(k_i,c)$ can be defined as follows:

$$\chi^2(k_i, c_j) = \frac{N \times (AD - CD)^2}{(A + C) \times (B + D) \times (A + B) \times (C + D)}$$

Based on $\chi^2(k_i, c_j)$, we could require to discriminate well across all classes. Then we could compute the expected value of for each candidate keyword as follows:

$$\chi^2_{avg}(k_i) = \sum_j Pr\,(k_i) \times \chi^2(k_i, c_j)$$

After computing the expected values for each candidate keyword, the candidate keywords with top-n χ^2_{avg} value are selected to be the representative keywords, say $\{t_1, t_2, \ldots, t_n\}$.

3.3.2 Determining the Importance of Representative Keywords

In this step, TF-IDF is used to determine the importance of representative keywords. TF-IDF is the product of two statistics, *term frequency* and *inverse document frequency*. For ease of presentation, t represents a representative keyword, d represents a product title, and D represents the set of product titles.

For the term frequency TF(t,d), the simplest choice is to simply use the raw frequency of a keyword in a product title. However, to prevent a bias towards longer product title, the normalized frequency is used. Let the raw frequency of t be f(t,d), the normalized frequency is defined as follows:

$$TF(t, d) = \frac{f(t, d)}{\max\{f(w, d) | w \in d\}}$$

The inverse document frequency IDF(t,D) is a measure of whether the representative keyword t is common or rare across the set of product titles D. It is obtained by dividing the total number of product titles by the number of product titles containing the representative keyword, and then taking the logarithm of that quotient. Formally, the inverse document frequency IDF(t,D) can be defined as follows:

$$IDF(t, D) = \log \frac{|D|}{|\{d \in D | t \in d\}}$$

Finally, the value of TF-IDF is defined as follows:

$$TFIDF(t, d, D) = TF(t, d) \times IDF(t, D)$$

A high weight in TF–IDF is reached by a high term frequency in the given product title and a low document frequency of the representative keyword in the whole collection of product titles. As a representative keywords appears in more product titles, the ratio inside the logarithm approaches 1, bringing the idf and tf-idf closer to 0.

To put it together, a product title *d* can be represented as a vector <TFIDF(t_1,d,D), TFIDF(t_2,d,D),…, TFIDF(t_n,d,D)> where t_i is the *i*-th representative keyword.

3.4 Classification Strategy

This section describes a possible classification strategy to use the features generated by the previous step. Here, we do not claim that this strategy is the best among all others, but it is just a reasonable strategy. Our feature generation methodology has good usability for the following reasons. First, it is neutral to classifiers. That is, it can be used for any classifiers, including decision trees, rule-based classifiers, and support vector machines. Second, it can team up with other feature generation methodologies. Products may have multiple attributes, including prices, description, category information, and so on. Some of these attributes may be able to transform into as a single value, an interval, or a sequence of values per product. Handling numerical attributes is beyond the scope of this paper. In our study, three classifiers are built using the naïve Bayesian classifier, decision tree, and support vector machine (SVM) [4]. According to the experimental results and the characteristic of e-commerce, SVM is implemented in our current system. This design decision stems from two characteristics of the feature vectors generated. First, they are high-dimensional since many features may be generated. Second, they are sparse since each product title has only a few of these features. The SVM is well-suited for such high-dimensional and sparse data [5].

4 Experimental Results

4.1 Environment Settings

In the following experiments, three datasets are used: Shopping, Auction(small), and Auction(big). These three datasets are used to test the performance of the proposed mechanism in different conditions. In these three datasets, the products in the *laptop* category during 2013/3/11 to 2013/3/17 are extracted to evaluate the proposed mechanism. The characteristics and the statistic information of each dataset are provided as follows:

Shopping dataset contains the products of Shopping Center in Yahoo! Taiwan which is a B2C platform. The suppliers describe the characteristics of laptop clearly in the product title. The product title usually contains at least the brand name, the model name, and specification of the laptop. Thus, we can observe that the product titles in this dataset precisely describe information about the laptop without noise. Moreover, almost all the products under the laptop category are actually products of laptops. In this dataset, we totally collect 2906 products with ten major brands of laptop. For each brand, there are at least 50 products. The number of products of each class is listed in Table 2.

Table 2. Statistics of Shopping Datasets (2013/3/11~2013/3/17)

Brand Name	Number of Products	Brand Name	Number of Products
Acer	904	HP	297
Apple	94	Lenovo	210
Asus	516	MSI	78
Dell	153	Sony	95
Fujitsu	83	Toshiba	476

Auction(small) and *Auction(big)* are the datasets from Yahoo! Auction, Taiwan. Auction(small) provides an ideal case that the number of products of each brand is uniformly distributed whereas Auction(big) provides the real situation that the number of products of each brand exists some bias. In both datasets, most of the product titles do not describe the characteristics of laptops very clearly. To increase the exposure rate, the sellers may describe unrelated information in the title. Besides laptops, there are many irrelative products which are related to maintenance service, notebook accessories products and the remaining unrelated products are probably in other categories. We classify products into 15 classes where 12 classes are brands of laptops which each brand also contains at least 50 products. The remaining three classes are "maintenance", "accessories" and "others" which refer to maintenance service providers, accessories and products not in the above classes respectively. The number of products for each brand is shown in Table 3.

Table 3. Statistics of Auction(small) and Auction(big) Datasets (2013/3/11~2013/3/17)

Brand Name	Auction(small) Number of Products	Auction(big) Number of Products
Acer	50	54
Apple	50	132
Asus	50	169
Clevo	50	50
Dell	50	153
Fujitsu	50	126
Gigabyte	49	49
HP	50	135
Lenovo	50	171
MSI	50	189
Sony	50	136
Toshiba	50	202
Other Brands	50	74
Maintenance	50	295
Accessories	50	925

In this experiment, three classifiers are used: Naïve Bayes, J48, and SVM. These classifiers are from the WEKA library []. *Precision* is the metric used to evaluate the performance of these classifiers under different datasets. Formally, the precision of a classifier is defined as $\frac{1}{n}\sum_{k=1}^{n}\frac{N_{k,c}}{N_k}$, where N_k is the number of the products in class k and $N_{k,c}$ is the number of the products that are in class k and successfully classified as class k. Ten-fold cross validation is used to evaluate the effectiveness of each classifier in the proposed mechanism. Specifically, the dataset will be randomly partitioned into ten complementary subsets of near equal size, and one of the subsets will be assigned as the testing data while the remaining are used as the training data.

4.2 Precision in Three Datasets

In this section, we conduct the experiments that test the precision of three classifiers in three datasets.

Fig. 5 shows the results of shopping dataset. It can be seen that the precision of each classifier exceeds 97%. In addition, J48 and SVM achieve the best performance that precisions of these two classifiers are over 99%. The reason is that the product title of each product in this dataset not only points out product characteristics clearly but also has not any interfering information. Thus, this result shows that the proposed method can work well when the given product titles are of less noise.

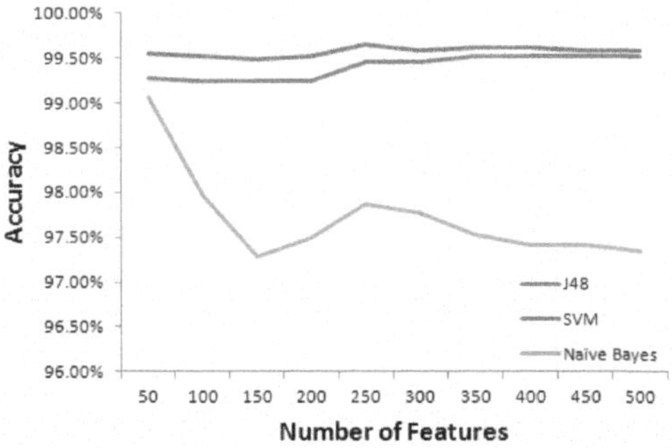

Fig. 5. Precision with different classifiers: Shopping Dataset

Fig. 6(a) shows the results of Auction(small) dataset. In this case, J48 outperforms SVM and Naïve Bayes. The precision of each classifier is at least 70%. Specifically, the precision of J48 exceeds 80% when the number of features is between 100 to 350. Thus, it can be concluded that J48 can honor the advantage that the size of each brand are uniformly distributed in training data. On the other hand, Fig. 6(b) shows the results of Auction(big) dataset. It can be seen that SVM can achieve the best precision in most cases. Interestingly, the precision of SVM increases from 74.42% to 76.53% while feature number increases from 200 to 500. To find out the root cause, we investigate the features and the classification results when the number of features is 200 and 500. Some critical features appear when the number of features is 500, which do not appear when the number of features is 200. For example, there are 10 more features related to products which is labeled "Maintenance", such as 風扇(fan), 檢測費(testing fee), 壞掉(out of order), and so on. We can observe the heat maps

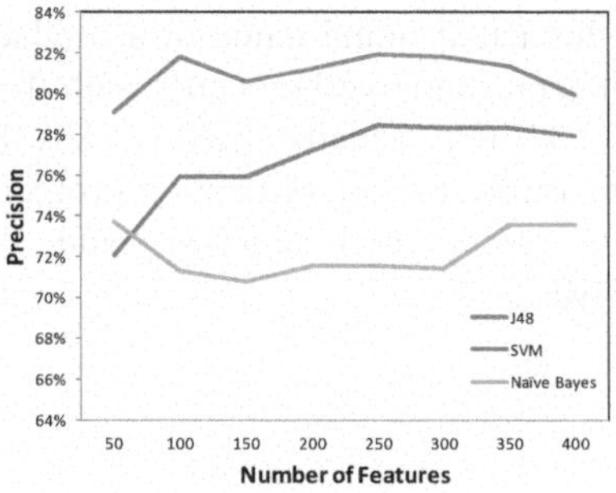

(a) Auction (small)

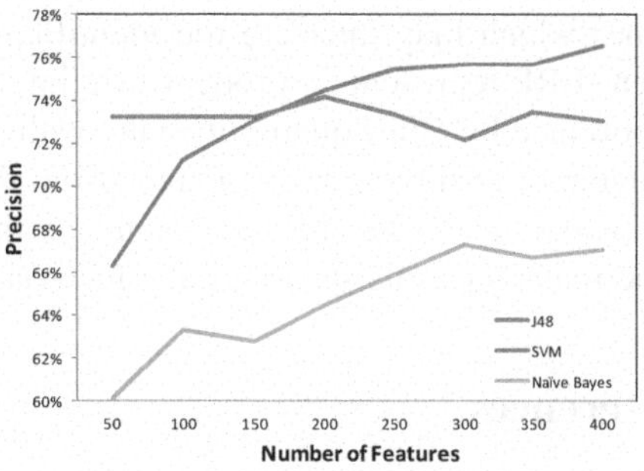

(b) Auction(big)

Fig. 6. Precision with different classifiers: Auction(small) and Auction(big) datasets

	a	b	c	d	e	f	g	h	i	j	k	l	m	n	o	p
a	83	0	2	2	0	1	0	0	1	1	1	0	0	8	0	0
b	15	57	0	6	0	0	0	0	0	11	2	2	0	2	0	6
c	30	0	68	0	0	0	0	0	0	1	0	0	0	1	1	0
d	12	0	0	78	0	0	0	0	1	2	0	1	1	4	1	0
e	16	0	0	0	84	0	0	0	0	0	0	0	0	0	0	0
f	13	0	0	1	0	84	0	0	0	1	0	0	0	1	0	0
g	18	0	0	1	0	0	79	0	0	2	0	0	0	0	0	0
h	0	0	0	0	0	0	0	100	0	0	0	0	0	0	0	0
I	21	0	0	1	1	0	0	0	73	1	0	0	1	1	1	1
g	26	1	0	0	0	0	0	0	1	72	0	1	0	0	0	0
k	11	0	0	1	0	0	0	0	0	1	86	1	0	0	1	0
I	66	3	0	9	0	1	1	0	3	4	0	3	3	5	0	1
m	59	1	4	7	1	0	0	0	3	0	1	0	16	6	2	0
n	36	0	0	3	0	0	0	0	1	0	1	0	0	57	0	0
o	10	0	0	0	0	0	1	0	1	1	0	0	0	0	88	0
p	5	0	0	1	0	0	0	0	0	1	0	0	0	0	0	92

(a) Number of Features: 200

	a	b	c	d	e	f	g	h	i	j	k	l	m	n	o	p
a	82	0	3	2	0	1	0	0	1	1	0	1	1	9	0	0
b	9	70	0	4	0	0	0	0	2	0	0	9	0	2	0	4
c	30	0	68	0	0	0	0	0	0	0	0	0	2	1	0	0
d	12	0	0	79	0	0	0	0	1	1	0	1	1	5	1	0
e	10	0	0	0	82	0	0	0	2	2	2	2	0	0	0	0
f	10	0	0	0	0	88	0	0	0	0	1	1	0	1	0	0
g	12	0	0	0	0	0	83	0	0	1	1	2	0	0	1	1
h	0	0	0	2	0	0	0	98	0	0	0	0	0	0	0	0
I	15	1	0	1	0	0	0	0	80	1	0	0	1	1	1	0
g	15	1	0	1	0	0	0	0	2	80	0	0	0	1	1	0
k	9	0	0	1	0	0	1	0	0	1	87	1	0	0	0	1
I	61	3	0	5	0	0	1	0	9	1	0	12	3	4	0	0
m	44	2	4	6	1	1	0	0	3	0	0	0	33	6	2	0
n	31	0	0	3	0	0	0	0	0	0	1	0	1	62	0	0
o	10	0	0	0	0	0	0	0	1	1	0	1	2	0	85	1
p	6	0	0	1	0	0	0	0	1	0	0	1	0	0	0	89

(b) Number of Features: 500

Fig. 7. Heat maps of SVM

in Fig. 7. These features improve the classification result in label "Maintenance Service (m)" and "Other Brands (n)" in SVM. For J48, these features also improve the precision of "Maintenance" class. However, these features diminish the precision of label "Other Brands" class. Consequently, the precision does not increase significantly in J48 when the feature number increases from 200 to 500.

5 Conclusion

In this paper, we target at the problem of identifying the brand name of a product in auction sites. To solve this problem, we first made observations from real datasets in the auction site of Yahoo! Taiwan. The root causes are classified into False-Use Problem, Accessory/Repair-Related Problem, and Brand-Name-Omission Problem. To deal with these three problems, a framework BRF is proposed to retrieve brand names from product of auction sites. BRF first eliminates those brand and model names which may interfere the identification of the actual brand name of a product. Then, BRF represents a product title into a set of representative keywords with their importance by Chi-Square attribute evaluation and TF-IDF. Finally, BRF models the problem of retrieving brand names from the product titles as a classification problem. Extensive experiments are then conducted by using real datasets, and the experimental results showed the effectiveness of BRF.

References

1. Hung, C.-C., Peng, W.-C.: A regression-based approach for mining user movement patterns from random sample data. Data Knowledge Engineering 70(1), 1–20 (2011)
2. Liu, H., Setiono, R.: Chi2: Feature selection and discretization of numeric attributes. In: IEEE 7th International Conference on Tools with Artificial Intelligence, pp. 338–391 (1995)

3. Baye, M.R., De los Santos, B., Wildenbeest, M.R.: The evolution of product search. Journal of Law, Economics & Policy 9(2), 201–221 (2012)
4. Vapnik, V.N.: Statistical Learning Theory. John Wiley & Sons (1998)
5. Han, J., Kamber, M.: Data Mining: Concepts and Techniques, 2nd edn. Morgan Kaufmann (2006)
6. Hall, M., Frank, E., Holmes, G., Pfahringer, B., Reutemann, P., Witten, I.H.: The WEKA Data Mining Software: An Update. SIGKDD Explorations 11(1) (2009)

An Adaptive Social Influence Propagation Model Based on Local Network Topology

Haifeng Liu, Zheng Hu, Hui Tian, and Dian Zhou

Key Laboratory of Universal Wireless Communications
(Beijing University of Posts and Telecommunications), Ministry of Education
haifengliu2011@gmail.com

Abstract. With the wide application of all kinds of social network services, social recommendation has attracted many attentions from academia and industry. Different from traditional recommender systems, social influence plays a significant role in social recommendation. However, many existing approaches cannot effectively simulate the influence propagation and the computation of social influence is complex. This leads to the low prediction accuracy. Hence, this paper proposes an adaptive social influence propagation model to address this problem. Moreover, we present a simple and fast social influence computation method according to the local network topology, which can provide distinguishing influences for one user depending on its neighbors. To demonstrate the performance, we design the shortest path with maximum propagation strategy and experiments are conducted to compare our model with other social influence propagation approaches on the real data set. Empirical results show that both the quality of prediction and coverage have remarkable improvement, especially with few ratings.

Keywords: Social Influence, Propagation Model, Local Network Topology, Social Recommendation.

1 Introduction

With the development of the Internet, the Internet of Things and the extensive application of all kinds of intelligent terminals, common people can generate, share and propagate any contents at any time and any place. People can also express their thoughts or ideas freely. The collective wisdom has been widely demonstrated and utilization, such as Wikipedia[1]. However, there are huge amount of contents on the Web, which make more difficult for users to obtain their required information. Traditional search engine fails to meet requirements on convenience and efficiency, especially when users do not know how to describe their demands by only a few search terms. In this case, the recommender system (RS)[2] has been presented and applied widely[3][4].

However, the traditional recommendation approaches have faced many challenges, such as data sparsity, cold start, scalability and so on. In recent years, all kinds of social network services have been widely applied in many domains[5],

C. Huemer and P. Lops (Eds.): EC-Web 2013, LNBIP 152, pp. 14–26, 2013.

such as Facebook, Twitter, LinkedIn, Instagram, Flickr etc. Social network can provide more information about users, especially social relationships. Researchers have demonstrated that the network can propagate many things, for instance, information, disease, emotion and even fat. At the same time, the decisions of user are also affected by their social relationships. Hence, social recommendation emerges and it is the use of social relationships as well as the contents on the social network to mine user's interest, preferences, and thus to recommend appropriate objects for the user.

Social influence and its propagation is very important to the performance of social recommendation. While the existing social influence propagation models and the computations of social influence generate low prediction accuracy. Hence, this paper focuses on social influence propagation on social network. We research and analyze the existing social influence propagation models and the computational methods of social influence. Then, we propose an adaptive social influence propagation model, in which the computation of social influence of one node is based on its local network topology.

The contributions of the paper are as follows:

1) We propose an adaptive social influence propagation model. In our model, social relationships and social influence will be propagated through the network. Especially, social influence is dynamic with the change of network topology.

2) We design a simple and fast method to compute social influence of user. It relies on the network topology related to each user. It assigns different social influence measures depending on the user's neighbor in bounded computational time.

3) We adopt the shortest path with maximum social influence propagation strategy and compare our model with other two social influence propagation approaches on the real data set. The experimental results demonstrate that the proposed model can improve the prediction accuracy effectively.

The rest of this paper is organized as follows. In section 2, related research work is introduced. The proposed social influence propagation model and the computation of social influence is formulated in section 3 and empirical results are reported in section 4. Finally, we provide some final remarks and a conclusion in section 5.

2 Related Work

Since the abundant and huge amount of social network data can provide more information about users and alleviate many problems with which the traditional recommender systems encounter, such as cold start, data sparsity and so on. Social recommendation has been presented and applied widely. Sigrubjörnsson *et al.*[6] proposed a tag recommendation method based on the collective knowledge. The tags described the contents of the photo and provided additional contextual and semantical information. The paper firstly analyzed the tag characteristic, that is, how users tag photos and what kind of tags the users provide. Then, they presented four different tag recommendation strategies to help users annotate photos. Tan *et al.*[7] built a hypergraph model for music recommendation by using the rich social media information (such as user, music, tag, relation etc.). The model includes more sophisticated relations than pairwise relation. They proposed a novel music recommendation algorithm which used both multiple kinds of social media information and music acoustic-based content.

Social relationships are the most important information in social network. The behavior of user is influenced by its social relationships and the influence is not only from the direct friends, but also from indirect friends. Christakis and Fowler[8] indicates that the behavior, interest and decision of the user is influenced by users who are in your three degree distance. The influence becomes very small, when the distance is more than three. The innovation, disease, idea, trust, social influence and even fat can be propagated along with the social relationships. Yang *et al.*[9] researched the interest propagation in social networks. They presented a friendship-interest propagation model which was used to predict friendship. Trust propagation has also used in social recommendation. Massa and Avesani[10] proposed a trust-aware recommender system. They proposed to replace the finding similar user with the use of a trust metric, which can propagate trust over the trust network. This system can alleviate the sparsity of the rating matrix. In social network, not only the trust can be propagated, but also the distrust. Guha *et al.* [11] developed a framework of trust and distrust propagation schemes. In this framework, it was first to incorporate distrust in the computational trust propagation setting.

Many propagation models have also been proposed. The Linear Threshold Model and Independent Cascade Model[12] are two most widely used propagation models. The former assumes that each node has a threshold. The node becomes the active state (i.e. it is influenced) when the sum of influence of its neighbors exceeds this threshold. While, the latter assumes that each neighbor of one node has some probability to activate the node. Moreover, epidemic model[13] and probabilistic generative model[14] are also proposed. In social influence propagation model, the key is to compute the social influence. Social influence is a measure which denotes the degree of affecting the behavior of others. Generally, influence metrics may basically be subdivided into global and local. The global influence is based upon complete social network information. PageRank[15] is a global influence metric. However, it is too time consuming and the influence of one node is equal to its neighbors. While, local influence is able to operate on partial social network information. Sun *et al.*[16] presented a fixed decay factor method to transfer the similarity in network. They assume that the influence is proportional to the distance. The greater the distance is, the smaller the influence is. Massa and Avesani[17] presented a linear distance propagation method. They evaluate every user's trust based on its minimum distance from the source user. If the user is not reachable within the maximum propagation distance, it has not predicted trust value.

3 Proposed Social Influence Propagation Model

3.1 Motivations

All kinds of social relationships, such as friendship, colleagues, schoolmate etc., can influence user's behavior, decision, thought. For example, if your friends recommend a movie to you, you probably will watch it on Sunday. However, users do not usually follow each recommendation provided by their friends. That is, different friends may generate different trusts and influences to you.

However, many existing influence propagation models and computation methods cannot obey the principle. Sun *et al.*[16] assumes that the influence decreases as a fixed decay factor with the increase of propagation distance. In [17], the author defines a linear function, the influence decreases linearly with the increase of propagation distance. In both methods, the direct neighbors of node have not influence decay, that is, each direct neighbors will generate same influence. This is not reasonable obviously.

The motivations of this paper are as follows:

1) Influence does not only from our direct friends. In practice, our behaviors will be influenced not only from our direct friends, but also from the indirect friends. However, not all other users on social network can influence our behaviors. According to [8], our behaviors will be influenced from the users who are within our three degree distance. The influence is very small if the distance is more than three.

2) Your social influence is dynamic with your friends. In fact, every person has many friends, however, your social influence is not equal to all your friends. Your influence is larger to your good friends than to the common friends.

3) The local network topology of the node can affect its size of social influence. That is, the social influence is local, which is related to its local friends, is not very relevant to other nodes of the network.

3.2 Adaptive Social Influence Propagation Model

A social network can be denoted as $G = (V, E, W)$. V is the user set. E represents the social relationships, such as $(u, v) \in E, u, v \in V$. W is the weight matrix between each pair of users. For example, it is the similarity matrix if G is a user similarity network. If G is undirected network, the matrix is symmetric and each element $w \in W$ is set 1. In directed network, W is a non-symmetric matrix, that is, $w = (u, v) \neq w' = (v, u)$.

In this section, we present an adaptive social influence propagation model. Fig. 1(a) shows the illustration of the model. w denotes the weight between two nodes and SI represents the social influence (SI) of the node. In our propagation model, different neighbors of one node have different social influences, which is determined by its local network topology (it will be introduced in section 3.3). Assume that $P_{u,v}$ represents the path set between node u and v. $P_{u,v}^k \in P_{u,v}$ denotes the k path and $P_{u,v}^k = \{(v_1, v_2), ..., (v_{n-1}, v_n)\}$. The formalization of the proposed social influence propagation model is as follows:

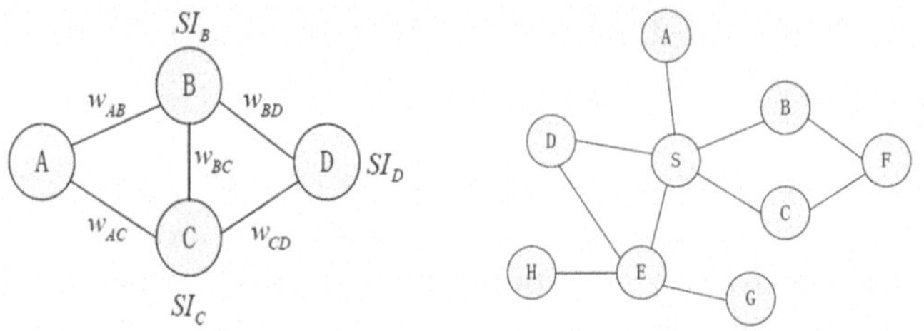

(a) Illustration of the presented social influence propagation model

(b) An example of computation of social influence based on local network topology.

Fig. 1. The illustration of the proposed social influence propagation model and the computation of the social influence

$$SI_{u,v} = \prod_{(v_i,v_j)\in P_{u,v}^k} (w_{v_iv_j} \cdot SI_i) \tag{1}$$

Where, $SI_{u,v}$ represents the influence of node u to node v. Take the $SI_{D,A}$ for example, one of the path between node D and node A is $P_{D,A}^1 = \{(v_D, v_B), (v_B, v_A)\}$. The influence of node D to node A is $SI_{D,A} = (w_{DB} \cdot SI_D) \cdot (w_{BA} \cdot SI_B)$.

In fact, there are many paths between two nodes. Hence, we should aggregate all path to obtain the final social influence from one node to another. In [18], the author intruduces two aggregation methods. One of the methods considers only the best propagation path between two nodes, i.e., the path where the influence propagation is maximum. Another considers all possible paths between two nodes and the social influence is computed by weighted all paths. Golbeck *et al.*[19] introduces the maximum and minimum length path strategies. These path length functions can return the full chains of weighted edges which make up the maximum and minimum length paths.

In this paper, we design the shortest path with maximum propagation methods(SPMPM) by aggregating the previous two methods. We first find all the shortest path between two nodes. Then, the social influence propagation of each path will be computed. The maximum propagation path is selected as the final result. Assume $SP_{u,v}$ represents the shortest path set between node u and v. The formalization is defined as follows:

$$SI_{u,v} = \max\left\{ \prod_{(v_i,v_j)\in SP_{u,v}^k} (w_{v_iv_j} \cdot SI_i), k = 1, 2, ..., m \right\} \tag{2}$$

Where, m denotes the number of the shortest path between node u and v. $SP_{u,v}^k$ is the k shortest path.

Take the influence of $SI_{D,A}$ for example in Fig. 1(a), there are two shortest paths between node D and A. That is $SP_{D,A}^1 = \{(v_D, v_B), (v_B, v_A)\}$ and

$SP^2_{D,A} = \{(v_D, v_C), (v_C, v_A)\}$. $SI^1_{D,A} = (w_{DB} \cdot SI_D) \cdot (w_{BA} \cdot SI_B)$, $SI^2_{D,A} = (w_{DC} \cdot SI_D) \cdot (w_{CA} \cdot SI_C)$. The maximum propagation value between $SI^1{}_{D,A}$ and $SI^2{}_{D,A}$ will be selected as the final social influence between node D and A.

3.3 Computation of Node Social Influence

Social influence is an intuitive concept. It refers to the behavioral change of individuals affected by others in the social network. The strength of social influence depends on many factors, such as node attribution, the strength of relationships between users, the distance between users, temporal effects and so on. It is difficult to measure the social influence, but the social influence has been accepted in social network.

Granovetter[20] states that the more common neighbors a pair of nodes may have, the stronger the tie between them, further, the stronger the mutual influence will be. The disadvantage is that it cannot compute the social influence if they don't have any common neighbors. However, any pair of nodes has some influence so long as they are connected. Node centrality[21] can measure the importance of one node in social network and it can also be used to represent the social influence of one node, such as degree centrality, closeness centrality, betweenness centrality, Katz centrality. However, the computation of node centrality need the global network topology and it is time consuming.

In this section, we introduce a simple and fast method to compute the social influence based on the local network topology of the node which is called local node centrality (LNC) method. The social influence of one node to another is related to the local information, and is irrespective with other nodes. The formalization can be defined as follows:

$$SI_{v_k,u} = \frac{degree\,(v_k)}{\max\{degree\,(v_i)\,, i = 1, ..., n\}} \tag{3}$$

Where, $SI_{v_k,u}$ is the social influence of node v_k to node u. $degree\,(v_i)$ represents the node degree of v_i. n is the number of neighbors of the node u. The formula indicates that the social influence $SI_{v_k,u}$ is only related to the neighbors of the node u. This method doesn't need the global information of network.

Fig. 1(b) gives an example of the computation of social influence based on the local network topology. The node S has five neighbors. The maximum degree of the neighbor is the neighbor $E(degree(E) = 4)$. Hence, the social influence of each neighbor is:

$SI_{A,S} = degree(A)/degree(E) = 1/4 = 0.25$
$SI_{E,S} = degree(E)/degree(E) = 1/1 = 1$
$SI_{B,S} = SI_{C,S} = SI_{D,S} = degree(B)/degree(E) = 2/4 = 0.5$

There are three advantages of this methods. First, it can generate different social influences for each neighbor of one user when their degrees are different. In practice, your friends will impact you in varying degree. Second, for the same node, its social influence is varying depending on its neighbors. This reflect the adaptiveness of our model. Third, it does't need the global network information, hence its computation is simple and fast.

4 Experiments and Analysis

4.1 Data Set

In our experiments, we adopt the most widely used Epinions (http://www.epinions.com/) data set. It is collected from epinions.com. Epinions founded in 1999 is a product and shop review site where users can review items (such as movies, books, software, etc.) And users can also assign items numeric ratings in the range 1 to 5. Moreover, users can express their trust to other users, i.e. reviewers whose reviews and ratings are helpful and valuable to me.

The Epinions data set consists of 49289 users who have rated a total of 139738 different items at least once. There are 40163 users who have rated at least one item. The total number of reviews is 664824. The sparseness of the data set is hence more than 99.99%. The total number of trust statements is 486985. The number of users who have rated items less than 5 is more than 52.8%. For example, the number of users who have rated three and four items is 2917 and 2317 respectively.

4.2 Evaluation Measures

The MAE (Mean Absolute Error)[22] and RMSE (Rooted Mean Squared Error) [23] are the two most widely used metrics to measure the performance of algorithm.

However, MAE and RMSE are not always informative about the quality of an recommender systems[17]. Usually, in the computations of MAE and RMSE, for the users who have rated many items (called heavy rater), the results will have small errors; for the users who have rated little (called cold user), the results will have big errors. But, since heavy raters provide many ratings, these small errors will be counted many times, while the few big errors made for cold users count few times. For this reason, we need adopt other two measures: Mean Absolute User Error (MAUE) and Rooted Mean Squared User Error (RMSUE). Take the MAUE for example, we first compute the mean error for each user and then these user errors are averaged over all the users. In this case, every user is taken into account only once and the cold users are influenced as much as the heavy raters. The MAUE and RMSUE can be defined as follows:

$$\begin{aligned} \text{MAUE} &= \frac{1}{N_T} \sum_{k=1}^{N_T} \text{MAE}(u_k)' \\ \text{MAE}(u_k)' &= \frac{1}{R_N(u_k)} \sum_{i=1}^{R_N(u_k)} |r_i - r_i'| \end{aligned} \tag{4}$$

$$\begin{aligned} \text{RMSUE} &= \frac{1}{N_T} \sum_{k=1}^{N_T} \text{RMSE}(u_k)' \\ \text{RMSE}(u_k)' &= \frac{1}{R_N(u_k)} \sum_{i=1}^{R_N(u_k)} (r_i - r_i')^2 \end{aligned} \tag{5}$$

Where, N_T is the testing user number. MAE$(u_k)'$ and RMSE$(u_k)'$ denotes the mean absolute error and rooted mean squared error of user u_k respectively. $R_N(u_k)$ represents the number of ratings by user u_k. r_i is the real rating of item i and $r_i{}'$ is the predicted value.

In practice, it is often the case that the recommender systems can give a good performance in predicting all the ratings for a user who gave many ratings and provide a worse predicting to a user who has rated few items. Hence, except the MAUE and RMSUE, we should measure how many users can be predicted(*user coverage*) and how many ratings are able to be predicted among all the ratings (*item coverage*). The *user coverage* can be defined as the portion of users for which the system is able to predict at least one rating. The *item coverage* is defined as the portion of items for which the system can predict. The formalization of the user coverage (UC) and the item coverage (IC) can be defined as follows:

$$UC = \frac{N_T{}'}{N_T}, IC = \frac{R_N{}'}{R_N} \tag{6}$$

Where, $N_T{}'$ denotes the number of users who can be predicted at least one rating by the system. $R_N{}'$ represents the number of items which can be predicted.

4.3 Compared Methods

In order to demonstrate the performance of the proposed social influence propagation model, we compare our model with three other approaches.

Collaborative filtering (CF) is the traditional prediction approach. The user-based nearest neighbor algorithm is used in this paper. It includes two steps: the computation of each pair of users and recommendation according to the nearest neighbors. Pearson's correlation coefficient[4] is the most used similarity measure. The formula is as follows:

$$sim(u,v) = \frac{\sum_{p \in I} (r_{u,p} - \bar{r}_u) \cdot (r_{v,p} - \bar{r}_v)}{\sqrt{\sum_{p \in I} (r_{u,p} - \bar{r}_u)^2 \cdot (r_{v,p} - \bar{r}_v)^2}} \tag{7}$$

Where, I is the common rating set between user u and v. $\bar{r}_u$ and $\bar{r}_v$ is the average rating of user u and v respectively. The similarity will be sorted according to descending order and the M most similar users are selected as the nearest neighbors. The prediction of item p by user u can be obtained by aggregating the rating of nearest neighbors.

$$pre(u,p) = \bar{r}_u + \frac{\sum_{i \in M} (w_{u,i} \cdot r_{i,p})}{\sum_{i \in M} w_{u,i}} \tag{8}$$

Another benchmark is the method which is proposed in [16]. It assumes that the propagation of social influence decreases as a fixed decay factor. This method is named decay factor (DF). Assume $SP_{u,v}^k$ is the k shortest path from node u to

v except the last hop. According the shortest path with maximum propagation strategy, the formalization the social influence from u to v is as follows:

$$SI_{u,v} = \max \left\{ \varepsilon \cdot \prod_{(i,j) \in SP^k_{u,v}} w_{i,j}, k = 1, ..., m \right\} \tag{9}$$

The third benchmark is proposed in [17], the author defines a linear function according to the maximum propagation distance, the social influence decreases linearly with the increase of propagation distance. We call this method as linear decrease (LD) method. Assume the maximum propagation distance is d, user u at distance n from the user v. The social influence from u to v can have a predicted value:

$$SI_{u,v} = \frac{d - n + 1}{d} \tag{10}$$

From equation 9 and 10, we note that the direct neighbors of node v have the same and maximum social influence. However, our approach (equation 3) can make up this drawback.

4.4 Performance Comparison

In this section, we compare the performance between our model and the benchmarks. We choose the Leave One Out evaluation technique to measure the performance. Leave one out technique involves hiding each rating and trying to predict them successively. We compare the predicted rating with the real rating and the difference (such as absolute value and rooted squared value) is the prediction error. Averaging the error over every prediction gives the overall MAUE and RMSUE respectively. Moreover, we also compute the user coverage (UC) and item coverage (IC) to compare these methods comprehensively.

According to [8], the behavior of user will be influenced within three degree distance, that is, your behavior is influenced by your friends of friends of friends. The influence is very small if the users are more than three degree and it can be ignored. Hence, in our experiments, the social influence propagation is limited within three degree distance. Moreover, since the optimal performance of fixed decay factor method can be obtained when the decay factor ε is set 0.006 in [16], we also set this value in our experiments.

In order to predict one rating, we first compute the user similarity matrix after hiding the rating. Then the social similarity network can be built according to the similarity matrix. The network is weighted and undirected in our experiments. Moreover, we make the comparison for the users who only give three and four ratings(because user similarity cannot be computed when rating number is two) in our experiments.

Fig. 2 shows the comparisons between our model and the benchmarks when the users only give three and four ratings. We can see that the approaches based on social influence propagation are better than the traditional collaborative filtering (CF). In Fig. 2(a), the performance of our model (LNC) is better than

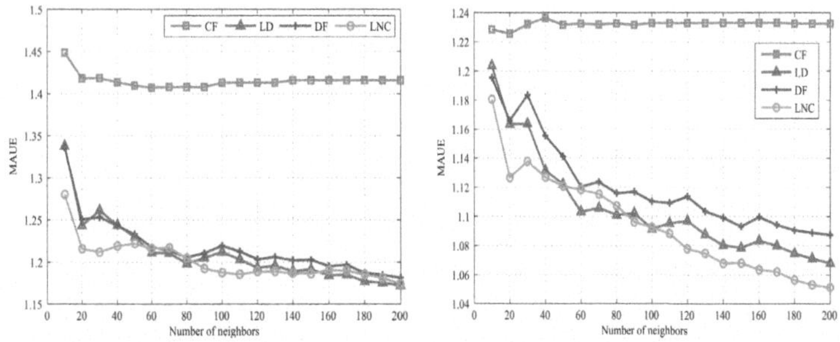

(a) Rating number:3 (b) Rating number:4

Fig. 2. The comparison on mean absolute user error (MAUE) between our model (LNC) and collaborative filtering(CF), linear decrease (LD), decay factor (DF) with the condition of users only give three and four ratings respectively

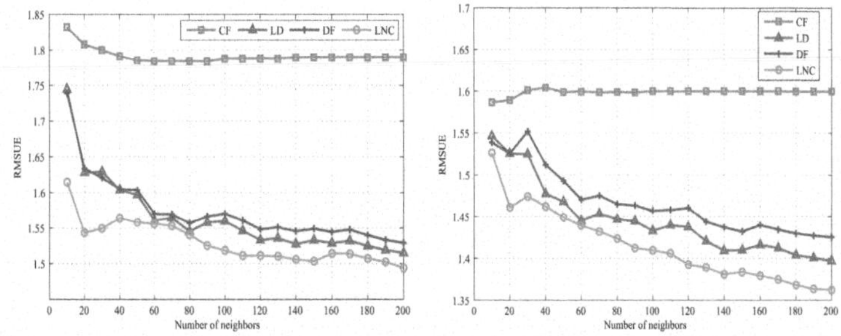

(a) Rating number:3 (b) Rating number:4

Fig. 3. The comparison on rooted mean squared user error (RMSUE) between our model (LNC) and collaborative filtering(CF), linear decrease (LD), decay factor (DF) with the condition of users only give three and four ratings respectively

the linear decrease (LD) and decay factor (DF) methods when the number of neighbors is less than 50 and it is between 90 and 170. When the number of neighbors is more than 40, the LD will be better than DF. While in Fig. 2(b), the performance of our model is not better than LD only when the number of neighbors is between 50 and 80. The LD can surpass DF except when the number of neighbors is less 20. From the Fig. 2, we also can see that the mean absolute user error (MAUE) of the social influence propagation approaches is less when the rating number given by users is more(the maximum MAUE is less than 1.21 in Fig. 2(b) and the best MAUE is more than 1.18 in Fig. 2(a)).

The performance on rooted mean squared user error (RMSUE) between our model and other approaches is given in Fig. 3. We also see that the RMSUE of the social influence propagation approaches is more small than the collaborative filtering. We can note that our model (LNC) can obtain the best performance within the range of entire neighbors. The linear decrease (LD) method is also better than decay factor (DF) method except when the number of neighbors

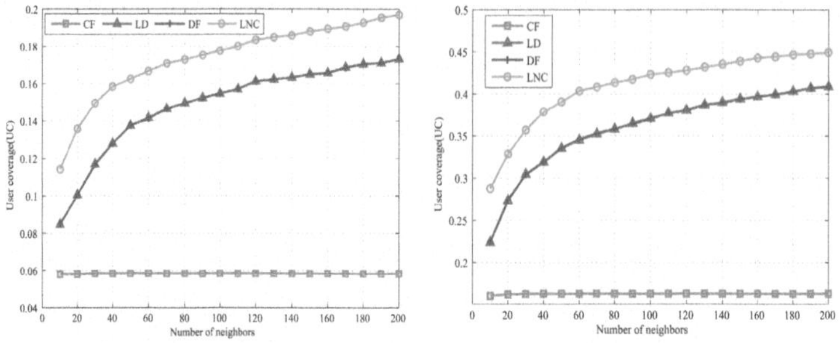

(a) Rating number:3 (b) Rating number:4

Fig. 4. The comparison on user coverage (UC) between our model (LNC) and collaborative filtering(CF), linear decrease (LD), decay factor (DF) with the condition of users only give three and four ratings respectively

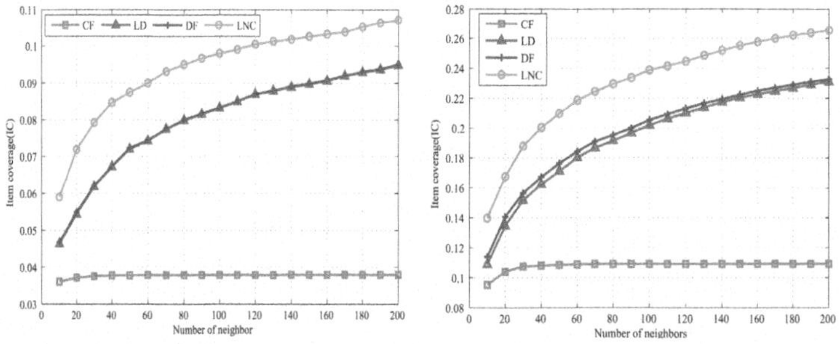

(a) Rating number:3 (b) Rating number:4

Fig. 5. The comparison on item coverage (IC) between our model (LNC) and collaborative filtering(CF), linear decrease (LD), decay factor (DF) with the condition of users only give three and four ratings respectively

is small, such as 10. In Fig. 2, the advantage of our model is not obviously. However, it is very notable in Fig. 3. This phenomenon explains that our model can produce many small error data and other two methods generate more large error data. Since the rooted mean squared user error (RMSUE) can magnify those large errors, our model is more accurate and stable than the benchmarks.

Moveover, we also compare the user coverage (UC) and item coverage (IC) except the MAUE and RMSUE. Fig. 4 shows the comparison results on the user coverage evaluation measure between our model and other three methods. We can see that the three social influence propagation methods can give better UC than the traditional collaborative filtering (CF). Moveover, the linear decrease (LD) and the decay factor (DF) methods have the same performance. We note that our model can give better results than LD and DF methods evidently. It obtains the best performance. We also see that the performance is better when users give more ratings. For example, the optimal user coverage is less than 0.2 in Fig. 4(a), while the worst result is more than 0.2 in Fig. 4(b).

Fig. 5 presents the comparison results on the item coverage evaluation measure between our model and the benchmarks. Just like the Fig. 4, the three social influence propagation approaches obtain better item coverage (IC) than the traditional collaborative filtering (CF) and our model can also achieve the best performance. The decay factor (DF) method obtain better item coverage than the linear decrease method and the users give more ratings, the distinction is larger. Similarly, the three social influence propagation approaches can give better item coverage if the users provide more ratings. For instance, the optimal item coverage is less than 0.11 in Fig. 5(a), while the worst performance is more than 0.11 in Fig. 5(b).

From Fig. 2 to Fig. 5, we can conclude that our model is not only able to obtain the less prediction error, but also it can have the best user coverage and item coverage. This demonstrates that the proposed model can improve the prediction performance effectively.

5 Conclusions

In order to improve the prediction performance in social recommendation, this paper proposes an adaptive social influence propagation model in which the computation of social influence of one node is based on its local network topology. There are three advantages of this method. First, different neighbors of nodes can generate different social influences. Second, one node can produce different social influences depending on its neighbors. Third, it does't need the global information about social network, hence its computation is very fast. We conduct experiments on Epinions data set and compare our model with other methods. The experimental results show that the proposed model can obtain the least prediction error and largest coverage. The performance of social recommendation is able to be improved effectively.

Acknowledgements. This work is partially supported by the National 3rd Key Program project (No. 2011ZX03005-004-02 and No.2012ZX03005008-001), National Natural Science Foundation of China (61101119), Key Project of the National Research Program of China (No. 2012BAH41F00), Funds for Creative Research Groups of China (61121001) and Program for Changjiang Scholars and Innovative Research Team in University (IRT1049).

References

1. Wikipedia, `http://zh.wikipedia.org/`
2. Resnick, P., Varian, H.R.: Recommender systems. Communications of the ACM 40, 56–58 (1997)
3. Linden, G., Smith, B., York, J.: Amazon.com recommendations: Item-to-item collaborative filtering. Internet Computing 7, 76–80 (2003)
4. Resnick, P., Iacovou, N., Suchak, M., Bergstrom, P., Riedl, J.: GroupLens: an open architecture for collaborative filtering of netnews. In: Proceedings of the ACM Conference on Computer Supported Cooperative Work, pp. 175–186. ACM (1994)

5. Dong, W., Tao, Z., Cimini, G., Pei, W., Weiping, L., Yicheng, Y.: Effective mechanism for social recommendation of news. Physica A: Statistical Mechanics and its Applications 390, 2117–2126 (2011)
6. Sigrubjörnsson, B., Van Zwol, R.: Flickr tag recommendation based on collective knowledge. In: Proceedings of the International Conference on World Wide Web, pp. 327–336 (2008)
7. Shulong, T., Jiajun, B., Chun, C., Bin, X., Can, W., Xiaofei, H.: Using rich social media information for music recommendation via hypergraph model. ACM Transactions on Multimedia Computing, Commuications, and Applications 7, 1–20 (2011)
8. Christakis, N.A., Fowler, J.H.: Connected. Little Brown (2010)
9. Yang, S.H., Long, B., Smola, A., Sadagopan, N., Zheng, Z.H., Zha, H.Y.: Like like alike: joint friendship and interest propagation in social networks. In: Proceedings of the International Conference on World Wide Web, pp. 537–546. ACM (2011)
10. Massa, P., Avesani, P.: Trust-aware Recommender Systems. In: Proceedings of the ACM Conference on Recommender Systems, pp. 17–24. ACM (2007)
11. Guha, R., Kumar, R., Raghavan, P., Tomkins, A.: Propagation of trust and distrust. In: Proceedings of the International Conference on World Wide Web, pp. 403–412. ACM (2004)
12. Kempe, D., Kleinberg, J., Tardos, E.: Maximizing the spread of influence through a social network. In: Proceedings of the ACM SIGKDD International Conference on Knowledge Discovery and Data Mining, pp. 137–146. ACM (2003)
13. Wu, F., Huberman, B.A., Adamic, L.A., Tyler, J.R.: Information Flow in Social Groups. Physica A: Statistical Mechanics and its Applications 337, 327–335 (2004)
14. Ye, M., Liu, X.J., Lee, W.C.: Exploring Social Influence for Recommendation - A Probabilistic Generative Model Approach. arXiv preprint (2011)
15. Page, L., Brin, S., Motwani, R., Winograd, T.: The pagerank citation ranking: Bringing order to the web. Technical report. Stanford, USA (1998)
16. Duo, S., Tao, Z., Jianguo, L., Runran, L., Chunxiao, J., Binghong, W.: Information filtering based on transferring similarity. Physical Review E 80, 017101 (2009)
17. Massa, P., Avesani, P.: Trust-aware collaborative filtering for recommender systems. In: Meersman, R., Tari, Z. (eds.) CoopIS/DOA/ODBASE 2004. LNCS, vol. 3290, pp. 492–508. Springer, Heidelberg (2004)
18. Richters, O., Peixoto, T.P.: Trust Transitivity in Social Networks. PLOS One 6, e18384 (2011)
19. Golbeck, J., Parsia, B., Hendler, J.: Trust Networks on the Semantic Web. In: Klusch, M., Omicini, A., Ossowski, S., Laamanen, H. (eds.) CIA 2003. LNCS (LNAI), vol. 2782, pp. 238–249. Springer, Heidelberg (2003)
20. Granovetter, M.S.: The strength of weak ties. American Journal of Sociology, 1360–1380 (1973)
21. Scott, J.: Social network analysis. SAGE Publications Limited (2012)
22. Bobadilla, J., Ortega, F., Hernando, A.: A collaborative filtering similarity measure based on singularities. Information Processing & Management 48, 204–238 (2012)
23. Deepa, A., Kamal, K.B.: Utilizing various sparsity measures for enhancing accuracy of collaborative recommender systems based on local and global similarities. Expert Systems with Applications 38, 5101–5109 (2011)

A Rule Based Personalized Location Information System for the Semantic Web

Iosif Viktoratos[1], Athanasios Tsadiras[1], and Nick Bassiliades[2]

[1] Department of Economics
[2] Department of Informatics,
Aristotle University of Thessaloniki, GR-54124 Thessaloniki, Greece
{viktorat,tsadiras,nbassili}@auth.gr

Abstract. In this paper, an innovative Personalized Location Information System for the Semantic Web (called SPLIS) is presented. The proposed system adopts schema.org ontology and combines it with rule-based policies, to deliver fully contextualized information to the user of a location-based system. Owners of points of interest can add their own rule-based policies to SPLIS to expose and deploy their marketing strategy on special offers, discounts, etc. These rules are combined at run-time with information about relevant place properties and user (people) profiles. Additionally, owners of points of interest can extend the ontology by adding dynamically specific properties. Rules are encoded in RuleML for interchangeability and to Jess in order to be executed. All data and rules are stored in the form of triples, using Sesame. Rules are evaluated on-the-fly to deliver personalized information according to the rules that fired within the current user-location-time context. In the paper, a demonstration of SPLIS is given using data from Google Places API and Google map for visualization.

Keywords: Rules, Ontologies, Location Based Services, Context.

1 Introduction

Over the last few years Location Based Services (LBS) have become an important part of everyday life, used daily by millions of people for navigation, traffic reporting, sightseeing, etc [1]. Due to the fact that LBS user's environment changes rapidly, it is really important for a successful application to conceive these changes and deliver up-to-date personalized and contextualized information to users [2-6]. If we take as examples a LBS user who is driving and looks for a restaurant close to him, or a LBS user who is looking for a taxi, it becomes apparent that a successful LBS should be capable of offering emerging information retrieval to users, relevant to their needs and preferences. As a result, researches and industries focus on the delivery of such capabilities by developing a) relevant hardware such as GPS, sensors and b) software structures such as semantically annotated metadata for describing the information.

Semantic technologies such as ontologies, gave a huge boost by offering the ability to represent complex user concepts. They enable context perception of higher quality by representing related concepts such as time, location etc. RDFS and OWL are

C. Huemer and P. Lops (Eds.): EC-Web 2013, LNBIP 152, pp. 27–38, 2013.

developed to represent the structure of physical entities and the connections between them [7-10]. Furthermore, by providing a general representation standard [8-10], they offer flexibility and interoperability between systems. Connecting and sharing data from various sources (people, places, offers) enables applications that operate on a global data layer and provide more flexible querying as new data appear at runtime.

Ontologies often require reasoning capabilities and they are combined with rule based approaches. Rule-based systems are more autonomous because they are capable of conceiving context changes and respond accordingly without user intervention [11, 12]. Such a capability is important in interactive LBS applications where the user environment is exposed to rapid changes. “Automatic contextual reconfiguration”[2], the ability of a system to keep track of environmental changes and adapt to the current context, is important and leads to high quality services instead of just providing simple information [13-16].

The aim of our work is to combine semantics with LBS to deliver personalized and contextualized information services to users. A system called Semantic Personalized Location Information System (SPLIS)[1] is implemented for this purpose. SPLIS uses an “open” data model by discovering data at run-time. An early version of SPLIS called PLIS has been presented in [17] that implemented a fixed-set of “closed” data model. The use of an “open” data model is achieved by making SPLIS fully compatible with the popular schema.org ontology (also adopted by Google, Bing and Yahoo), incorporating dynamically its RDF Schema version[2]. Because of the variety and the amount of linked data found on the web, a consistently used and widely accepted ontology such as the above is crucial for the success of the system. Additionally in SPLIS, end users and/or place owners are able to enrich the schema dynamically at run time by adding their own properties. Furthermore, SPLIS has a user-friendly form-based web interface for the creation of rules. Another advantage of SPLIS is that its data and knowledge are completely open and interoperable with other systems, being in RDF/S (data and knowledge/schema) and RuleML (knowledge/rules).

After a short review on related work, a detailed presentation of the system is included in the following sections. In sections 3 and 4 the design of our system and the implementation details are described. In section 5 the system operation process is illustrated in detail. In section 6 the functionally of our system is exhibited by the use of a number of examples. Finally, section 7 presents the conclusions of our work and discusses future directions.

2 Related Work

Some works from various scientific areas that use semantics are the following:

Point of Interest (POI) Recommendation. Serrano et al.[18] proposed a tourist information service which combines RDF data taken from sources such as foaf profile with rules in SWRL format to recommend POIs related with user profile. Noguera

---

[1] SPLIS can be accessed at `http://tinyurl.com/splis-login`

[2] `http://schema.org/`

et al. [19] combined recommendation techniques such as collaborative and knowledge based filtering with smartphones visualization capabilities (e.g. 3D).

Personalized Recommendations Based on Social Media Data. Savage et al. [20] used foursquare data to make POI recommendations based on a pattern-matching scoring algorithm while Patton et al. [21] implemented a mobile agent for wine and food recommendation. Data from social media such as facebook and twitter are stored in RDF triples format and retrieved for personalized recommendations.

Search Optimization. Nowadays, LBS offer high quality mobile search capabilities by personalizing query results or search tag recommendations. Choi et al. [22] proposed a personalized mobile information retrieval system, while Bouidghaghen et al. [23] optimized web search by re-ranking results according to position. Arias et al. [24] proposed a thesaurus-based semantic context-aware auto completion mechanism.

Applications that Take Advantage of Smartphones Capabilities. Woensel et al. [25] proposed a person matching application based on data retrieved from foaf profile and identification techniques such as RFID, Bluetooth etc. Furthermore, Keßler et al. [26] combined data collected from sensors with ontologies and rules in SWRL format for utilizing complex context information. *Venezia et al. [27],* adopted a dynamic rule based approach for personalizing mobile experiences, by offering user the capability to choose from a set of rules (concerning mobile preferences) or add one manually.

Applications to other Areas. Except from LBS applications semantic technologies are used in other domains, such as health, e-commerce etc. For example, Bayrhammer et al. [28] used a rule based service bus for controlling data flows in patient centric hospital information systems.

SPLIS is not in contrast with similar works and could easily be combined with most of existing approaches. It offers service providers-place owners the capability to expose their marketing strategy in a direct way. A rule-based approach was followed for SPLIS implementation, based on the advantages discussed in the previous section. Most rule based LBS support a static rule base. Our proposed system differs by enabling a fully dynamic rule base that offers users the option to add rules at run time. By offering users the ability to add rules dynamically SPLIS becomes more intelligent and autonomous. Additionally, a user-friendly interface layer provides proactive personalized information to the regular user.

3 Design and General Idea

In everyday life, POIs, as businesses, adopt a rule-based policy in order to deploy their specific marketing strategy (e.g. a coffee shop offers 20% discount to students). On the other hand, LBS users search for such kind of information according to their profile, preferences and needs. For example, someone searches for a cheap coffee shop close to his/her location, or a restaurant having an offer for pizza. SPLIS aim is to provide a direct interaction platform between POI owners and users - potential customers. This can be done by combining business policies with user context and needs in order to deliver up-to-date, personalized information.

Every time a user logs into the system to search for a place, SPLIS gets user's context, evaluates the rules-offers associated with nearby POIs and delivers proactive personalized information to the user, presented on Google Maps[3]. On the other hand, owners of POIs can expose their marketing strategy by inserting their own rule base policy. They are able to assert data concerning the places they own (data based on the ontology referred above, or even new data, by extending the ontology) and rules related to these data (such as reduced prices for unemployed users). SPLIS is currently able to handle rules concerning: a) Every existing property of a POI, b) User's occupation (e.g. a museum offers discount to students), c) User's gender (a pub has special prices for women), d) User's age (free entrance for children under 12 years), e) User's location (a coffee shop decreases coffee price for users who are less than 400 meters away), f) Time (a restaurant is closed on Sundays or a coffee shop has special prices between 17:00-19:00).

4 Implementation and Technical Details

SPLIS implementation is based on Java Server Pages (JSP) technology, a web development technology based on Java programming language [29]. It was chosen due to the fact that the vast majority of available rule engines are java-based. Furthermore, JSP could be easily integrated with technologies used for RDF, RDFS and OWL storage and querying such as Sesame, Jena, Protégé etc [30, 31]. Another core component of the proposed system is Sesame, which is a very popular choice for RDF data manipulation, such as storing, querying and inferring large sets of RDF triples [30]. Additionally, it can easily be embedded into java-based applications.

An important part of our system is the rule execution process. A rule representation language is necessary to represent human understandable policies. In our case, RuleML and being more specific, Reaction RuleML (a clone of RuleML) was adopted. RuleML (launched August 2000) is a family of sublanguages which are used to publish rules on the web [32, 33] and their main objective is to provide a general rule markup approach for semantic web applications [34]. It is a powerful markup language (XML with a predefined schema) which supports various types of rules such as deductive, reactive and normative. It also addresses the issues of interoperability and flexibility among different systems on the web, by allowing rules to be encoded in a standard way [32]. Moreover, there are attempts to translate natural language to an XML representation [35], therefore the development of a user-friendly interface is foreseeable. Before adopting RuleML we have considered alternative web rule languages, such as SWRL. However, SWRL employs open world reasoning without default negation, while our approach needs close world reasoning. RIF-PRD is also a candidate, currently not supported by tools as much as RuleML [36]. A rule representation language has to be translated into a machine readable language. Rule engines such as Jess, Drools, Prova [37] are used for this purpose. Jess was chosen to implement the core of SPLIS, because of the fact that it is a lightweight rule engine that connects well with web technologies, which were needed for SPLIS system

[3] `http://maps.google.com`

implementation [38]. Rules in RuleML format are transformed to Jess rules by using XSLT. Additionally, apart from the PC browser-based version of SPLIS, a lightweight mobile version for Android devices has been implemented. The mobile application supports all functionalities concerning regular user operations (e.g. search for POIs, rating, etc.) which are described in the following section.

5 SPLIS Operation Process

The SPLIS operation process includes the following layers (Fig. 1):

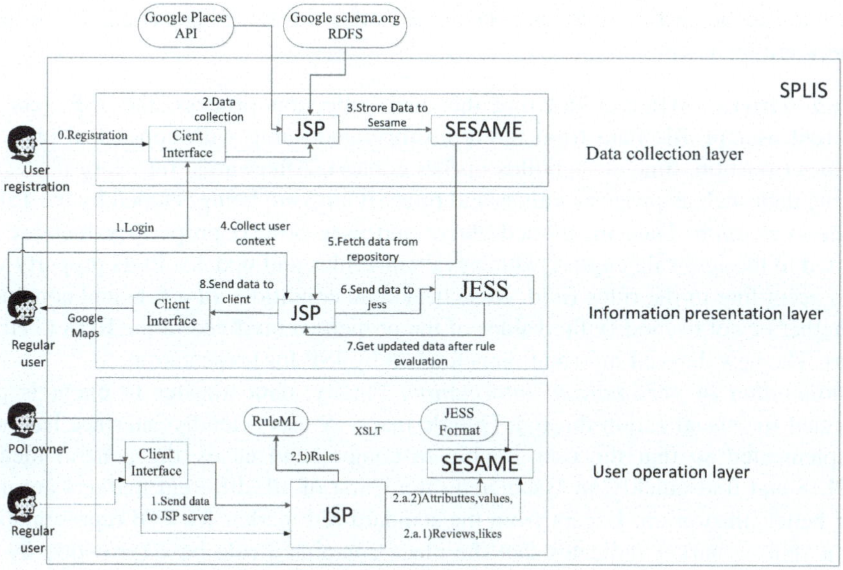

Fig. 1. SPLIS operation process

Layer 1: Data Collection. This layer is responsible for gathering and adding new data into the system repository. Concerning user-related data, users are capable of registering to the system by completing a registration form. Form fields are inferred dynamically from the ontology related classes and after submission property values are stored as triples in the repository. After completing the registration process, the user is able to log into the system and (if authentication is successful) a process concerning POI data collection begins. Two steps are included:

1. *Ontology loading.* The ontology is loaded dynamically into Sesame so that the system is always up-to-date with the latest official updates of the RDF Schema.
2. *Data update.* After the completion of ontology loading step, the system obtains user's position (via GPS in mobile or via IP address in desktop) and retrieves the nearest POIs (for reduced computational cost) from external sources such as Google Places API. We manually designed a mapping between the schema.org

RDFS ontology classes/properties and Google Places API categories/attributes based on terms similarities. Specifically, every category is assigned to a related schema.org class (e.g. API "lodging" is matched with schema.org "LodgingBusiness" etc.) and every attribute which is being parsed from the API is mapped to the related schema.org property (e.g. "name" with http://schema.org/name). Data from Google Places API are stored into the RDF repository. If a POI was already stored into the system by a previous use, SPLIS updates its related data with the latest information. For optimization, SPLIS compares existing data with the new one and updates them only if they are different.

Layer 2: Information Presentation Layer. In this layer, the information is presented to the end user according to his profile and the rules that have been fired. The following steps are included:

1. *Data retrieval.* After completing the data collection process, the JSP gets the current user profile data from the repository, and along with contextual property values (location, time etc.), builds his/her context. Afterwards, for every place, existing data such as property values and rules (if any) are being fetched by the JSP.
2. *Rule evaluation.* Data mentioned above and user context property values are asserted to the Jess rule engine, which evaluates rules and updates POIs property values according to the rules fired. Jess checks the conditions of a rule and concludes whether or not to modify the values of the properties involved in the RHS (THEN) part. The new derived information is fetched by JSP for presentation.
3. *Presentation of personalized information.* Finally, data transfer to client is performed for visualization through Google maps. A user-friendly interface has been implemented so that the user is able to comprehend easily the general idea of SPLIS and find quickly an associated offer. First of all, different markers are used for better illustration. Except from the standard red marker for POI representation, a) a yellow marker indicates that the place contains a rule base (provided by the owner) but no rule was fired for the user, b) a green marker indicates that the place contains a rule base and at least one rule was fired, and c) a crown over the marker indicates that the current user is the POI owner. Moreover, by clicking in a marker, the user can obtain additional information explaining either which rules were fired and why or (if no rule was fired) which rules exist for the place (if any). Additionally, the user can directly execute a number of operations (described in layer 3 below) by clicking the corresponding buttons on the available menu.

Layer 3: User Operation Layer. In this layer, all supported operations of SPLIS are provided to the user. These operations are related to two different types of users, a) the regular user and b) the user who owns a POI and is able to modify it (POI owner).

1. *Regular user operations.* To begin with, a regular user, apart from seeking for information, can also directly interact with the available POIs. He/she can contribute by writing a review, rating them, or adding "likes". In other words, users not only provide useful information to other people, but they also create information that can be used during rule creation (e.g. place average rating, number of likes).

In addition, users are able to report abuse (e.g. for fake prices) for security and reliability. Moreover, a user is able to insert his/her own POIs (if any).

2. *POI owner operations.* If a user is POI owner, then he/she can update POI's profile by adding new data to its properties through a form-based interface. Properties are dynamically generated from the RDF Schema depending on the place type. Except from asserting data such as property values, the user can also extend the RDFS ontology by adding new properties through a simple form interface. Beside the name, the user can choose through a drop down menu if the added property is related only to a specific place (it is stored as a triple) or if it should be attached to a POI category and its subcategories (it is stored as a property of the related place type-class). An owner can also choose the type of the property among text, number and date.

One of the core functionalities of SPLIS is rule creation. A user-friendly form-based rule editor has been implemented so that users can easily create rules through completing web forms. More specifically, users are able to create rules which pose conditions that relate any property of the specific POI with any property regarding user context. Data collected from the forms are being transformed to RuleML, so that policies and SPLIS knowledge can be re-used by other systems. Afterwards RuleML is transformed to Jess in order to become machine executable, as discussed above.

For example the rule "If day is Tuesday and person jobTitle is student then entrance fee is 5 euro" is represented in Jess as:

```
(defrule for_students
  (declare (salience 10))
  (person ( day Tuesday)( jobTitle student))
=>
  (modify ?fact (entrance_fee 5))
  (store EXPLANATION "entrance fee for Students on Tuesday's is 5 euro"))
```

In detail, the JESS salience operator is used for resolving rule conflict issues, "modify" changes the values of the related properties and "EXPLANATION" is a variable for storing the explanation and presenting it afterwards to the end user.

Place owners are able to repeat this process and add multiple rules. In case of rule conflict, a LIFO system is used. Furthermore, the same form-based interface is provided to owners for updating directly the existing rules. Alternatively, using RuleML, a POI owner can develop a rule base outside the system and upload it to SPLIS via a URL. Concerning security issues, it's worth mentioning that the editing of the POIs rule base is authorized only to the owner. Additionally, files containing the rules are securely kept to the server.

6 Demonstration of SPLIS

To demonstrate the functionalities of SPLIS, let's imagine user "Peter" who is the owner of POI "Hotel el Greco". After entering SPLIS, "Peter" receives the information presented in Figure 2a. He can edit all properties of "Hotel el Greco" as it can be seen in Figure 3. For the correct insertion of data, property types are pulled directly from the RDF Schema and displayed next to each field of the form. Additionally, the POI owner can click on the info icons to receive a textual comment (fetched by schema.org) for the specific property. Notice that data collected from the Google Places API are read-only. By filling the corresponding fields in a web-form, an owner can also add new properties, as discussed above. Let's assume that "Peter" added a new property called "room price per night", which is a number, has domain only "Hotel el Greco" and default value 80.

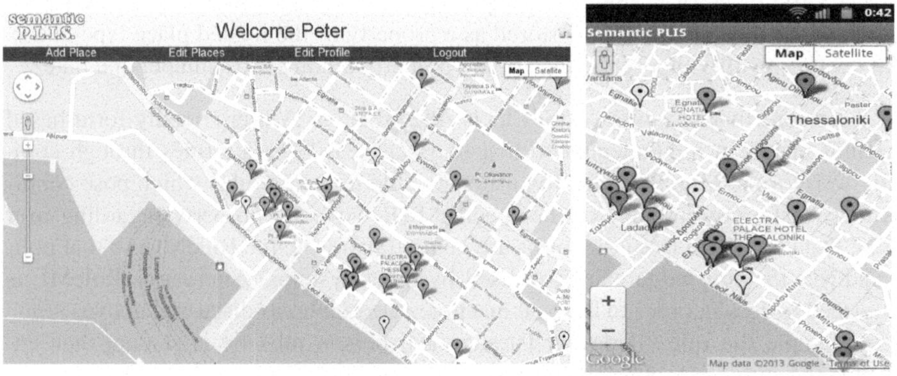

a) PC browser-based version for "Peter" b) mobile version for "John"

Fig. 2. SPLIS personalized information

Fig. 3. Editing form of POI properties in SPLIS

After completing the relevant data entry, "Peter" is able to use the rule editor and add rules. A demonstration of rule creation in SPLIS is given in Figure 4, where the owner is ready to assert the rule "*If a person is a student and day is Saturday and distance is less than 1000m then room price per night is 50€ and payment accepted is cash, credit card and check*". The rule editor is horizontally split into two parts, the "IF" part and the "THEN" part. "IF" part elements consist of a property field (place- or user-related), an operator ("is" for text and "<",">" for numbers and dates) and a value field. "THEN" part elements consist of a place property, an assignment operator "is" (or a predefined function "discount" for numbers) and the value field. Additionally, in order SPLIS to provide comprehensible information to the end-user, the web interface provides fields for entering a rule title and a textual explanation of the rule. Also a preview is provided so as the user to check the rule before submitting it.

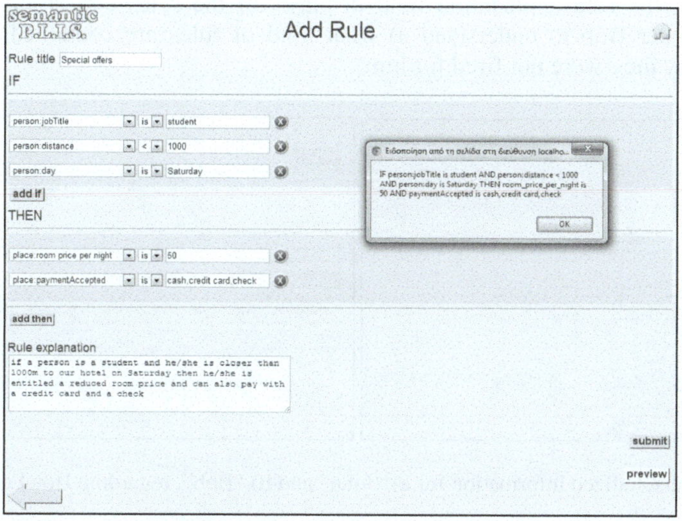

Fig. 4. Web based rule editor of SPLIS

Let now connect POI "Hotel el Greco" with two random regular user profiles who logged in. The following two different profiles snapshots are considered.

1. User A ("John") is a 20-year old student, his current environmental snapshot is taken on Saturday, at 15:14 and we assume his current location (a random location A) is closer than 1000 meters to "Hotel el Greco".
2. User B ("Bob") is 36, unemployed, and has logged in the system on Sunday at 21:15 at a location B (hypothetically closer than 1000m to "Hotel el Greco").

As soon as "John" logs into the system, SPLIS gets his profile, evaluates rules and displays proactive personalized information according to which rules were fired (Figure 2b illustrates the starting screen). By clicking into green markers (POIs where at least one rule is fired) or yellow markers (POIs that contain at least one rule, with no rule to have been fired) he can easily see which rules were fired and why.

For example, if "John" clicks on the green marker of "Hotel el Greco", he receives all the information that is presented in Figure 5a. Because of the fact that "John" is a student, it is Saturday, and John's current location is closer than 1000m from the hotel, the corresponding rule is fired. As a result, a) the room price per night value for

"John" has been changed to 50 euro and b) payment accepted options are not only cash (as it is for the default customer) but he can also pay by credit card or check. Additionally "John" receives information about the hotel such as the currency that it accepts, the date that it was founded, average rating etc. "John" can also add a "like" to the POI, add a review and a rate to the POI or view reviews and rates for the hotel that have been submitted by other SPLIS users.

Similarly, when User B - "Bob" logs into the system, no rule is fired for him for this place, because he is neither a student, nor it is Saturday. As a result, the hotel is displayed with a yellow marker and if it is clicked the information presented in Figure 5b appears. Bob is entitled for the standard room price and payment options. Additionally, the rule explanation field displays all the rules concerning "Hotel el Greco" in order Bob to understand a) what kind of rules are contained and b) the reason(s) why they were not fired for him.

Fig. 5. Personalized information for a) "John" and b) "Bob", regarding Hotel el Greco

7 Conclusions and Future Work

SPLIS was designed and implemented, offering a boost to the quality of delivered information, by giving users the opportunity to add rules dynamically to a location-based information system. On one side, owners add data and rules-offers, and on the other regular users enjoy proactive contextualized information. The capability of adding rules on the fly can not only lead to powerful, autonomous and intelligent services, but also to the evolution of these services. All the above has been achieved by SPLIS that is an "open" system that a) uses the schema.org ontologies, b) uses web based rule editor to create rules that initially are in RuleML format and then they are transformed to Jess rules in order to be able to be executed by the Jess inference engine, c) stores data and rules in the form of triples using the Sesame repository, d) retrieves data using Google Places API and e) display information using Google map. Experimental testing, confirmed SPLIS evolution without developers intervention, as more and more users add rules to the system. The more rules were added to the system, the more interesting and intelligent it becomes.

SPLIS implementation can evolve in various ways. One such way is SPLIS to crawl into POI websites in order to retrieve related RDF data so as POI owners will be able to add data without even logging into SPLIS. Furthermore, not only POI owners but also regular users should be able to have rules-contextualized preferences, as in [39]. Last but not least, in order to resolve possible rule abuse issues, system will check at compile-time the uniqueness and the firing scope of the rule.

References

1. Steiniger, S., Moritz, N., Alistair, E.: Foundation of Location Based Services. Lecture Notes on LBS (2006)
2. Abowd, G.D., Dey, A.K.: Towards a Better Understanding of Context and Context-Awareness. In: Gellersen, H.-W. (ed.) HUC 1999. LNCS, vol. 1707, pp. 304–307. Springer, Heidelberg (1999)
3. Liu, Y., Wilde, E.: Personalized Location-Based Services. In: Proc. of the iConference (2011)
4. Bouidghaghen, O., Tamine, L., Boughanem, M.: Context-Aware User's Interests for Personalizing Mobile Search. In: 12th IEEE Int. Conference on Mobile Data Management (2011)
5. Hosseini-Pozveh, M., Nematbakhsh, M., Movahhedinia, N.: A multidimensional approach for context-aware recommendation in mobile commerce. (IJCSIS) International Journal of Computer Science and Information Security 3(1) (2009)
6. Kwon, K., Kim, C.: How to design personalization in context of customer retention: Who personalizes what and to what extend? Electronic Commerce Research and Applications (11), 101–116 (2012)
7. Hwang, H., Shin, S., Kim, K., Lee, S., Kim, C.-S.: Context-aware System Architecture using Personal Information based on Ontology. In: 5th ACIS International Conference on Software Engineering Research, Management & Applications (2007)
8. Bizer, C., Heath, T., Berners-Lee, T.: Linked data - the story so far. International Journal on Semantic Web and Information Systems 5(3), 1–22 (2009)
9. Tryfona, N., Pfoser, D.: Data Semantics in Location-Based Services. In: Spaccapietra, S., Zimányi, E. (eds.) Journal on Data Semantics III. LNCS, vol. 3534, pp. 168–195. Springer, Heidelberg (2005)
10. Ilarri, S., Lllarramendi, A., Mena, E., Sheth, A.: Semantics in Location-Based Services. IEEE Internet Computing 15(6), 10–14 (2011)
11. Wu, S., Chang, C., Ho, S., Chao, H.: Rule based intelligent adaptation in mobile information systems. Expert Systems with Applications 34, 1078–1092 (2008)
12. Lassila, O.: Applying Semantic Web in Mobile and Ubiquitous Computing: Will Policy-Awareness Help? In: Semantic Web and Policy Workshop (2005)
13. Emmanouilidis, C., Koutsiamanis, R., Tasidou, A.: Mobile Guides: Taxonomy of Architectures, Context Awareness, Technologies and Applications. Journal of Network and Computer Applications, 103–125 (2012)
14. Etter, R., Dockhorn Costa, P., Broens, T.: A rule-based approach towards context-aware user notification services. In: ACS/IEEE Int. Conference on Pervasive Services, PERSER (2006)
15. Goix, L., Valla, M., Cerami, L., Felcarin, P.: Situation Inference for Mobile Users: A Rule Based Approach. In: Int. Conference on Mobile Data Management, pp. 299–303 (2007)
16. Wu, S., Chang, C., Ho, S., Chao, H.: Rule based intelligent adaptation in mobile information systems. Expert Systems with Applications 34, 1078–1092 (2008)
17. Viktoratos, I., Tsadiras, A., Bassiliades, N.: Personalizing Location Information through Rule-Based Policies. In: Bikakis, A., Giurca, A. (eds.) RuleML 2012. LNCS, vol. 7438, pp. 215–223. Springer, Heidelberg (2012)

18. Serrano, D., Hervás, R., Bravo, J.: Telemaco: Context-aware System for Tourism Guiding based on Web 3.0 Technology. In: International Workshop on Contextual Computing and Ambient Intelligence in Tourism (2011)
19. Noguera, J.M., Barranco, M.J., Segura, R.J., Martinez, L.: A Mobile 3D-GIS Hybrid Recommender System for Tourism. TR-1 (2012)
20. Savage, N.S., Baranski, M., Chavez, N.E., Höllerer, T.: I'm feeling LoCo: A Location Based Context Aware Recommendation System. In: 8th Int. Symposium on LBS, Vienna (2011)
21. Patton, E.W., McGuinness, D.L.: The Mobile Wine Agent: Pairing Wine with the Social Semantic Web. In: 2nd Social Data on the Web Workshop (2009)
22. Choi, O., Kim, K., Wang, D., Yeh, H., Hong, M.: Personalized Mobile Information Retrieval System. Int. Journal of Advanced Robotic Systems (2012)
23. Bouidghaghen, O., Tamine, L., Boughanem, M.: Personalizing Mobile Web Search for Location Sensitive Queries. In: 12th IEEE Int. Conference on Mobile Data Management (2011)
24. Arias, M., Cantera, J.M., Vegas, J.: Context-Based Personalization for Mobile Web Search. In: Very Large Data Bases Conference, Auckland, New Zealand, August 23-28 (2008)
25. Van Woensel, W., Casteleyn, S., De Troyer, O.: Applying semantic web technology in a mobile setting: The person matcher. In: Benatallah, B., Casati, F., Kappel, G., Rossi, G. (eds.) ICWE 2010. LNCS, vol. 6189, pp. 506–509. Springer, Heidelberg (2010)
26. Keßler, C., Raubal, M., Wosniok, C.: Semantic rules for context-aware geographical information retrieval. In: Barnaghi, P., Moessner, K., Presser, M., Meissner, S. (eds.) EuroSSC 2009. LNCS, vol. 5741, pp. 77–92. Springer, Heidelberg (2009)
27. Venezia, C., Licciardi, C.A., Salmeri, A.: Rule based dynamic adaptation of mobile services based on context. In: ICIN (2008)
28. Bayrhammer, K., Grechenig, T., Köstinger, H., Fiedler, M., Schramm, W.: Using a Rule-Based Service Bus for Controlling Dataflows in Patient Centric Hospital Information Systems. In: Proc. of the AMA IEEE Medical Technology Conference 2011. IEEE (2011)
29. Fields, D.K., Kolb, M.A., Bayern, S.: Web Development with Java Server Pages. Manning Publications (2001) ISBN:193011012X
30. Broekstra, J., Kampman, A., van Harmelen, F.: Sesame: An architecture for storing and querying RDF data and schema information. In: Lieberman, H., Fensel, D., Hendler, J., Wahlster, W. (eds.) Semantics for the WWW. MIT Press (2001)
31. Horridge, M., Bechhofer, S.: The OWL API: A Java API for Working with OWL 2 Ontologies. In: OWLED 2009, 6th OWL Experienced and Directions Workshop, Chantilly (2009)
32. Hu, Y.-J., Yeh, C.-L., Laun, W.: Challenges for Rule Systems on the Web. In: Governatori, G., Hall, J., Paschke, A. (eds.) RuleML 2009. LNCS, vol. 5858, pp. 4–16. Springer, Heidelberg (2009)
33. Paschke, A., Kozlenkov, A., Boley, H.: A Homogenous Reaction Rule Language for Complex Event Processing. In: 2nd International Workshop on Event Drive Architecture and Event Processing Systems (EDA-PS 2007), Vienna, Austria (2007)
34. Boley, H., Tabet, S., Wagner, G.: Design Rationale of RuleML: A Markup Language for Semantic Web Rules. In: Proc. SWWS 2001, Stanford (July/August 2001)
35. Hirtle, D.: TRANSLATOR: A TRANSlator from LAnguage TO Rules. In: Proceedings of the Canadian Symposium on Text Analysis, CaSTA (2006)
36. de Sainte Marie, C., Hallmark, G., Paschke, A.: RIF Production Rule Dialect, 2nd edn. W3C Recommendation (February 5, 2013), `http://www.w3.org/TR/rif-prd/`
37. Liang, S., Fodor, P., Wan, H., Kifer, M.: OpenRuleBench: An Analysis of the Performance of Rule Engines. In: WWW 2009, Madrid (2009)
38. Friedman-Hill, E.: Jess in Action. Rule-Based Systems in Java, pp. 32–33. Manning Publications (2003) ISBN-10: 1930110898
39. Giurca, A., Tylkowski, M., Muller, M.: RuleTheWeb!: Rule-based Adaptive User Experience. In: 6th Int. Symposium on Rules, RuleML 2012@ECAI Challenge, Montpellier (2012)

DIESECT: A DIstributed Environment for Simulating E-commerce ContracTs

Damian Wood, Özgür Kafalı, and Kostas Stathis

Department of Computer Science
Royal Holloway, University of London
Egham, TW20 0EX, UK
{damian.wood.2010,ozgur.kafali,kostas.stathis}@cs.rhul.ac.uk

Abstract. We study the development of a distributed, agent-based, simulation environment where autonomous agents execute e-commerce contracts. We present a multi-agent architecture in which contracts are represented as a set of commitments that an agent must be capable of monitoring and reason with in order to be able to verify that the contract is not violated during interaction. We employ the JADE agent platform to build the multi-agent simulation infrastructure, and the Reactive Event Calculus to provide agent reasoning for monitoring and verification of contracts. We then experimentally evaluate the performance of our system by analysing the time and memory requirements as the number of agents increases, and by looking whether the behaviours of agents have any significant effect on the system's overall performance.

Keywords: Agent Technology for E-Commerce, Contracts and Commitments, Distributed Simulation.

1 Introduction

Contracts are normally construed as agreements describing the terms of how two or more parties should act in exchanges between or among them. When a customer wants to buy a book from an online store, the terms of the contract describe how the payment should be done as well as the deadline for the delivery of the book. Unless the customer pays, the contract is not binding for the store. After customer payment the contract is fulfilled - if the store delivers the book on time, or violated - if the store delivers late.

In open environments where autonomous agents collaborate to do business together, contracts describe how agents should act to fulfil their duties. The fulfillment of contracts depends on how agents behave and communicate in the environment. Previous work has considered contract execution either in a centralised manner where a central authority manages contract monitoring for all agents, or without taking into account the effect of agent autonomy for contract outcomes. There has been a plethora of work in the literature for formal modeling of electronic contracts: preparation, negotiation, monitoring [1,2,3,4,5]. Among others, commitments are a widely accepted formalisation of representing contracts in agent-based environments [6]. A commitment binds two agents (e.g. a customer and a store) with a property (e.g. deliver), in which one agent is committed to the other (e.g. by paying) for bringing about the property. For the above example a commitment is represented as:

C. Huemer and P. Lops (Eds.): EC-Web 2013, LNBIP 152, pp. 39–50, 2013.

$$C^{c}_{store,customer}(pay, deliver)$$

That is, the store is committed to deliver the book after payment is completed. The commitment is in conditional state (denoted with the superscript c) until the customer makes the payment. As a result, to effectively monitor and verify contracts amounts to effectively monitoring and verifying commitments.

There has been considerable effort to provide several logic-based tools for monitoring and verification of commitments [7,8,9]. While these tools allow significant results to be achieved in terms of contract execution, e.g., detect violations, diagnose the cause of exceptions, predict future problems, they normally assume the existence of a trace representing the agents' interactions; they are used offline. However, a realistic system should take into account different agent behaviours as well as environmental effects online, when considering contract execution.

Our contribution in this work is two-fold: (i) we integrate agent autonomy with contract execution in order to provide a simulation environment for electronic contracts, (ii) we provide a practical implementation based on the widely-used JADE agent development framework and evaluate our system's performance via experiments. We build upon previous work with commitments to provide an agent-based distributed environment, which we call $\mathcal{DIESECT}$, for the simulation of contract executions in e-commerce. We use the JADE agent platform to build agents, and the Reactive Event Calculus to provide contract monitoring and verification. Our approach combines the strengths of object-oriented programming to provide the infrastructure and network operations for distribution and communication of agents, and logic programming to provide a declarative and efficient way to deal with agent reasoning for contracts. We describe the general architecture and the components for $\mathcal{DIESECT}$. Each agent has a partial view of the environment concerning its own contracts. We use commitments to represent agent contracts. Our contribution is the integration of agent autonomy with contract execution accompanied by a practical implementation.

We provide two sets of experiments to evaluate the performance of our system. The first set is designed to test the system by increasing the number of agents. The second set focuses on the agent behaviour. We take a fixed number of agents and change the agents' behaviours to see whether it has an effect on the system's performance. We record the time it takes to complete simulation and the peak memory usage for the system, and comment on the results.

The rest of the paper is organised as follows. Section 2 reviews relevant background on JADE, commitments and the Reactive Event Calculus. Section 3 introduces a delivery protocol from e-commerce as our running example. Section 4 describes the distributed multi-agent architecture for simulating contract execution. Section 5 shows the performance results for our system. Section 6 reviews related work and concludes the paper.

2 Background

We describe next the background for the infrastructure and main components of our system, by explaining their main characteristics.

2.1 JADE Agent Platform

The JADE[1] agent platform is a distributed Java-based middleware for developing multi-agent systems [10]. We have chosen JADE to develop our agents since it is the most widely used agent platform that provides reliable agent communication and documentation support. JADE consists of a runtime environment, a library of classes which to develop agents, and a set of graphical tools to allow agent administration and monitoring. JADE agents use the FIPA[2] specification to communicate with each other via messages. The platform provides a set of behaviours to describe agent tasks, which the developers can extend to implement their own agent behaviours. It also provides a yellow page service for publish & subscribe type services, allows mobile agents to be developed for J2ME, and has graphical tools for debugging agents during run-time execution. JADE allows agents to be distributed over a network via containers, possibly located in a separate physical machine and holding agents connected to a main container where JADE is initiated from.

2.2 Commitments

A contract describes how the participants should act in a business dealing. We represent contracts with commitments between two agents: the debtor agent commits to the creditor agent about a specific property [6]. Definition 1 defines a commitment formally. Below, X and Y denote agents, Ant and $Cons$ are propositions (either atomic propositions or conjunctions of them).

Definition 1 A commitment $C^S_{X,Y}(Ant, Cons)$ denotes the commitment between the agents X and Y, where S is the state of the commitment. Four commitment states are meaningful for our work: conditional, active, fulfilled and violated. The above is a conditional commitment; if the antecedent Ant is satisfied (i.e., becomes true), then the debtor X becomes committed to the creditor Y for satisfying the consequent $Cons$, and the commitment becomes active. If Ant is already $True$ (denoted $\top$), then this is an active base-level commitment; X is committed to Y for satisfying $Cons$ unconditionally. ▮

We follow the idea and notation of [11] to represent commitments (i.e., every commitment is conditional). A base-level commitment is simply a commitment with its condition being true. Commitments are live objects; we always consider a commitment with its state. The commitment states are demonstrated in Fig. 1. Further details on the use of commitments in multi-agent systems can be found in [6,3,11].

2.3 $\mathcal{R}$eactive $\mathcal{E}$vent $\mathcal{C}$alculus

The Reactive Event Calculus ($\mathcal{REC}$) [12,8] is a logic programming tool that extends the Event Calculus [13] for run-time monitoring, including commitments. When used for monitoring the states of commitments the $\mathcal{REC}$ engine takes as input the following:

[1] `http://jade.tilab.com/`

[2] `http://www.fipa.org/`

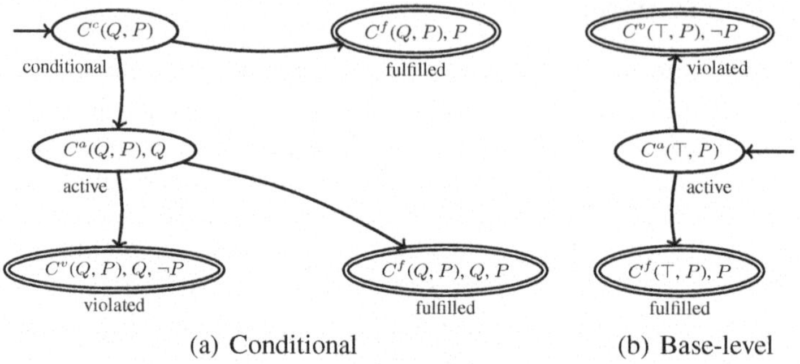

Fig. 1. Commitment states

- a *commitment theory* that contains the rules on how commitments are manipulated, e.g., a commitment is fulfilled when its consequent is satisfied within its deadline. This rule-base is shared amongst all agents. Listing 1 shows part of the implementation for the commitment theory.
- a *protocol description* that contains rules describing the consequences of the agents' actions as well as domain facts, e.g., customer payment makes the commitment for delivery active. This is agent and domain dependent rule-base; each agent has a separate protocol description that relates to its own view. For example, a courier does not know the rules between the customer and the store.
- an *event trace* that contains the actions performed throughout time, e.g., the customer has paid at time 4 , the courier has delivered at time 7. Like protocol descriptions, event traces are also agent-dependent. That is, each agent is aware of only the events that are related to it, but does not see the events that might take place among other agents.

Once the $\mathcal{REC}$ engine is run with above input, it produces an outcome that demonstrates the fluents the agent is aware of through time (e.g., states of commitments). A detailed explanation of how $\mathcal{REC}$ manipulates commitment states can be found in [12].

```
% create as conditional
initiates(E, status(C, conditional), T):- ccreate(E, C, T).

% conditional to active
terminates(E, status(C, conditional), T):- detach(E, C, T).

initiates(E, status(C, active), T):- detach(E, C, T).

detach(E, c(X, Y, property(e(T1, T2), Q), P), T):-
   conditional(c(X, Y, property(e(T1, T2), Q), P), T),
   T >= T1, T =< T2, initiates(E, Q, T).
```

Listing 1. Commitment theory in $\mathcal{REC}$

Commitment tracking with $\mathcal{REC}$ is extended in [2] to integrate exception handling behaviour for agents using an *exception theory* in addition to the above input.

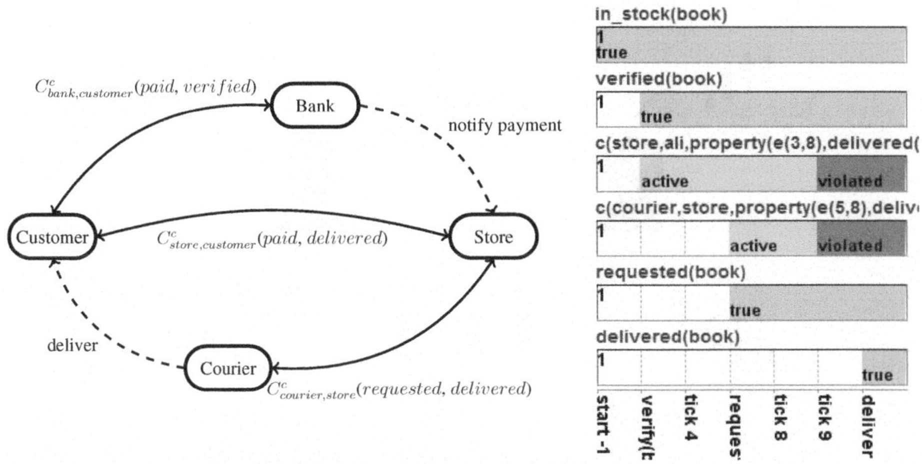

(a) Delivery protocol. (b) $\mathcal{REC}$ output.

Fig. 2. E-commerce protocol

3 Running Example

In the sequel we use a delivery protocol [14] from e-commerce to demonstrate our simulation environment. Figure 2(a) shows the delivery protocol with four parties. In a desired execution, first the customer sends the payment to the bank regarding its purchase of a book from the store (*pay*). Then, the bank verifies the payment of the customer (*verify*), and informs the store about the payment (*notify payment*). Upon receiving the payment, the store requests the delivery of the book from the courier (*request*). Finally, the courier delivers the book to the customer (*deliver*).

```
% payment
initiates(exec(pay(Customer, Bank, Item)), paid(Item), _).

% verification of payment
initiates(exec(verify(Bank, Customer, Item)), verified(Item), _).

% commitment for payment
create(exec(pay(Customer, Bank, Item)), Bank,
   c(Bank, Customer, property(e(Ts, Te), verified(Item))), Ts):-
   Te is Ts + 3.
```

Listing 2. Domain dependent $\mathcal{REC}$ rules for the customer

There are three commitments among the parties that regulate their interactions:

- $C^c_{store,customer}$ $(paid, delivered)$: if the customer pays, the store commits to deliver.
- $C^c_{bank,customer}$ $(paid, verified)$: the customer uses a bank for payment.
- $C^c_{courier,store}$ $(requested, delivered)$: the store delivers via a courier.

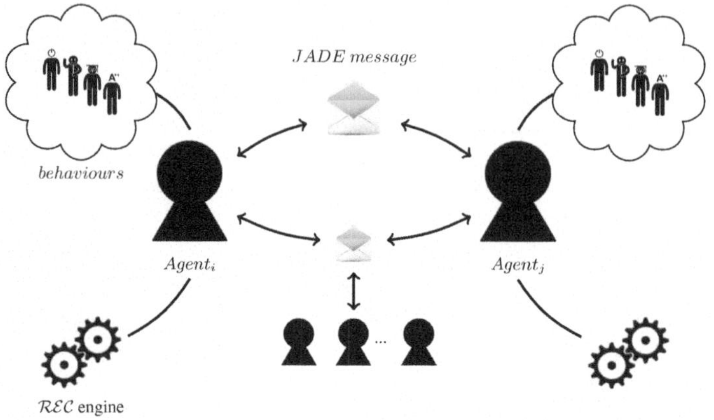

Fig. 3. Distributed architecture for contract execution and monitoring

Listing 2 shows the $\mathcal{REC}$ rules that describe the interaction between the customer and the bank. Fig. 2(b) shows the output of $\mathcal{REC}$ for a sample trace of the protocol. The horizontal axis shows the events that happened throughout time, and the vertical axis demonstrates how fluents (i.e., predicates and commitments) evolve due to the events happened.

4 Multi-agent Simulation Architecture

$\mathcal{DIESECT}$ is a distributed agent-based architecture to simulate e-commerce contracts. Previous work has paid little attention on environments where agents can track down their contracts while they autonomously act within the environment and interact with each other. That is, there are either distributed agent platforms that do not deal with contract execution, or systems that support offline contract monitoring, i.e., given a trace of agent actions that accounts to a predefined scenario designed prior to execution. Among others, the most similar work to ours is that of Faci *et al.* 's [4]. Their focus is on normative multi-agent systems where contracts are described by a set of norms, while we deal with commitment-based protocols. In addition, they provide centralised entities for monitoring of contracts such as observer, manager, contract store. In contrast, execution in our system is fully distributed such that each agent monitors and verifies its own contracts using its partial knowledge of the environment.

Our proposal enables the simulation of distributed contract execution and monitoring for e-commerce protocols by following two directions: (i) we develop a fully distributed multi-agent system using JADE and provide agents with distinguished behaviours (e.g., strategies) that lead to different contract executions, (ii) we enable agents to reason on their contacts throughout execution using logic programming. Fig. 3 depicts the proposed multi-agent architecture. Agents are developed using JADE libraries and combined with logic programming capabilities. The underlying JADE infrastructure enables distributed execution and inter-agent communication (e.g., social aspect) while the powerful temporal reasoning capability allows the agent to perform reasoning on its commitments through time (e.g., individual aspect). Different agent behaviours can be associated with the roles in the protocol, leading to different contract outcomes, as if the agents have a personality that affect how the agent acts during the protocol (e.g., a courier that always delivers on time) [15].

Agents in JADE communicate via messages. Messages correspond to executed actions among agents. For example, when the customer pays for a book, this corresponds to a message from the customer agent to the bank agent with the content payment. Actions have consequences in terms of changes in the environment: (i) they cause fluents to be initiated or terminated, e.g., the payment action causes the fluent *paid* to be initiated, (ii) they also caused related commitments to change states, e.g., the payment action causes the commitment of store to become active since its antecedent is satisfied. These are handled by the $\mathcal{REC}$ reasoner component of an agent. At certain points in time, the agent may run its $\mathcal{REC}$ engine to check the states of its commitments. In order to do so, the agent creates a trace of events using its message history. Each agent has a separate $\mathcal{REC}$ engine that it can run at any time throughout the execution. Thus, an agent operates only with partial information that it has gained through messages in the environment.

```
<simulation>
 <agents>
  <customer name="bob" eagerness="0.3" lateness="0.0">
   <wanteditems><product name="ipad"/></wanteditems>
  </customer>

  <store name="ebay" eagerness="0.0" lateness="0.0" bank="hsbc" courier="ups">
   <inventory>
    <product name="ipad" deliveryCost="5" price="450"/>
    <product name="iphone" deliveryCost="5" price="350"/>
   </inventory>
  </store>

  <bank name="hsbc" eagerness="0.0" lateness="0.0"/>

  <courier name="ups" eagerness="0.0" lateness="0.2"/>
 </agents>
</simulation>
```

Listing 3. A simulation profile

A simulation can then be run in one of three modes:

- *Manual* mode: where the user increments the simulation clock and selects what actions the agents should perform at each timestep. Note that with this mode, we can simulate what has already been proposed by existing systems, e.g., test specific execution traces offline that would lead to different contract outcomes.
- *Simulation* mode: where agents schedule their actions to be executed at a specific timestep and perform them autonomously according to a customised simulation profile. A sample profile is given in Listing 3. Note that this mode can be used to test different agent behaviours online, and see how contract execution is affected.

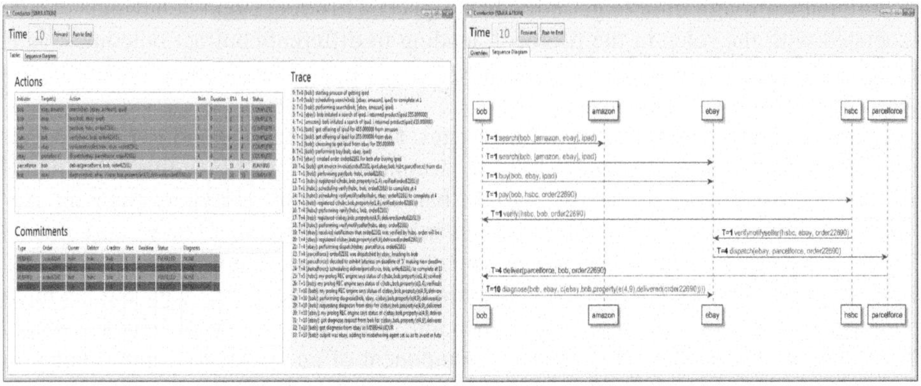

Fig. 4. $\mathcal{DIESECT}$ simulation panel

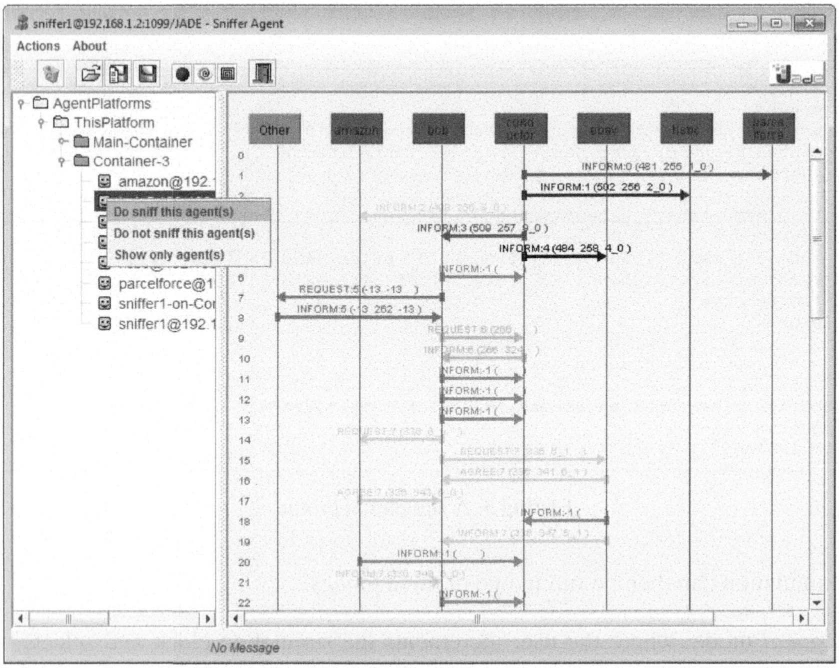

Fig. 5. JADE sniffer agent used in $\mathcal{DIESECT}$

– *Silent* mode: where the user again initiates the simulation by selecting a profile and the system carries it out automatically. In this mode, the interface is not shown but rather text-based statistics are logged after the simulation is finished. We use this mode to evaluate performance.

The manual and simulation modes provide a graphical demonstration of how the protocol is executed. Fig. 4 demonstrates this simulation panel after the execution is started. The current simulation time is displayed at the top left. The user can press the "Forward" button to advance simulation time. In simulation mode, the user can press the "Run to End" button to make the simulation cycle through each timestep until the end of it.

The "Actions" panel shows running actions in yellow and completed in green, while the "Commitments" panel shows active commitments in yellow, fulfilled commitments in green and violated commitments in red. The status column of the "Commitments" panel shows the status of the commitment that the agent's $\mathcal{REC}$ engine has determined[3].

The sequence diagram shows the ordering of agents' actions through time. Completed actions are represented in green text, while running actions are represented with blue. If operating in manual mode, the user may either click a blue action text on the sequence diagram to trigger its completion, or double click the action in the top table. Note that the underlying JADE environment also allows us to utilise the *sniffer* agent which helps debug and diagnose certain exceptions regarding the messaging of agents, see Fig. 5.

5 Experimental Evaluation

We carry out two sets of experiments to test the performance of our agents: (i) with increasing number of agents, (ii) with different agent behaviours. We run simulations in silent mode on an Intel Core2 Quad 2.40 GHz computer with 4 GB of memory running Windows 7 64-bit OS. We repeat each experiment five times and record the average statistics for (i) the time it takes for the agents to complete the simulation, and (ii) the peak memory usage of the system.

5.1 Increasing Agents

For the first set of experiments, we gradually increase the number of agents to test how it affects the system's overall performance. Fig. 6 shows the performance results for 10 to 140 customer agents with the addition of two store agents, one bank agent and one courier agent. We record the time it takes in seconds to complete simulation, and the peak memory usage in megabytes. It can be seen that there is a linear increase for memory usage, and the time requirements stay within reasonable values for a considerable number of agents executing an e-commerce protocol. Note that these results are compatible with the performance of $\mathcal{REC}$ discussed in [16].

5.2 Different Agent Behaviours

For the second set of experiments, we take 30 customer agents (again with the addition of other agents as above), and change the simulation profile by assigning different behaviours to the agents. Fig. 7 shows the performance results for changing behaviours of each agent type. It can be seen that there is no significant difference in performance, and the results are compatible with the previous one with 30 customer agents.

[3] The complete implementation with sample simulation profiles for 𝒟ℐℰ𝒮ℰ𝒞𝒯 can be downloaded from `http://dice.cs.rhul.ac.uk/article.php?id=7`.

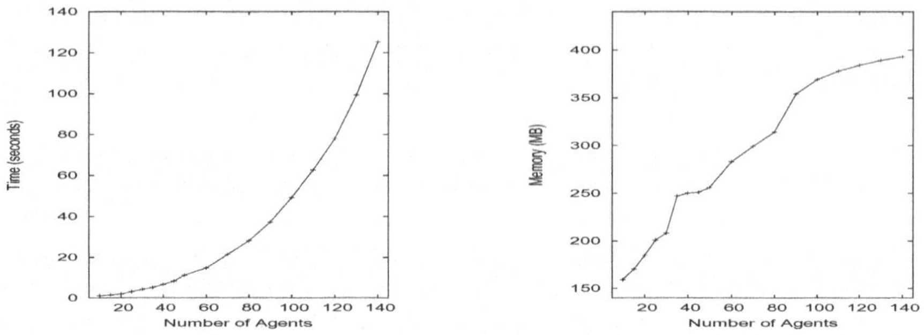

Fig. 6. Performance of $\mathcal{DIESECT}$ for increasing number of agents. The figure on the left shows time it takes to complete simulation while the figure on the right shows peak memory usage.

Agent behaviour	Time (s)	Memory (mb)
Customer eagerness 100%	5.62	218
Customer eagerness 50%	4.63	207
Bank lateness 100%	3.87	208
Bank lateness 50%	4.02	211
Store lateness 100%	3.41	217
Store lateness 50%	4.30	213
Courier lateness 100%	3.98	208
Courier lateness 50%	4.27	210

Fig. 7. Performance of $\mathcal{DIESECT}$ for different agent behaviours. The time and memory values are recorded for full and half eagerness / lateness.

6 Discussion

In this paper, we have presented $\mathcal{DIESECT}$ to provide a distributed simulation environment for contract execution and monitoring. Contracts have been discussed extensively in the literature in the context of business workflows [17,1,18], modeling, execution and exceptions [19,7,2], and ontologies [20]. However, most of these work have either approached contract monitoring in a centralised manner ignoring the distributed aspect of open systems where the contents of a contract should be kept private among its participants, and thus be managed individually by each agent, or they have failed to the take into account the relation between agent autonomy and contract outcomes in their systems. Here, we present a simulation environment where the autonomous behaviour of an agent may lead to different contract outcomes during execution.

Commitments are proven to be effective in modeling multi-agent interactions [6,3]. In central monitoring systems, tracking the states of individual commitments is an effective way to detect protocol exceptions [8], since all the interactions of agents are observable. However, this is not a valid assumption for realistic e-commerce scenarios. In our system, each agent has forms a partial view of its environment via interacting with other agents through JADE messages.

Normative multi-agent systems are an alternative to commitment-based protocols, where artificial institutions and organisations are modeled via norms rather than commitments [21,22,4]. Similar to commitments, norms represent obligations for agents to follow, but they also possess additional properties like power, which is needed to represent the hierarchical behaviour in organisations, e.g., whether an agent possessing a certain role can enforce a norm. In this paper, we do not consider power or the hierarchy among agents when managing commitments.

We have shown via two sets of experiments that (i) our systems performs well under increasing number of agents (with a linear increase in memory usage and reasonable simulation times), and (ii) the changing of agent behaviours does not have a significant effect on the system's performance. We plan to extend 𝒟ℐℰ𝒮ℰ𝒞𝒯 with the following possible extensions:

- We aim for a generic contract execution and monitoring environment where protocols can be described by defining commitment templates and the associated agent roles. We are currently working on this direction so that new e-commerce protocols can be created and tested in our platform.
- We use ℛℰ𝒞 as the current reasoning mechanism for agents to detect and diagnose commitment violations. Another interesting direction for contract execution is to predict that a commitment might be violated in the future. One powerful tool for such prediction is model checking [23,9]. Model checking is based on temporal logic, and creates possible future worlds given an initial world model and a set of transition rules. We plan to integrate the model checking capability besides ℛℰ𝒞 into the agents' reasoning. By doing so, we could report on the soundness of the system, i.e., whether commitments reach their final states.
- We plan to extend our performance evaluation by distinguishing between the time spent on JADE side and the time spent for executing ℛℰ𝒞. This will provide insight on how to improve the system's overall performance, e.g., agents might not execute ℛℰ𝒞 at each timestep. We also plan to run experiments with larger agent populations and report the communication costs among agents.

References

1. Krishna, P.R., Karlapalem, K., Chiu, D.K.W.: An erec framework for e-contract modeling, enactment and monitoring. Data Knowl. Eng. 51(1), 31–58 (2004)
2. Kafalı, Ö., Torroni, P.: Exception diagnosis in multiagent contract executions. Annals of Mathematics and Artificial Intelligence 64(1), 73–107 (2012)
3. Yolum, P., Singh, M.P.: Flexible protocol specification and execution: Applying event calculus planning using commitments. In: Proceedings of the 1st International Conference on Autonomous Agents and Multiagent Systems (AAMAS), pp. 527–534 (2002)
4. Faci, N., Modgil, S., Oren, N., Meneguzzi, F., Miles, S., Luck, M.: Towards a monitoring framework for agent-based contract systems. In: Klusch, M., Pěchouček, M., Polleres, A. (eds.) CIA 2008. LNCS (LNAI), vol. 5180, pp. 292–305. Springer, Heidelberg (2008)
5. McGinnis, J., Stathis, K., Toni, F.: A formal model of agent-oriented virtual organisations and their formation. Multiagent and Grid Systems 7(6), 291–310 (2011)
6. Singh, M.P.: An ontology for commitments in multiagent systems: Toward a unification of normative concepts. Artificial Intelligence and Law 7, 97–113 (1999)

7. Kafalı, Ö., Yolum, P.: A distributed treatment of exceptions in multiagent contracts. In: Proceedings of the 9th International Workshop on Declarative Agent Languages and Technologies, DALT (2011)
8. Chesani, F., Mello, P., Montali, M., Torroni, P.: Commitment tracking via the reactive event calculus. In: Proceedings of the 21st International Joint Conference on Artifical Intelligence (IJCAI), pp. 91–96 (2009)
9. El Menshawy, M., Bentahar, J., Qu, H., Dssouli, R.: On the verification of social commitments and time. In: Proceedings of the 10th International Conference on Autonomous Agents and Multiagent Systems (AAMAS), pp. 483–490 (2011)
10. Bellifemine, F., Poggi, A., Rimassa, G., Turci, P.: An object-oriented framework to realize agent systems. In: WOA Workshop: From Objects to Agents, pp. 52–57 (2000)
11. Chopra, A.K., Singh, M.P.: Multiagent commitment alignment. In: Proceedings of the 8th International Conference on Autonomous Agents and Multiagent Systems (AAMAS), pp. 937–944 (2009)
12. Chesani, F., Mello, P., Montali, M., Torroni, P.: Monitoring time-aware social commitments with reactive event calculus. In: 20th European Meeting on Cybernetics and Systems Research, 7th International Symposium "From Agent Theory to Agent Implementation" (AT2AI-7), pp. 447–452 (2010)
13. Kowalski, R., Sergot, M.: A logic-based calculus of events. New Generation Computing 4(1), 67–95 (1986)
14. Malone, T.W., Crowston, K., Herman, G. (eds.): Organizing Business Knowledge: The MIT Process Handbook. MIT Press, Cambridge (2003)
15. Kakas, A.C., Mancarella, P., Sadri, F., Stathis, K., Toni, F.: Declarative agent control. In: Leite, J., Torroni, P. (eds.) CLIMA 2004. LNCS (LNAI), vol. 3487, pp. 96–110. Springer, Heidelberg (2005)
16. Bragaglia, S., Chesani, F., Mello, P., Montali, M., Torroni, P.: Reactive event calculus for monitoring global computing applications. In: Artikis, A., Craven, R., Kesim Çiçekli, N., Sadighi, B., Stathis, K. (eds.) Sergot Festschrift 2012. LNCS (LNAI), vol. 7360, pp. 123–146. Springer, Heidelberg (2012)
17. Grefen, P., Aberer, K., Ludwig, H., Hoffner, Y.: Crossflow: Cross-organizational workflow management in dynamic virtual enterprises. International Journal of Computer Systems Science & Engineering 15, 277–290 (2000)
18. Urovi, V., Stathis, K.: Playing with agent coordination patterns in MAGE. In: Padget, J., Artikis, A., Vasconcelos, W., Stathis, K., da Silva, V.T., Matson, E., Polleres, A. (eds.) COIN 2009. LNCS, vol. 6069, pp. 86–101. Springer, Heidelberg (2010)
19. Molina-jimenez, C., Shrivastava, S., Solaiman, E., Warne, J.: Contract representation for run-time monitoring and enforcement. In: Proc. IEEE Int. Conf. on E-Commerce (CEC), pp. 103–110. IEEE (2003)
20. Grosof, B.N., Poon, T.C.: Sweetdeal: Representing agent contracts with exceptions using xml rules, ontologies, and process descriptions, pp. 340–349. ACM Press (2003)
21. Sadri, F., Stathis, K., Toni, F.: Normative KGP agents. Computational & Mathematical Organization Theory 12(2-3), 101–126 (2006)
22. Fornara, N., Colombetti, M.: Specifying and enforcing norms in artificial institutions. In: Proceedings of the 7th International Joint Conference on Autonomous Agents and Multiagent Systems (AAMAS), pp. 1481–1484 (2008)
23. Kafalı, Ö., Günay, A., Yolum, P.: $\mathcal{PROTOSS}$: A run time tool for detecting $\mathcal{PR}$ivacy vi$\mathcal{O}$la$\mathcal{T}$ions in $\mathcal{O}$nline $\mathcal{S}$ocial network$\mathcal{S}$. In: IEEE/ACM International Conference on Advances in Social Networks Analysis and Mining (2012)

Semi-automated Structural Adaptation of Advanced E-Commerce Ontologies

Marek Dudáš[1], Vojtěch Svátek[1], László Török[2], Ondřej Zamazal[1], Benedicto Rodriguez-Castro[2], and Martin Hepp[2]

[1] University of Economics Prague, Nám. W. Churchilla 4, 13067 Praha 3, Czech Rep.
{xdudm12,svatek,ondrej.zamazal}@vse.cz

[2] Univ.der Bundeswehr Munich, W.-Heisenberg-Weg 39, 85579 Neubiberg, Germany
{laszlo.toeroek,bene.rodriguez,martin.hepp}@unibw.de

Abstract. Most ontologies used in e-commerce are nowadays taxonomies with simple structure and loose semantics. One exception is the OPDM collection of ontologies, which express rich information about product categories and their parameters for a number of domains. Yet, having been created by different designers and with specific bias, such ontologies could still benefit from semi-automatic post-processing. We demonstrate how the versatile *PatOMat* framework for pattern-based ontology transformation can be exploited for suppressing incoherence within the collection and for adapting the ontologies for an unforeseen purpose.

Keywords: ontology, e-commerce, GoodRelations, transformation, ontology pattern, linked data.

1 Introduction

The idea that well-designed, structurally rich ontologies would allow to partially automate e-commerce operations has been around for years [1]. Nevertheless, even nowadays, most ontologies exploited in this field are plain taxonomies with imprecise semantics. Proposals for sophisticated modeling remain at the level of academic prototypes, or, at most, are used in closed B2B settings [5].

The *GoodRelations* (GR) ontology [3] has been conceived, as an attempt to balance expressiveness and practical usability, with size comparable to popular linked data vocabularies[1], OWL ontology language[2] expressivity and stress on favorable learning curve thanks to a cookbook with a number of recipes.[3] As 'vertical' extensions to GR, ontologies for specific product/service categories then started to be developed, most recently within the *Ontology-Based Product Data Management* (OPDM) project.[4] This family of ontologies already enjoyed

[1] http://lov.okfn.org/dataset/lov/

[2] http://www.w3.org/TR/owl2-overview/

[3] http://wiki.goodrelations-vocabulary.org/Cookbook

[4] http://www.opdm-project.org/

C. Huemer and P. Lops (Eds.): EC-Web 2013, LNBIP 152, pp. 51–58, 2013.

industrial adoption, such as the car sales ontology used by a major automotive manufacturer.[5]

In this paper we focus on two aspects of such product ontologies for which further enhancement is possible. First, the rapid pace of creation of the ontologies and involvement of multiple designers in parallel occasionally leads to *incoherence* in modeling patterns and naming conventions, both within a single ontology and across a set of them. Second, some of their features are compromises between the best practices for publishing linked data [2] and somewhat different requirements imposed by the e-commerce and web engineering worlds, given they are to be used in direct integration with web-based product catalogs. Therefore they need to be adapted in order to be used in a 'canonical' linked data setting.

As either kind of structural adaptation potentially involves a wide scope of restructuring and renaming operations, it can benefit from application of a user-friendly ontology transformation framework. Such framework has been recently developed under the name of *PatOMat* [6,8]. In the rest of the paper we first describe the material, i.e., the GoodRelations ontology and the product ontologies based on it (Section 2). Then we present the incoherence problems of both types discovered in the product ontologies (Section 3). Next, the principles of the PatOMat framework and its user interfaces are briefly reviewed (Section 4), and its application on the OPDM ontologies is described (Section 5). Finally, the paper is wrapped up (Section 6).

2 GoodRelations and Product Ontologies

GoodRelations (further GR) is a generic ontology for e-commerce, which offers conceptual elements to capture facts that are most relevant for exchanging arbitrary goods and services. The core model revolves around the abstraction that an *agent* offers to transfer certain *rights* related to a *product* or *service* [3]. This model is independent of a particular e-commerce domain, since the agent can be any commercial entity making the offer, and rights transferring can range from simple *sale* to *rental* or *leasing*. GR includes generic conceptual elements for products and services and their properties (including prices, delivery or warranty conditions etc.), but no domain-specific product classes or taxonomies.

A premier use case for GR is adding semantic annotation to of e-commerce *web sites*. Aside the website-level application, there are also domain-specific extensions of GR that can be used within e-commerce *business information systems* as a common data schema that all software services support. Product data available in many systems is often unstructured or incomplete. As sophisticated automated business processes require precise, highly structured data, they are likely to benefit from ontologies capturing data about products from particular domains. *OPDM ontologies*, designed to fulfil this need, extend a subset of GR: domain-specific *product classes* are subclasses of `gr:ProductOrService`, *product properties* are subproperties of `gr:quantitativeProductOrServiceProperty`

[5] `http://www.w3.org/2001/sw/sweo/public/UseCases/Volkswagen/`

or its 'quantitative' or 'datatype' counterparts,[6] and a few *generic properties* such as color, dimension or weight are directly reused from the GR ontology. The ontologies are self-contained, and capture the most frequently occurring properties of each particular product type.

3 Incoherence Problems in OPDM Ontologies

3.1 Incoherence Types Considered

When an OWL ontology is being developed, there is often more than one option how to model a specific concept or structure, due to high expressiveness of the language. Modeling incoherence may thus arise when such modeling options differ for concepts/structure of similar nature. The fact that OPDM ontologies are all grafted upon the GR ontology somewhat alleviates this problem. Nevertheless, there is still space for incoherence; both at *structural* level, e.g., using a datatype property instead of object property, or at the level of *naming conventions*, such as arbitrarily switching between synonymous lexical constructs.

Another way of incoherence classification is according to the situation in which a particular part of an ontology is considered 'incoherent'. Due to the large number of OPDM ontologies and involvement of multiple designers, *intrinsic incoherence* may easily occur, which is a term we suggest for unintentional heterogeneous modeling occurring either within a single ontology or within a collection of ontologies typically presented together (such as the OPDM collection). On the other hand, if the ontologies are to be used outside the original context, it is likely that one will run into what we call *export-based extrinsic incoherence*. Finally, we could also consider *import-based extrinsic incoherence*, which occurs when legacy ontologies have to be adapted to a 'canonical' modeling style (here, the style pre-supposed by GR).[7] In the rest of this section we discuss examples[8] of different types of incoherence in the context of OPDM ontologies.[9]

3.2 Intrinsinc Incoherence

Intrinsic structural incoherence. One example of intrinsic structural incoherence is related to modeling the support of various media data types (e.g., GIF, JPEG, AVI etc.) available in an electronic device. There are several ontologies in the OPDM project that cover the described concept (ontologies of computers, cameras, bluray players, portable media players etc.), and as the OPDM ontologies

[6] We omit their full names for typographic reasons – excessive length.

[7] Pre-cursor work on resolving import-based extrinsic incoherence (though not labeled by this term) at a generic level – with 'canonical' modeling defined by ontology content design patterns – is described in [9].

[8] A longer version of this article with more examples is available at`http://nb.vse.cz/svabo/patomat/tp/opdm/ecweb13su.pdf`.

[9] In all examples, local entities from the individual OPDM ontologies are without prefix, while the GR ontology entities are presented with their usual `gr` prefix.

are not modular and are designed to be used independently, the same concept has been designed separately in each ontology. In most of the ontologies there is a class `MediaFormat`, with instances JPEG, GIF, AVI etc., as well as an object property `playbackFormat`, which has the class `MediaType` as its range. In one of the ontologies, however, a different approach is used: there is a boolean data property for each of the media data types. So, for example, the fact that a hypothetical portable media player supports AVI would be expressed as `player playbackFormat AVI` in the former case and as `player AVI true` in the latter. We will refer to this incoherence pattern as to 'boolean vs. instance'.

3.3 Extrinsic Structural Incoherence

An example of extrinsic structural incoherence comes from considerations of using OPDM ontologies in an 'orthodox' linked data environment. A very relevant opportunity for advanced product ontologies is, for example, their use by an application for *public contracts* management. The *Public Contracts Ontology*[10] designed within the EU LOD2 project, as well as the processing tools that provision RDF data according to this ontology [4], strictly adhere to the linked data principles, which suggest using object properties rather than data properties.[11] Each OPDM ontology is meant to be used independently, outside the linked data cloud, and barriers for their usage by practitioners (unfamiliar with semantic web technologies) is lowered as much as possible, hence most of the properties are datatype properties. This makes them easy to populate with 'instances' in the form of literals; however, in the linked data environment, the benefits of *interlinking* could not be exploited.

4 PatOMat Framework for Ontology Transformation

The central notion in the *PatOMat* framework[12] is that of *transformation pattern* (TP). A TP contains two *ontology patterns* (the source OP and the target OP) and the description of transformation between them, called *pattern transformation* (PT). The representation of OPs is based on the OWL 2 DL profile, except that *placeholders* are allowed in addition to concrete OWL entities. An OP consists of *entity declarations* (of placeholders and/or concrete entities), *axioms* and *naming detection patterns* (NDP); the last capture the naming aspect of the OP, which is important for its detection. A PT consists of a set of *transformation links* and a set of *naming transformation patterns* (NTP). Transformation links are either *logical equivalence relationships* or *extralogical relationships* (holding between two entities of different type, thus also called 'heterogeneous equivalence').

[10] `http://code.google.com/p/public-contracts-ontology/`

[11] The use of object properties allows for explicitly referring to resources (ontological instances) from external datasets.

[12] [8] provides details about the initial version of the framework, [6] about the user-oriented tools, and at `http://owl.vse.cz:8080/tutorial/` there is a fully-fledged tutorial for the current version.

Naming transformation patterns serve for generating names for target entities. Naming patterns range from *passive naming operations*, such as detection of a head noun for a noun phrase, to *active naming operations*, such as derivation of verb form of a noun. Syntactically, the patterns are expressed according to an XML schema[13] However, the patterns needn't be edited manually, as a graphical editor is available for their authoring.[14] The framework prototype implementation is available either as a *Java library* or as three *RESTful services*.[15] The Java library is used by the GUIPOT tool[16] and other transformation GUIs.

The framework has already been used in multiple use cases, such as:

- Adaptation of the style of an ontology to another one to which it is to be *matched* [8]
- Adaptation of the style of a legacy ontology to a best-practice content pattern being *imported* into it [9]
- *Repair* use cases, including downgrading of an ontology to a less expressive dialect of OWL [7] or entity naming canonicalization [10].

5 Pattern-Based Transformation of OPDM Ontologies

5.1 Selected Transformation in Depth

Transformation patterns were designed for all of the previously described incoherence cases. One of them[17] is presented in this section in detail.

Transformation for 'boolean vs. instance' This incoherence case requires a transformation of boolean data properties to instances of a new `MediaFormat` class, while also adding a property such as `playbackFormat`, whose range is this class. It can be achieved using the transformation pattern in Fig. 1.[18] The source pattern thereof fits all boolean (as specified in the first axiom) subproperties of `gr:datatypeProductOrServiceProperty` (specified in the second axiom), of which those representing media types have to be selected (currently, manually). The rest of the transformation is performed automatically according to the target ontology pattern and the pattern transformation parts of the transformation pattern, as shown below. The role of the two axioms concerning annotations (labels and comments) is to transfer them to the target transformed ontology. The purpose of the last axiom in the source pattern is to keep the information about the domain of the transformed data property (i.e., some product class) in the placeholder `?pc`. It will be used to set the domain of the newly created object property `playbackFormat`, whose range will be the newly created `MediaFormat`

[13] `http://nb.vse.cz/~svabo/patomat/tp/tp-schema.xsd`
[14] `http://owl.vse.cz:8080/tpe/`
[15] All accessible via the web interface at `http://owl.vse.cz:8080/`.
[16] `http://owl.vse.cz:8080/GUIPOT/`
[17] All patterns are in full extent at `http://nb.vse.cz/~svabo/patomat/tp/opdm/`.
[18] The | symbols are not part of the code: they only mark elements that are referred to in the explanatory text.

```
<op1>
   <entity_declarations>
    <placeholder type="DatatypeProperty">?m</placeholder>
    <placeholder type="Literal">?a1</placeholder>
    <placeholder type="Literal">?a2</placeholder>
    <placeholder type="Class">?pc</placeholder>
    <entity type="Class">&xsd;boolean</entity>
    <entity type="DatatypeProperty">
         &gr;datatypeProductOrServiceProperty</entity>
    <entity type="AnnotationProperty">&rdfs;label</entity>
    <entity type="AnnotationProperty">&rdfs;comment</entity>
   </entity_declarations>
   <axioms>
    <axiom>DataProperty: ?m Range: boolean</axiom>
    <axiom>DataProperty: ?m SubPropertyOf:
         datatypeProductOrServiceProperty</axiom>
    <axiom>DataProperty: ?m Annotations: label ?a1</axiom>
    <axiom>DataProperty: ?m Annotations: comment ?a2</axiom>
    <axiom>DataProperty: ?m Domain: ?pc</axiom>
   </axioms>
 </op1>
<op2>
   <entity_declarations>
    <placeholder type="Individual">?OP2_m</placeholder>
    <placeholder type="Class">?OP2_C</placeholder>
    <placeholder type="ObjectProperty">?OP2_p</placeholder>
    <placeholder type="Literal">?OP2_a1</placeholder>
    <placeholder type="Literal">?OP2_a2</placeholder>
    <placeholder type="Class">?OP2_pc</placeholder>
    <entity type="ObjectProperty">
         &gr;qualitativeProductOrServiceProperty</entity>
   </entity_declarations>
   <axioms>
    <axiom>Individual: ?OP2_m Types: ?OP2_C</axiom>
    <axiom>ObjectProperty: ?OP2_p SubPropertyOf:
         qualitativeProductOrServiceProperty</axiom>
    <axiom>Individual: ?OP2_m Annotations: label ?OP2_a1</axiom>
    <axiom>Individual: ?OP2_m Annotations: comment ?OP2_a2</axiom>
    <axiom>ObjectProperty: ?OP2_p Domain: ?OP2_pc</axiom>
    <axiom>ObjectProperty: ?OP2_p Range: ?OP2_C</axiom>
   </axioms>
 </op2>
 <pt>
   <eqHet op1="?m" op2="?OP2_m"/> <eq op1="?a1" op2="?OP2_a1" />
   <eq op1="?a2" op2="?OP2_a2" /> <eq op1="?pc" op2="?OP2_pc" />
   <ntp entity="?OP2_C">MediaFormat</ntp>
   <ntp entity="?OP2_p">playbackFormat</ntp>
   <ntp entity="?OP2_a1">"+?a1+"</ntp>
   <ntp entity="?OP2_a2">"+?a2+"</ntp>
 </pt>
```

Fig. 1. Pattern for transforming (media type) boolean properties to instances

class; its instances arise from the transformed data properties. All the datatype properties `?m` selected in the previous step are transformed into instances `?OP2_m` of class `MediaFormat`, which is created as a new entity. The selected properties `?m` are removed from the ontology and replaced with instances `?OP2_m`. Axioms describing `?m` are also removed except labels and comments (as mentioned above), which are connected to the newly created instances `?OP2_m`. The `playbackFormat` object property (represented by placeholder `?OP2_p`) is created, its domain set to `?OP2_pc` – the domain of the transformed data property – and its range to `?OP2_C` – the newly created `MediaClass`.

5.2 Transformation Pattern Application Using GUIPOT

As one of the user-oriented add-ons [6] to the PatOMat framework we developed the Graphical User Interface for Pattern-based Ontology Transformation (GUIPOT), as means for comfortable application of transformation patterns. GUIPOT is a plugin for Protégé.

After loading a transformation pattern it displays a list of pattern instances of the source OP detected in the given ontology: see the upper-center of the screen in Fig. 2, for an application of the 'boolean vs. instance' pattern. By selecting one or more instances, the detected entities are highlighted in the hierarchical view of the ontology in the left part of the plugin window. The right part of the window shows the ontology after the transformation with entities that were affected (changed or added) by the transformation marked with red arrows.

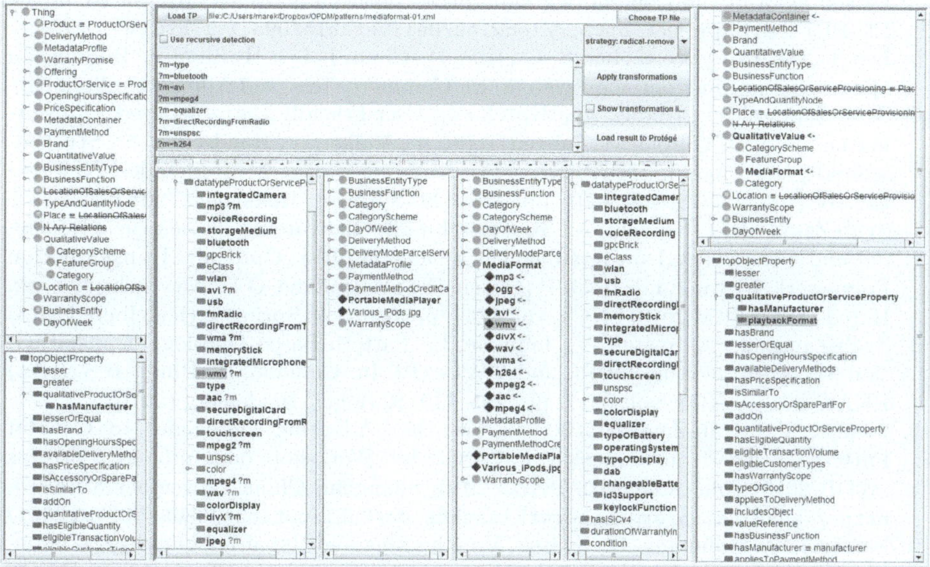

Fig. 2. Processing of 'boolean vs. instance' pattern by GUIPOT

6 Conclusions and Future Work

The presented research leverages on several years of research on both e-commerce ontology principles and ontology transformation techniques. It aims to provide collections of product ontologies with better internal coherence as well as external reusability, in particular, in the linked data world.

In the future, we also plan to address *import-based extrinsic incoherence*, i.e., adaptation of various legacy ontologies to GR-based modeling. Presumably, the design of ontologies for *novel domains* of products and services (such as the building industry, which plays an important role in public procurement) will also bring into light novel kinds of pattern, thus leading to enrichment of the transformation pattern library. The proliferation of specific transformation patterns will also need to be backed by a user-friendly *pattern portal* integrated with the mainstream ontology pattern portal.[19]

References

1. Ding, Y., Fensel, D., Klein, M., Omelayenko, B., Schulten, E.: The role of ontologies in e-Commerce. In: Handbook on Ontologies. Springer (2004)
2. Heath, T., Bizer, C.: Linked Data: Evolving the Web into a Global Data Space, 1st edn. Morgan & Claypool (2011)
3. Hepp, M.: GoodRelations: An Ontology for Describing Products and Services Offers on the Web. In: Gangemi, A., Euzenat, J. (eds.) EKAW 2008. LNCS (LNAI), vol. 5268, pp. 329–346. Springer, Heidelberg (2008)
4. Klímek, J., Knap, T., Mynarz, J., Nečaský, M., Svátek, V.: Framework for Creating Linked Data in the Domain of Public Sector Contracts. Deliverable 9a.1.1 of the EU FP7 LOD2 project, `http://lod2.eu/Deliverable/D9a.1.1.html`
5. Lee, T., Lee, I.-H., Lee, S., Lee, S.-G., Kim, D., Chun, J., Lee, H., Shim, J.: Building an operational product ontology system. El. Commerce Res. and App. 5, 16–28 (2006)
6. Šváb-Zamazal, O., Dudáš, M., Svátek, V.: User-Friendly Pattern-Based Transformation of OWL Ontologies. In: ten Teije, A., Völker, J., Handschuh, S., Stuckenschmidt, H., d'Acquin, M., Nikolov, A., Aussenac-Gilles, N., Hernandez, N. (eds.) EKAW 2012. LNCS, vol. 7603, pp. 426–429. Springer, Heidelberg (2012)
7. Šváb-Zamazal, O., Schlicht, A., Stuckenschmidt, H., Svátek, V.: Constructs Replacing and Complexity Downgrading via a Generic OWL Ontology Transformation Framework. In: van Emde Boas, P., Groen, F.C.A., Italiano, G.F., Nawrocki, J., Sack, H. (eds.) SOFSEM 2013. LNCS, vol. 7741, pp. 528–539. Springer, Heidelberg (2013)
8. Šváb-Zamazal, O., Svátek, V., Iannone, L.: Pattern-Based Ontology Transformation Service Exploiting OPPL and OWL-API. In: Cimiano, P., Pinto, H.S. (eds.) EKAW 2010. LNCS, vol. 6317, pp. 105–119. Springer, Heidelberg (2010)
9. Svátek, V., Šváb-Zamazal, O., Vacura, M.: Adapting Ontologies to Content Patterns using Transformation Patterns. In: Workshop on Ontology Patterns (WOP 2010) collocated with ISWC 2010, Shanghai, China, November 8 (2010), `http://sunsite.informatik.rwth-aachen.de/Publications/CEUR-WS/Vol-671/`
10. Zamazal, O., Bühmann, L., Svátek, V.: Checking and Repairing Ontological Naming Patterns using ORE and PatOMat. In: WoDOOM 2013, Workshop at ESWC 2013 (2013)

[19] `http://ontologydesignpatterns.org`

SDRule-L: Managing Semantically Rich Business Decision Processes

Yan Tang Demey and Christophe Debruyne

Semantics Technology & Application Research Lab,
Department of Computer Science, Vrije Universiteit Brussel,
Pleinlaan 2, 1050 Brussels, Belgium
{yan.tang,christophe.debruyne}@vub.ac.be

Abstract. Semantic Decision Rule Language (SDRule-L) is an extension to Object-Role Modelling language (ORM), which is one of the most popular fact based, graphical modelling languages for designing information systems. In this paper, we want to discuss how SDRule-L models can be formalized, analysed and applied in a business context. An SDRule-L model may contain *static* (e.g., data constraints) and *dynamic* rules (e.g., sequence of events). A reasoning engine is created for detecting inconsistency. When an SDRule-L model is used to manage linked data, a feasible way is to align SDRule-L with Semantic Web languages, e.g. OWL. In order to achieve this, we propose to map dynamic rules into a combination of static rules and queries for detecting anomalies. In this paper, we will illustrate a model reification algorithm for automatically transforming SDRule-L models that contain dynamic rules into the ones containing static rules, which can be formalized in Description Logic.

Keywords: business process modelling, fact based modelling, Description Logic, semantic decision support.

1 Introduction

Ontologies can be applied in many fields, such as system engineering, requirement analysis, bioinformatics, information categorization and Semantic Web (SW). One interesting and appealing domain is semantic decision support (SDS) for business, which can be further considered as a means to enhance decision support using business domain knowledge. We call a system for SDS as SDSS, with which we can assist communications between decision makers by enhancing the shareability and improve interoperabilities among business decision tools and services.

A fundamental requirement of SDSS is that its business semantics that is important to make a decision must be properly captured. In order to fulfil this need, we use Semantic Decision Rule Language (SDRule-L, [1]), which is a dialect in the family of fact based modeling (FBM) languages [2] and an extension to Object-Role Modelling language (ORM [3]), to capture decisional semantics and graphically present it.

In this paper, we will discuss the SDRule-L constraints that do not exist in most FBM dialects, or, have different semantics. We also propose using SDRule-L for checking the consistency of linked business data. An SDRule-L model may contain

C. Huemer and P. Lops (Eds.): EC-Web 2013, LNBIP 152, pp. 59–67, 2013.

static rules (e.g., data constraints), *dynamic* rules (e.g., sequence of events), and *second-order* attributes (e.g., clusters). Unfortunately, current solutions of managing linked data are based on Description Logic (DL) family, which does not directly deal with dynamic rules. And, DL by default is first-order logic instead of second-order logic. In this paper, we will illustrate how SDRule-L models can be mapped into OWL (Web Ontology Language)-compatible SDRule-L model and DL. In order to check consistency of business data, we have implemented an SDRule-L engine.

It is organized as follows. Sec. 2 is the paper background. How to map dynamic rules into a combination of static rules and queries for detecting anomalies will be discussed in Sec. 3. We will show the implementation issues and present the discussions in Sec. 4. In Sec. 5, we will conclude.

2 Background and Related Work

For over three decades, FBM dialects, such as ORM [3], have been intensively studied for modeling business information. When comparing FBM dialects to the languages in the related work, FBM has many outstanding advantages as a modeling tool for ontologies. For example, Entity-Relationship diagrams (ER, [4]) and Unified Modeling Language (UML, [5]) cannot express relevant constraints on or between attributes. Business Process Models and Notations (BPMN, [6]) and its extensions (e.g., rBPMN that focuses on expression of constraints in BPMN, [7]) mainly focuses on processes and researchers pay less attention to other models, such as data models. Compared to Conceptual Graph (CG, [8]), FBM languages contain more semantically rich graphical notations and have *verbalization* mechanisms, which enable modelers to easily learn and communicate with domain experts. Hence, FBM is more suitable for conceptual analysis, especially when *non-technical* domain experts are involved. In the domain of business, this is an extremely important reason.

Since 1999, the FBM methodological principles have been adopted for modeling ontologies and supporting *verbalization* of ontology models in the paradigm of Developing Ontology-based Methodologies and Applications [9] [10]. Later on, ORM/ORM2 is extended for modeling ontologies. One extension is called Semantic Decision Rule Language (SDRule-L, [1]) and is used for modeling semantically rich decision support rules within the context of business. Its markup language – SDRule-ML – has been designed to store and exchange ontology-based decision rules.

3 Model Transformation

SDRule-L extends ORM by introducing contains, operators and corresponding graphical notations such as instance, sequence, cluster, negation, exception and modality. In this section, we will illustrate those graphical notations and explain their semantics. In the meanwhile, we will show how SDRule-L models can be transformed into OWL-compatible models and the SPARQL queries used for checking the consistency of business data.

Formalization of Objectification: Before going into the details of SDRule-L constraints and operators, it is necessary to explain objectification and the formalization.

Objectification is a way of treating a role pair as an object [3]. Graphically, it is represented as shown in Fig. 1 (O1), which is a minimum constrained fact type with an objectification. A and B are two object types, r1 and r2 are the roles that A and B can play with, and C is an objectified role pair r1/r2. The bar on r1/r2 is a uniqueness constraint, meaning that the populations of A and B with regard to r1/r2 are unique.

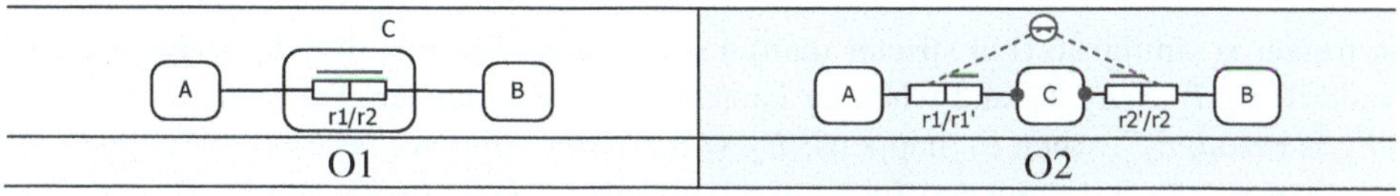

Fig. 1. Example of objectification and its equivalent owl-compatible model

The objectification from Fig. 1 (O1) can be mapped to Fig. 1 (O2) without losing any semantics. In Fig. 1 (O2), the objectified role pair r1/r2 is treated as a new object type C. Two new roles r1' and r2' are introduced for the issues of formalization and implementation. Two mandatory constraints (graphically represented as dots) are applied between C and A, and between C and B. The constraints on roles r1' and r2' ensures 1:1 population between C and A, and between C and B. The circled bar in Fig. 1 (O2) is an external uniqueness, which is a direct adaptation from the uniqueness constraint on r1/r2 from Fig. 1 (O1). We use $\mathcal{SOIQ}(D)$ – a DL dialect – to formalize Fig. 1 (O2) as follows:

$\exists r1.\top \sqsubseteq A \qquad r1^{-} \equiv r1' \qquad \exists r2.\top \sqsubseteq B \qquad r2^{-} \equiv r2'$

$\exists r1'.\top \sqsubseteq C \qquad \exists r2'.\top \sqsubseteq C \qquad C \equiv \leq 1r1'.\top \sqcap \exists r1'.\top \sqcup \leq 1r2'.\top \sqcap \exists r2'.\top$

In what follows, we will use objectification to objectify roles.

<u>Sequence</u> is a common constraint for an event. In SDRule-L, two events can have the relations as indicated in Table 1.

Table 1. SDRule-L Sequence (E_1: event on the right of the connector;E_2: event on the left)

ID	Name	Graphical Notation	Verbalization
1	Succession	——>>——▶	E_1 is before E_2
2	Continuation	——_ _——▶	E_1 is exactly before E_2
3	Overlap	◀——_-_——▶	E_1 and E_2 overlap
4	Trigger	>——>>——▶	E_1 triggers E_2
5	Terminator	——>>——○	E_1 is terminated by E_2
6	Coincidence	◀——|=|——▶	E_1 and E_2 are in parallel

Allow us to use E for denoting an event. An event contains two basic time indicators: *begin time stamp* (which we indicate as T_1) and *end time stamp* (indicated as T_2). E is a valid event iff $T_2 \geq T_1$. We use a dot "." to indicate the holder of an element. For example, for an event E_i, its begin time stamp is denoted by $E_i.T_1$. Given two events – E_1 and E_2 – a succession ($E_1$is before E_2) is valid iff $E_1.T_1 > E_2.T_1$. A continuation (E_1 is exactly before E_2) is valid iff $E_1.T_2 = E_2.T_1 + \alpha$ where α is a given time interval. An overlap is valid iff

- $E_1.T_1 \leq E_2.T_1$ and $E_1.T_2 > E_2.T_1$. Or,
- $E_2.T_1 \leq E_1.T_1$ and $E_2.T_2 > E_1.T_1$

A trigger is similar to (but stricter than) a succession. The fact that E_1 triggers E_2 is valid iff $E_1.T_1 > E_2.T_1$ and when E_1 happens, E_2 must happen. For a succession like "E_1 is before E_2", when E_1 happens, E_2 will possibly (but not necessarily) happen. A terminator – E_1 is terminated by E_2 – is valid iff $E_1.T_1 \geq E_2.T_2$ and $E_1.T_2 = E_2.T_2$. A coincidence is valid iff $E_1.T_1 = E_2.T_1$ and $E_1.T_2 = E_2.T_2$.

Fig. 2 shows an example containing all the six sequence constraints. Each role pair (see the rectangles) is constrained with a uniqueness constraint (graphically represented as a bar above role pairs). Without it, a role pair cannot be populated.

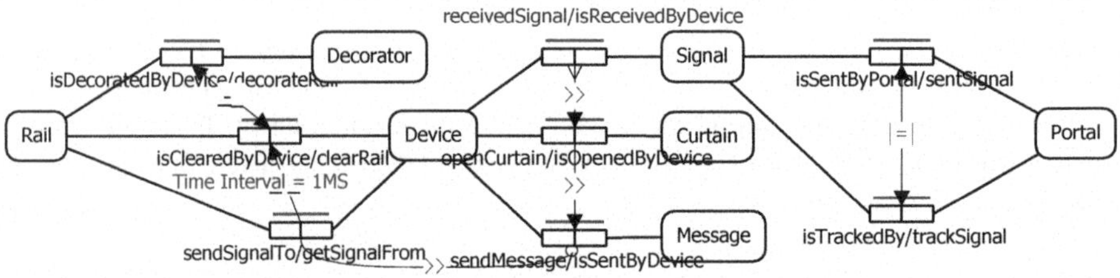

Fig. 2. An example of sequence

An example of the **verbalization**[1] of Fig. 2 is Device open(s) Curtain <u>before</u> Device send(s) Message.

We can transform the succession constraint modelled in Fig. 2 into an OWL-compatible model as illustrated in Fig. 3. Role pairs are objectified and new concepts concerning event and time stamps are added with mandatory constraints (graphically represented as dots). The part in Fig. 3 that contains extra concepts can be verbalized as "Open Curtain is a subtype of Event; Send Message is a subtype of Event; Event has Time Stamp T1; Event has Time Stamp T2".

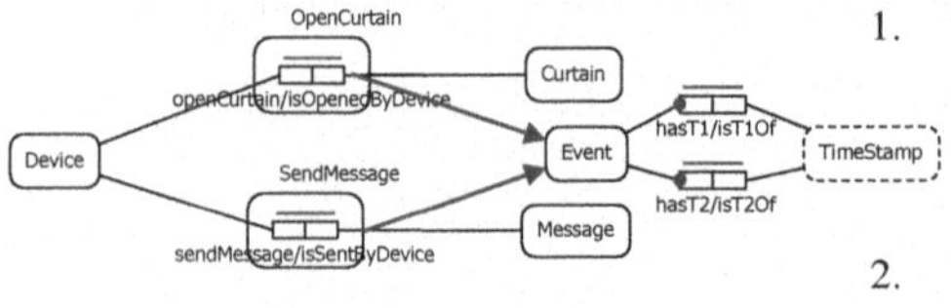

1. $OpenCurtain \sqsubseteq \exists openCurtain'.Device \sqcap \exists isOpenedByDevice'.Curtain \sqcap \leq 1 openCurtain'.Device \sqcap \leq 1 isOpenedByDevice.Curtain.$
2. $Event \sqsubseteq \exists hasT1.TimeStamp \sqcap \exists hasT2.TimeStamp$

Fig. 3. An OWL-compatible model transformed partly from **Fig. 2** and the DL axioms

[1] Verbalization is a process of mapping a graphical model to (or from) a few sentences in a controlled language.

Note that one part of the semantics of sequence from the original design in Fig. 2 and the discussed DL axioms is missing in Fig. 3. It does not specify that T1 of "Open Curtain" must be smaller than T1 from "Send Message". It is normal because it can be modelled neither in an OWL-compatible model nor in any DL dialects that are supported by OWL.

Such semantics is captured using a query language. We can check data consistency by querying linked data. In this paper, we adopt an approach similar to the one in [11] for checking constraints, namely to translate constraints into SPARQL ASK queries to check whether counterexamples (i.e. constraint violations) exist. In our engine, the ASK query looks for counterexamples and upon a positive answer, will return that this particular constraint has been violated.

Cluster is a way of treating a set of fact types as an object. By having clusters, we can reify a model by looking into the details of an object, or, we can abstract a model by hiding the design details of its objects. The graphical notation of cluster is a round-cornered box indicated with a cluster name. A cluster can be composed of another cluster, fact types and objectified roles. A composition can be possible or necessary, the graphical notations of which are shown inTable 2.

Table 2. SDRule-L Cluster

ID	Name	Graphical Notation	Verbalization
1	Possible composition	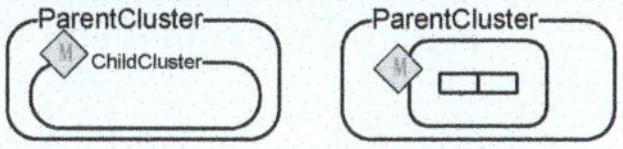	... possibly contains ...
2	Necessary composition	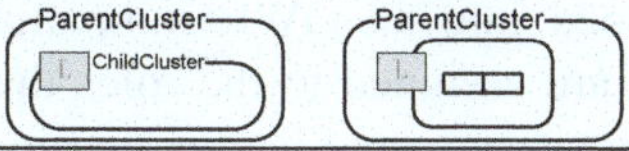	... must contain ...

The modality operators are used to specify whether it is necessary (or possibly) for a cluster to include a component. In SDRule-L, there are two modality operators – necessity and possibility. The graphical notation of necessity is a square marked with "L". A possibility operator is a diamond square marked with "M". Note that we shall not mistake M for mandatory. Since we want to align our graphical notations with the logical symbols from Modal Logic that are commonly accepted, we choose L ($\Box$) for necessity and M ($\Diamond$) for possibility.

Fig. 4 shows an example of cluster and the zoom-out view. The cluster "Opening Curtain" is composed of a necessary cluster "Listen and React" and a possible cluster "Sending Msg". The cluster "Listen and React" contains two fact types – Device received Signal and Device open(s) Curtain. The cluster "Sending Msg" contains one fact type – Device send(s) Message. The three clusters are subtypes of "Task".

If a role that is connected with a cluster is populated, then the necessary components of this cluster must be populated while it is not required to have its optional components populated. Each component of a cluster is by default optional.

With regard to design issues, when a necessary component of a cluster contains a possible component, then the necessary component is treated as if it were optional. Fig. 5 shows two models of cluster. Cluster C2 in the figure on the left is a necessary component for cluster C1, while C2 on the right is an optional component for C1. Their equivalence can be proven with a truth table.

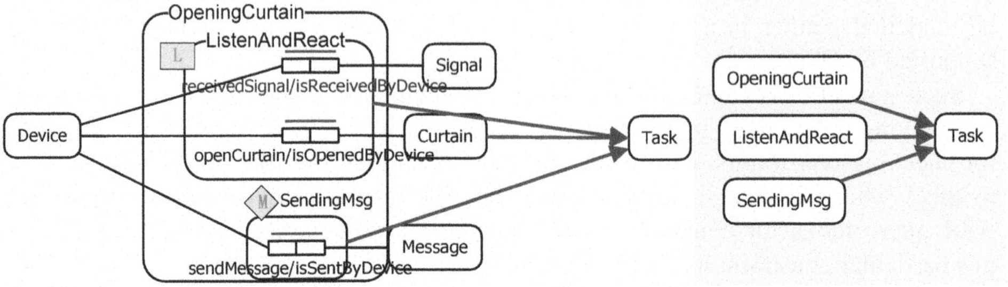

Fig. 4. Left: An example of cluster in SDRule-L; Right: a zoom-out view

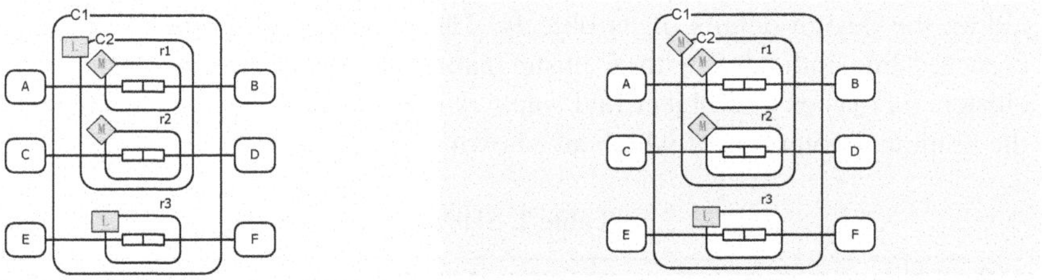

Fig. 5. Two equivalent models

Fig. 4 can be mapped into an OWL-compatible model as illustrated in Fig. 6. Mandatory constraints are assigned to the roles that come from a mandatory cluster. The semantics of composition from Fig. 4 is missing in Fig. 6.

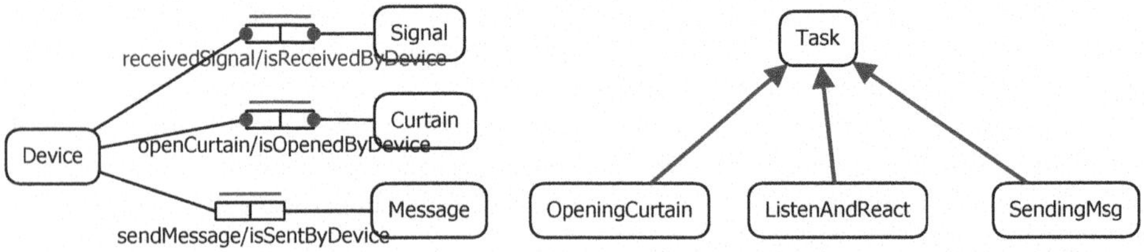

Fig. 6. OWL-compatible models partly transformed from Fig. 4

Other Constraints and Operators

In general, an implication is used to draw conclusions based on statements. In SDRule-L, we use it to control the population of a role based on alternatives. It is often used for modeling dynamic and non-monotonic decision rules.

Fig. 7 shows an example of implication and its verbalization. An arrow tipped bar indicated with ¬ is an operator of negation. When negation is applied on a role of the antecedent of an implication, it is a checksum of empty population. When it is applied on a role of the consequence of an implication, it is a denial of populating this role.

For instance in Fig. 7, if *openCurtain/isOpenedByDevice* is populated, then *isSentByDevice/sendMsg* must be populated; otherwise, the latter must not be populated.

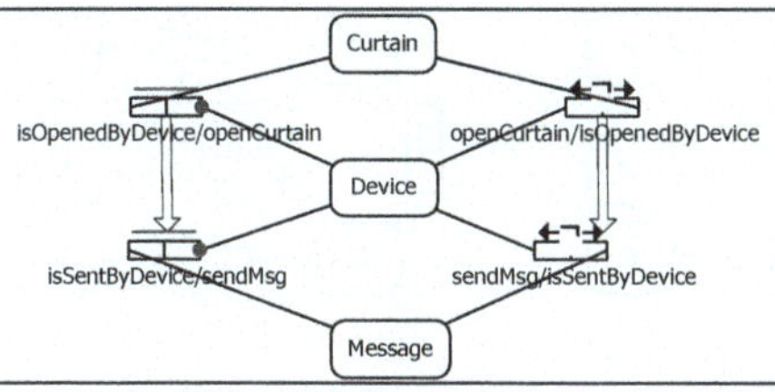

If Device does not open Curtain, then Device does not send Message.
If Device open(s) Curtain, then Device send(s) Message.
Each Device open(s) at least one Curtain.
Each Device send(s) at least one Message.

Fig. 7. An example of implication and its verbalization

Due to the limitation of DL, negation and conditional alternatives cannot be formalized. Implication could be partly modeled in DL as a subset. For instance, the non-negative part in Fig. 7 can be formalized as: $Device1 \sqsubseteq \exists\ openCurtain.\top$ $Device2 \sqsubseteq \exists openCurtain.\top$; and, $Device1 \sqsubseteq Device2$. However, we shall avoid this complicated construction and opt for queries to detect counterexamples instead.

When negation is used in a conditional statement, it is a constraint. When it is used in a conclusion, it is an operator. Another important operator in SDRule-L is skipper.

A skipper allows us to give an exception to the studied constraints. It is quite useful especially for the domains like law, which in most cases contains inconsistency. Fig. 8 shows the graphical notation of skipper.

Each Device send(s) exactly one Message [SKIP].

Fig. 8. An example of skipper (exception)

4 Implementation, Discussion and Future Work

The paper idea has been implemented in the SDRule-L engine, which can be downloaded from https://sourceforge.net/projects/sdrulel/.

An SDRule-L model is stored and shared in a mark-up language called SDRule-ML [1]. Our SDRule-L engine takes SDRule-ML files as inputs and generates analysis messages (e.g., whether all the constraints in a model are satisfied or not) as outputs. Including the method of model transformation that is discussed in Sec. 3, it is also required to specify any possible implicit constraints. Otherwise, it would be difficult to link the components in an XML file to the elements in a query.

In this paper, a sequence constraint (e.g., continuation) is applied on two fact types, which share at least one object entity. In general, we allow a sequence constraint to be applied on any two fact types that are indirectly connected. When we want to compare two facts from these two different fact types, we need to find the right connection between them; otherwise, we cannot compare them. Fig. 9 shows an example of sequence that is applied on indirectly connected and two possible paths of building the connection. The two different paths might lead to different conclusions. Finding right connections for indirectly connected fact types is a challenge, which we will study in the future.

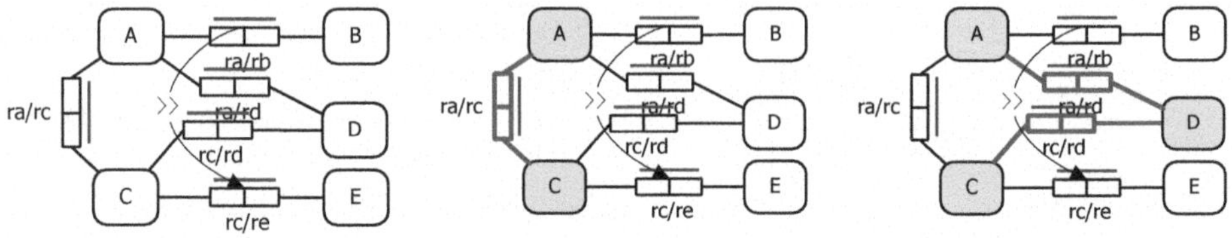

Sequence on unconnected fact types | Possible path 1 | Possible path 2

Fig. 9. An example of a sequence applied on unconnected fact types and two possible paths of connections

5 Conclusion

In this paper, we have discussed the most recent results concerning SDRule-L, which is a semantic decision support language. In particular, we have presented constraints of *sequence*, *cluster* and *implication*, and operators of *negation* and *skipper*. We have shown a method of mapping dynamic rules into a combination of static rules and queries for detecting model anomalies. This method is further implemented in the SDRule-L reasoning engine.

Acknowledgements. Our use case and experimental data from this paper are taken from the SBO OSCB project.

References

1. Tang, Y., Meersman, R.: SDRule Markup Language: Towards Modeling and Interchanging Ontological Commitments for Semantic Decision Making. In: Giurca, A., Gasevic, D., Taveter, K. (eds.) Handbook of Research on Emerging Rule-Based Languages and Technologies: Open Solutions and Approaches, sec. I, ch. V. IGI Publishing, USA (2008)
2. FBM: What is Fact Based Modeling? In: Fact Based Modeling Official Website, `http://www.factbasedmodeling.org/`
3. Halpin, T., Morgan, T.: Information Modeling and Relational Databases, 2nd edn. Morgan Kaufmann (2008)
4. Calì, A., Gottlob, G., Pieris, A.: The Return of the Entity-Relationship Model: Ontological Query Answering. In: Semantic Search over the Web, pp. 255–281. Springer, Heidelberg (2012)
5. Wang, X., Chan, C.: Ontology Modeling Using UML. In: Konstantas, D., Léonard, M., Pigneur, Y., Patel, S. (eds.) 7th International Conference on Object Oriented Information Systems Conference (OOIS 2001), Geneva. LNCS, vol. 2817, pp. 59–68 (2001)
6. Prater, J., Mueller, R., Beauregard, B.: An ontological approach to oracle BPM. In: Pan, J.Z., Chen, H., Kim, H.-G., Li, J., Wu, Z., Horrocks, I., Mizoguchi, R., Wu, Z. (eds.) JIST 2011. LNCS, vol. 7185, pp. 402–410. Springer, Heidelberg (2012)

7. Milanovic, M., Gasevic, D., Rocha, L.: Modeling Flexible Business Processes with Business Rule. In: The 15th IEEE International Enterprise Distributed Object Computing Conference, EDOC 2011, Helsinki, Finland, vol. 3.1, pp. 65–74 (2011)
8. Comparot, C., Haemmerlé, O., Hernandez, N.: Conceptual Graphs and Ontologies for Information Retrieval. In: Priss, U., Polovina, S., Hill, R. (eds.) ICCS 2007. LNCS (LNAI), vol. 4604, pp. 480–483. Springer, Heidelberg (2007)
9. Meersman, R.A.: Semantic Ontology Tools in IS Design. In: Raś, Z.W., Skowron, A. (eds.) ISMIS 1999. LNCS, vol. 1609, pp. 30–45. Springer, Heidelberg (1999)
10. Spyns, P., Tang, Y., Meersman, R.: An Ontology Engineering Methodology for DOGMA. Journal of Applied Ontology 3(1-2), 13–39 (2008)
11. Tao, J., Sirin, E., Bao, J., McGuinness, D.L.: Integrity Constraints in OWL. In: Fox, M., Poole, D. (eds.) AAAI, Atlanta, Georgia, USA (2010)

A Hybrid Approach for Business Environment-Aware Management of Service-Based Business Processes

Olfa Bouchaala[1,2], Samir Tata[1], and Mohamed Jmaiel[2]

[1] Insitut Mines-Telecom, TELECOM SudParis, CNRS UMR Samovar, Evry, France
{olfa.bouchaala,samir.tata}@it-sudparis.eu
[2] University of Sfax, ReDCAD Laboratory, Tunisia
mohamed.jmaiel@enis.rnu.tn

Abstract. Enterprises struggle to find a balance between adapting their business processes (BPs) against business environments and keeping competitiveness. Indeed, while the imperative nature of monolithic BPs is too rigid to adapt them at runtime, the declarative one of the purely rule-based BPs is very time-consuming. Therefore, in this paper, we focus on business environment-aware management of service-based business processes (SBPs) aiming at conciliating imperative and declarative techniques. Our challenge is to develop a hybrid management approach that (1) preserves standards to describe SBPs, (2) keeps non-dependency to a specific BP engine and (3) minimizes designers efforts. Based on a semantic modeling, we are able to synthesize a controller, itself modeled as a BP, connected to the BP to be monitored and configured. Using our approach does not impact any existing business process management system since controllers are BPs that can be deployed and enacted along with the managed processes.

1 Introduction

Business processes (BPs) represent a key concept for automating enterprises' activities. As enterprises encounter highly dynamic business environments, there is a great need for business process management (BPM) at run-time. By dealing with competitive and constantly changing business environments, enterprises' policies change frequently. Thus, they need to focus on adapting their processes from a business environment point of view. The business environment connotes all factors external to the enterprise and that greatly influence its functioning. It covers many factors such as economic, social ones (*e.g.* festive season).

Business environment-aware management (BEAM for short) [1,2,3,4] of BPs consists in configuring them in order to change their behaviors in reaction to business environment events (*e.g.* during a sales promotion, there is a decrease in clothes prices). There are two types of approaches of BEAM: imperative and declarative. Declarative approaches are based on ECA-rules [1,5] which are flexible, since they are well adapted for adding, removing and changing rules at

C. Huemer and P. Lops (Eds.): EC-Web 2013, LNBIP 152, pp. 68–79, 2013.

runtime. Nevertheless, they are inefficient since they are time consuming because of inference change in the business environment. In addition, they may not adopt standard notations for BP modeling such as BPMN or BPEL. On the other hand, imperative approaches consist in hard coding management actions into the BP. Consequently, they preserve standard notation for BP modeling and are very efficient, in terms of execution time. Nevertheless, they are too rigid due to over-specifying processes at design time.

An example depicting an online purchase order process of a clothing store is represented in Fig. 1. Upon receipt of customer order, the seller checks product availability. If some of the products are not in stock, the alternative branch "ordering from suppliers" is executed. When all products are available, the choice of a shipper and the calculation of the initial price of the order are launched. Afterwards, the shipping price and the retouch price are computed simultaneously. The total price is then computed in order to send invoice and deliver the order. During a sales promotion, a discount rule should be added and the relationships with the existing rules ought to be established [6]. In addition, they may require that BPs, to be monitored, are also described in terms of rules rather than standards such as BPEL and BPMN. On the contrary, imperative approaches require over-specifying processes by predicting all possible events.

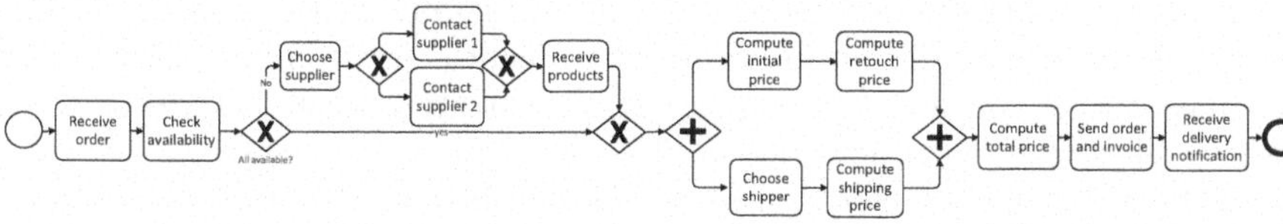

Fig. 1. Purchase order process

Given these limitations, in this paper, we address business environment-aware management of SBPs that mainly raises the following questions.

- How to conciliate between imperative and declarative techniques in an integrated hybrid approach aiming to strengthen their advantages?
- How to develop a hybrid management approach that (1) preserves industry standards to describe SBPs, (2) keeps non-dependency to a specific business process engine and (3) minimizes designers efforts?

In order to address these challenges, our approach models the management of an SBP as a process connected to it for its monitoring and configuration. Monitoring reads properties of services that compose the SBP while configuration alters values of these properties. Contrary to the imperative approaches, in our approach, the management process defines several management paths. Therefore, it can encapsulate different management behaviors. The choice of a management path is based on events of the business environment which are semantically described. Consequently, our approach presents a degree of flexibility inherited from declarative approaches.

The rest of this paper is organized as follows. Section 2 gives an overview of our technique for generating a management process as well as the required semantic modeling of SBPs, business environments and relationships between them. Based on this model, section 3 describes an algorithm enabling the management process construction. Then, section 4 presents the implementation and proves our concepts. In section 5, we present a literature review of business environment-aware management approaches. Finally, section 6 summarizes the main findings of our work and presents future directions.

2 A Hybrid Approach for BEAM of SBPS

2.1 Approach Overview

In our work, we consider that the management of a composition of services offering management operations is realized through the composition of the offered management operations. The enactments of management operations are triggered by events that are captured from the business environment. The composition of management operations and the business environment events constitute a BP that manages the original SBP. Fig. 2 illustrates the purchase order process and its corresponding generated management process. The management process uses the management operations to monitor and configure the original SBP.

In fact, in order to take into account the business environment changes into the managed SBP, we use service properties that are adjusted. Indeed, service properties allow for the configuration of an implementation with externally set values. The value for a service property is supplied to the implementation of the service each time the implementation is executed. In particular, the internal value of a property can be altered at any time through business management operations which enable its monitoring and configuration. The monitoring step reads properties while the configuration one updates them if necessary. When changing a property value, the corresponding service changes its behavior. For example, the service "Compute initial price" of Fig. 2 has a property named "Discount rate" which can change its behavior by a setter operation when a sales promotion is triggered. As we already mentioned, when changing a service behavior, the BP is reconfigured and its behavior is accordingly modified.

Thus, the first step towards the automation of the managing operations composition is to identify the semantic concepts of the services properties from the initial BP. The issue is how to modify these properties and in which order. To deal with this issue, we adopted a three-phase methodology:

- **Phase 1:** Events represent the glue between business environments and SBPs. Hence, events may trigger the update of service properties.
- **Phase 2:** Service properties may depend on each others. Accordingly, modifying a service property may engender changes on others depending on it.
- **Phase 3:** The structure of the initial BP gives an idea on the order of management operations that modify properties.

Consequently, this methodology requires appropriate semantic model. Therefore, we propose an upper management ontology which correlated with a domain ontology represents a declarative description of the company management strategy against dynamic business environment (section 2.2).

Based on the upper management ontology and the structure of the initial SBP, we design an algorithm for generating the management process (Section 3).

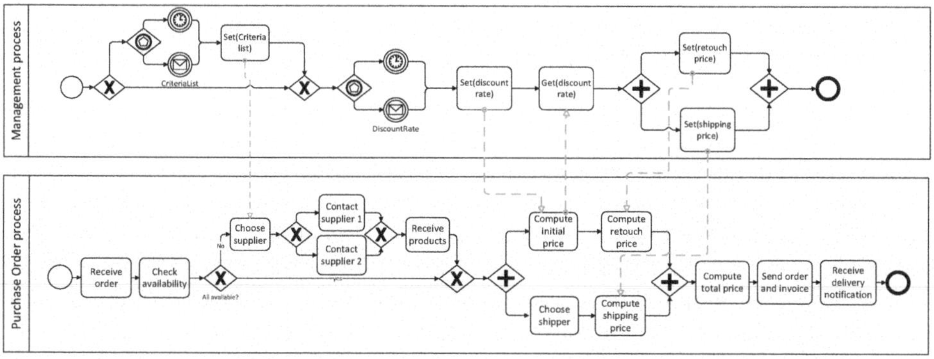

Fig. 2. Purchase order process with its corresponding management process

2.2 Semantic Modeling of SBPs and Business Environment

As shown in Fig. 3, there are three main actors in BEAM: business environment, BP and services. The BP has a service composition which is composed of activities and gateways. Activities are realized by services. Each service has a service property and management operations. Services interact with the business environment. This latter engenders **events** that trigger **management operations** which act in turn on **service properties**. These three concepts represented in grey ellipses in Fig. 3 represent the main concepts of the management ontology at a high level of abstraction.

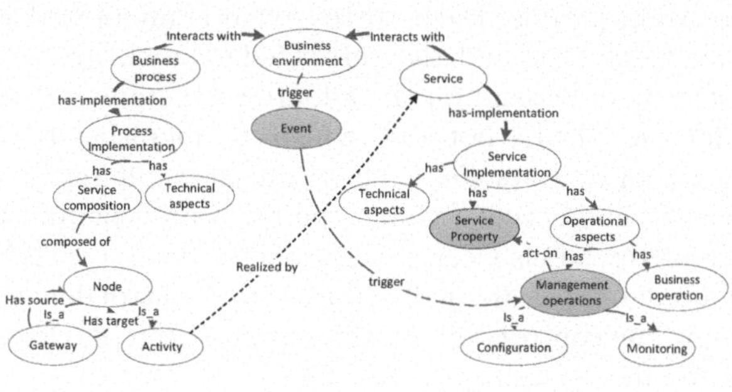

Fig. 3. Actors in the BEAM

Upper Management Ontology. Services properties, management operations and business environment events are described against a domain ontology. Such ontology is defined by domain experts. To facilitate the management process construction, we define an upper management ontology (Fig. 4). This ontology represents two main relationships:

- **Environment-Service relationship:** Events trigger Actions (management operations) which act on services properties.
- **Service-Service relationship:** Each service property has services properties that may depend on it.

Events play a prominent role in BEAM, since they are the glue between situations in the real world and SBPs. Thus, to be in line with standards, we base events semantics and definitions on the expressiveness of BPMN 2.0 [7]. Events are used to model something happening in the process lifetime. They affect the flow of the process by catching a trigger or throwing a result. Event definitions represent the semantics of events. In BPMN 2.0, there are 10 event definitions among them we use: Message, Signal, Timer and Conditional. Timer and Conditional events are implicitly thrown. When they are activated they wait for a time based or status based condition respectively to trigger the catch event (*e.g.* a timer event definition is used to detect that the promotion time date is reached). Some events (e.g. Message, Signal) have the capability to carry data (*e.g.* a Message event is used to define a Discount rate message in order to carry the discount Rate information).

The Structure of the Initial SBP. In SBPs, activities are realized by services. In this work, a semantic service S is mainly characterized by its property p, which, being adjusted, changes the service behavior. A service property has a name, a value and is annotated with a concept from the domain ontology. The initial SBP is a finite set of nodes representing activities, gateways and possibly events described using a BP standard (e.g. EPC, BPEL, BPMN, etc). Abstracting SBPs using graphs renders the management process generation possible for any BP standard language. Thus, SBPs and its corresponding management process are modeled using graphs. Each vertex/edge is annotated with a pair indicating the vertex/edge type and the vertex/edge label. As stated earlier, the available types of vertices depend on the adopted BP standard notation. In this paper, we consider the BPMN notation which distinguishes between activities ('a'), gateways ('g') and events ('e'). There are also different types of BPMN gateways and events. The activity name, the gateway type and the event type represent possible vertex labels (e.g. ('a', 'receive order'), ('g','AND-split'), ('e', 'start event')). The edge types are deduced from the control dependency graph of the BPMN process. The control dependency graph of the purchase order process (Fig. 1) is generated inspiring from [8,9] (Fig. 5).

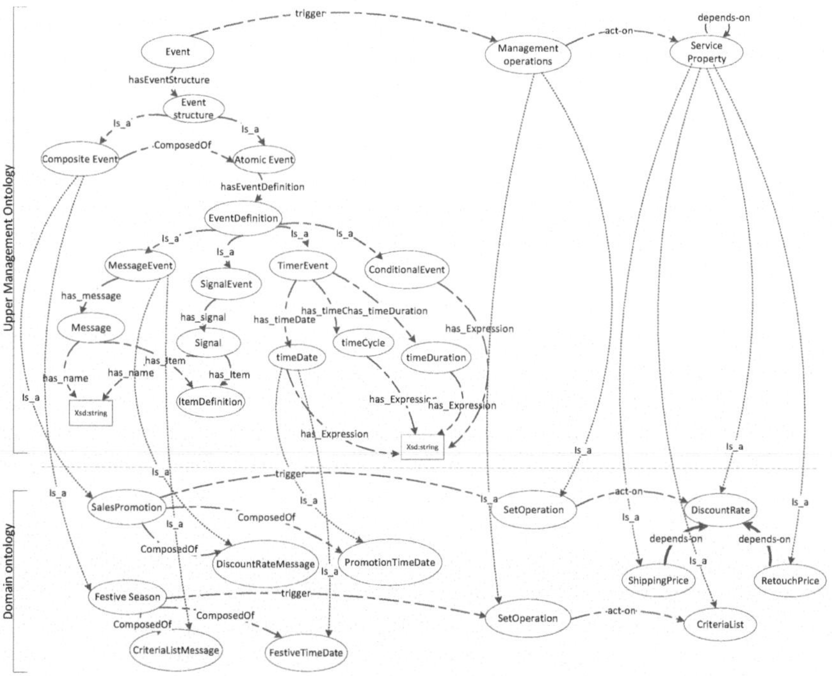

Fig. 4. Purchase order ontology

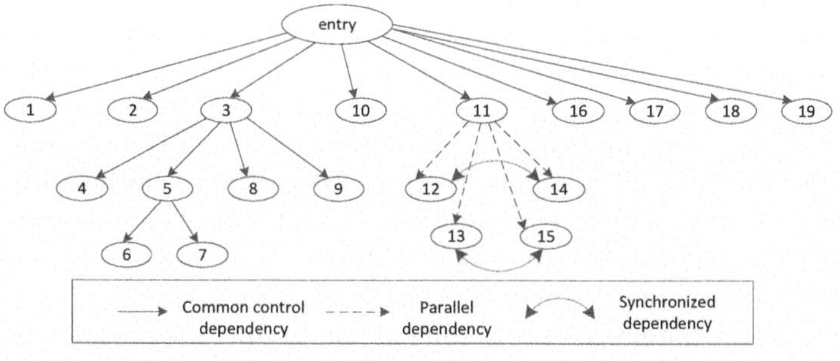

Fig. 5. Control dependency graph of the purchase order process (1: Receive order, 2: Check availability, 3: OR-split, 4: Choose supplier, 5: OR-split, 6: Contact supplier 1, 7: Contact supplier 2, 8: OR-join, 9: Receive products, 10: OR-join, 11: AND-split, 12: Compute initial price, 13: Compute retouch price, 14: Choose shipper, 15: Compute shipping price, 16: AND-join, 17: Compute total price, 18: Send order and invoice, 19: Receive delivery notification)

3 Generating Management Process

In the following, we define a management process to handle an SBP during its execution. We recall that services' properties frequently change due to business environment changes. When a new event in the business environment occurs, the adequate properties should be updated. Therefore, the management process consists in a composition of management operations that read and/or alter services' properties. At this level, we define a getter and a setter for each property.

The construction of the management solution (composition of management operations) is performed using semantic descriptions over domain ontology as well as the structure of the initial BP. Thereby, the construction of the composition comprises three main phases: (1) constructing sub-processes based on the Environment-Service relationship, (2) constructing sub-processes based on the Service-Service relationship and (3) connecting generated sub-processes.

Properties externalize the service behavior. Thus, the first step towards the automation of the managing operations composition is to capture the semantic concepts of the services properties from the initial BP. Each service property can have possible events that trigger the update of its value. Thus, Algorithm 1 is called with p as parameter for building sub-processes relating configuration operations with events (see section 3.1). Configuring a service property may engender the update of other properties related to it. Algorithm 2 is called in turn to build a sub-process connecting management operations with each other (see section 3.2). Finally, Algorithm 3 is performed to connect resulting subprocesses based on the structure of the initial SBP (see section 3.3).

3.1 Constructing Sub-processes Based on Environment-Service Relationship

In this first phase, the issue is to alter a service property based on the Environment-Service relationship introduced in section 2.2. Indeed, when an event occurs the corresponding service property is updated according to dependencies between business environment events and services. In accordance with the running example, when a "Sales promotion" happens, there is a decrease in clothes prices. Subsequently, the property named "Discount Rate" is altered. As stated in section 2.2, the event "Sales promotion" is composed of atomic events having event definitions: DiscountRateMessage and PromotionTimeDate.

In order to create subprocesses aiming at modifying a service property, Algorithm 1 is performed. These subprocesses relate a service management operation with possible events that can trigger it. Fig. 6(b) is the resulting subprocess for p="DiscountRate". Similarly, with p="CriteriaList" the subprocess described in Fig. 6(a) is generated.

The list of possible events as well as their definitions result from calling the procedure *FindEvents(p)* that executes the following SPARQL query (Line 1): "SELECT ?atomicEvent ?eventdefinition WHERE { ?event ns:trigger ?action. ?action ns:act-on ?property. ?property rdf:type ns:"+p+". ?event ns:hasEventstructure

?events. ?events ns:composedOf ?atomicEvent. ?atomicEvent ns:hasEventDefinition ?definition. ?definition rdf:type ?eventdefinition.}".

When an event occurs, the service property p will be altered automatically using a set operation. A vertex ("a", "$set(p)$") is added to the vertex-set of the managing graph MG (Line 3). If the list of possible events that can modify the property comprises only one event, we add this event to the set of vertices of MG graph (Line 5). A single edge between the event and the "set" operation is also added (Line 6). Otherwise, a node of gateway type labeled "*Event-based XOR*" is added (Line 8). Then, a node for each event and edges relating it to the gateway as well as the set operation are identified (Line 10, 11, 12).

Algorithm 1. *ConstructESR(ServiceProperty p, Managing Graph MG)*

Require: Managing Graph MG
Ensure: Managing Graph MG
1: List $L_1 \longleftarrow$ *FindEvents(p)*
2: **if** $L_1 \neq \emptyset$ **then**
3: $V_3(MG) \longleftarrow V_3(MG) \cup \{("a", "set(p)")\}$
4: **if** $L_1 = \{l_1\}$ **then**
5: $V_3(MG) \longleftarrow V_3(MG) \cup \{("e", "l_1")\}$
6: $E_3(MG) \longleftarrow E_3(MG) \cup \{(("e", "l_1"), ("a", "set(p)"))\}$
7: **else**
8: $V_3(MG) \longleftarrow V_3(MG) \cup \{("g", "Event - basedXOR")\}$
9: **for all** $l_1 \in L_1$ **do**
10: $V_3(MG) \longleftarrow V_3(MG) \cup \{("e", "l_1")\}$
11: $E_3(MG) \longleftarrow E_3(MG) \cup \{(("g", "Event - basedXOR"), ("e", "l_1"))\}$
12: $E_3(MG) \longleftarrow E_3(MG) \cup \{(("e", "l_1"), ("a", "set(p)"))\}$
13: **end for**
14: **end if**
15: **end if**
16: **return** MG

3.2 Constructing Sub-processes Based on Service-Service Relationship

A service property may depend on others. Hence, updating a service property may engender the modification of others depending on it. Therefore, in this second phase, the concern is to properly identify the semantic relationship holding between service properties. For instance, the service properties named "Shipping Price" and "Retouch price" depend on "Discount Rate" property (Fig. 4). Thus, if the property "Discount Rate" is updated, both "Shipping price" and "Retouch price" properties should be updated. The corresponding resulting subprocess is depicted in Fig. 6(c).

In order to generate this subprocess, Algorithm 2 explores the different dependency relationships between concepts of services' properties from the domain ontology. Two services properties have a relationship if they are related with "depends-on" relationship in the domain ontology. A SPARQL query is then sent to the domain ontology to enquire for the sources of the property p :

"SELECT ?sourceType WHERE ?source ns:depends-on ?a. ?a rdf:type ns:"+p+". ?source rdf:type ?sourceType. ?sourceType rdfs:subClassOf ns:ServiceProperty.".

The result of this query is performed by calling the procedure *ServiceSourceOfDepends-On(p)* (Line 1). If p has properties that depend on it (Line 2), then the $get(p)$ operation is automatically invoked (Line 3). As a result, a setter for each property depending on p is defined (Line 4-6). If there is only one property, then a simple edge links its setter with $get(p)$. Otherwise, the adequate gateway relating properties setters with $get(p)$ is identified based on the control dependency graph (Fig. 5). For example, the services "Compute retouch price" and "Compute shipping price" are synchronized according to the control dependency graph of the purchase order process. Therefore, a gateway labeled ('g','AND-Split) is added. As for a well structured BP, when starting with a gateway type, we finish by the same (Line 13, 16).

Algorithm 2. *ConstructSSR(ServiceProperty p, Managing Graph MG)*

Require: Managing Graph MG
Ensure: Managing Graph MG
1: List $L_2 \longleftarrow$ *ServiceSourceOfDepends-On(p)*
2: **if** $L_2 \neq \emptyset$ **then**
3: $V_3(MG) \longleftarrow V_3(MG) \cup \{("a","get(p)")\}$
4: **for all** $l \in L_2$ **do**
5: $V_3(MG) \longleftarrow V_3(MG) \cup \{("a","set(l)")\}$
6: **end for**
7: **if** $L_2 = \{l_2\}$ **then**
8: $E_3(MG) \longleftarrow E_3(MG) \cup \{(("a","get(p)"),("a","set(l_2)"))\}$
9: **else**
10: String GatewayType=$ChooseGateway(L_2, p)$
11: $V_3(MG) \longleftarrow V_3(MG) \cup \{("g", GatewayType)\}$
12: $E_3(MG) \longleftarrow E_3(MG) \cup \{(("a","get(p)"),("g", GatewayType))\}$
13: $V_3(MG) \longleftarrow V_3(MG) \cup \{("g", GatewayType)\}$
14: **for all** $l_2 \in L_2$ **do**
15: $E_3(MG) \longleftarrow E_3(MG) \cup \{(("g", GatewayType),("a","set(l_2)"))\}$
16: $E_3(MG) \longleftarrow E_3(MG) \cup \{(("a","set(l_2)"),("g", GatewayType))\}$
17: **end for**
18: **end if**
19: **end if**
20: **return** MG

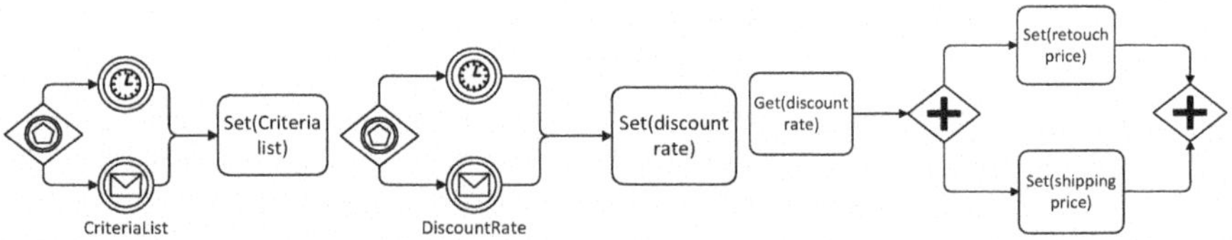

(a) Result of phase 1 for p="CriteriaList" (b) Result of phase 1 for p="DiscountRate" (c) Result of phase 2 for p="DiscountRate"

Fig. 6. Result of phase 1 and phase 2

3.3 Connecting Generated Sub-processes

So far, a set of sub-processes are created. Indeed, for each property sub-processes based on the Environment-Service and/or Service-Service relationship are built. How to connect their ends? How to determine their order?

Resuming with the running example, till now, three sub-processes are built (see Fig. 6). In order to connect them aiming to generate the whole management process (Fig. 2), in this phase, we add missing links and gateways based on the explicit semantic description of the initial BP. Doing so, we adopted the following steps: (1) identifying management process ends, (2) capturing their corresponding in the initial BP, (3) determining control dependencies for each activity in order to add corresponding gateways and (4) organizing results based on the control flow of the initial BP.

Algorithm 3 formalizes these steps as follows. The first step consists in finding nodes having no targets (set operations) and nodes having no sources (get operations) (Line 2). The second step is to identify nodes corresponding to these activities having p as property in the process graph (Line 3). Afterwards, the control dependency of each node is determined (Line 5). Control dependencies for each node are then compared in order to identify the existence or not of control dependency between subprocesses (Line 12-16). Then, with respect to control-flow relations between activities in the process graph, the subprocesses are organized and control flow edges are added to the managing graph.

As a final step, nodes which have no sources are linked to the start event (Line 19, 20). In addition, nodes having no targets are connected to the end event (Line 22, 23).

Algorithm 3. *ConnectSP(Process Graph PG, Managing Graph MG)*

Require: Managing Graph MG, Process Graph PG
Ensure: Managing Graph MG
1: **for all** $v \in V_3(MG)$ **do**
2:   **if** $(S(v) = \emptyset \wedge MG.\tau_3(v) =' a') \vee (T(v) = \emptyset \wedge MG.\tau_3(v) =' a')$ **then**
3:     Find v_1 in $V_1(PG)$ such that $v_1.p.concept = MG.\theta_3(v)$
4:     $v_2 \longleftarrow searchControldependencies(CDG, v_1)$
5:     **if** $PG.\omega_1((v_1, v_2)) = "commoncontrol - dependency"$ **then**
6:       $V_3(MG) \longleftarrow V_3(MG) \cup \{('g', "OR - Split")\}$
7:       $E_3(MG) \longleftarrow E_3(MG) \cup \{(('g', "OR - Split"), PG.\theta_1(v_1)\}$
8:     **end if**
9:     $Map \longleftarrow Map \cup (v_1, v_2)$
10:   **end if**
11: **end for**
12: **if** $\bigcap\{Map(i)\} = \varnothing$ **then**
13:   $V_3(MG) \longleftarrow V_3(MG) \cup \{('g', "OR - Join")\}$
14:   $E_3(MG) \longleftarrow E_3(MG) \cup \{PG.\theta_1(v_1), ('g', "OR - Join")\}$
15:   $E_3(MG) \longleftarrow E_3(MG) \cup \{('g', "OR - Split"), ('g', "OR - Join")\}$
16: **end if**
17: $V_3(MG) \longleftarrow V_3(MG) \cup \{(("e", "Startevent"), ("e", "Endevent"))\}$
18: **for all** $v \in V_3(MG)$ **do**
19:   **if** $S(v) = \emptyset$ **then**
20:     $E_3(MG) \longleftarrow E_3(MG) \cup \{(("e", "Startevent"), MG.\theta_3(v))\}$
21:   **end if**
22:   **if** $T(v) = \emptyset$ **then**
23:     $E_3(MG) \longleftarrow E_3(MG) \cup \{(MG.\theta_3(v), ("e", "Endevent"))\}$
24:   **end if**
25: **end for**
26: **return** MG

4 Implementation

As a proof of concept, we have implemented a business environment-aware management framework called BEAM4SBP. BEAM4SBP is a java library that intends to generate a management process connected to an initial business process allowing for its monitoring and configuration. The architecture and implementation details about BEAM4SBP can be found at: `http://www-inf.int-evry.fr/SIMBAD/tools/BEAM4SBP`.

5 Related Work

As business environment changes keep increasing, enterprises are always seeking for a balanced solution to manage their processes. However, most research has focused on efficiency or flexibility using either imperative or declarative techniques. Therefore, different approaches [2,10,3,4] try to integrate these two techniques in a joint approach by separating business logic (described by Business rules) and process logic (described by imperative BP).

Charfi et al. [11] focus on Aspect Oriented Programming in order to integrate Business rules and the process logic at run-time. Indeed, the business rules are proposed to be implemented in an aspect-oriented extension of BPEL called AO4BPEL. AO4BPEL is used to weave the adaptation aspects into the process at run-time. Although they preserve BP standards, the weaving phase can strongly limit the process efficiency at run-time since it can raises issues on maintainability and transformation. On the contrary, our management process is generated at deployment time and hence at run-time the managing process is connected to the managed process creating an imperative and efficient process.

Other approaches, such as [2] and [10], address management issue by process variants. When modeling process and their variants, one has to decide which control flow alternatives are variant-specific and which ones are common for all process variants. However, these process variants ought to be configured at configuration time which leads to a static instance of the process model at run-time. While in our case, the values of services properties are altered at run-time taking into account changes in the business environment.

Authors in [10], present an adaptation of BPEL language called VxBPEL. They emphasize on the lack of flexibility and variability when deploying BPEL processes. Thus, they propose to extend BPEL language by adding `Variation Points` and `Variants`. The former represents the places where the process can be configured, while the latter defines the alternative steps of the process that can be used. In this work, the variability is focused on BP aspects written in VxBPEL language. The designers should consider this extension and add their variation when designing the BP. However, in our work, variability are integrated in services and the process designer will not re-write its process.

Ouyang et al. [3] introduce an ECA-based control-rule formalism to modularize the monolithic BPEL process structure. Only one classification of rules is defined that handle the control flow part of the composition linking activities together. In this work, the designer should also take into account the defined ECA-control rule and specify its process accordingly.

6 Conclusion

In this paper, we proposed a novel hybrid approach for managing SBPs against highly dynamic business environments. This approach conciliate between imperative and declarative techniques while addressing the following issues: preserving standards for describing SBPs, minimizing designers efforts and non-dependency to a specific Business process engine. Our approach consists in generating, at deployment time, a management process for an initial SBP connected to it allowing its monitoring and configuring. The management process generation is performed thanks to a semantic model. This semantic model involves an upper management ontology, describing relationship between SBPs and business environments, and an explicit semantic description of the initial BP. This latter is based on identifying control dependencies to facilitate the organization of the whole management process.

However, data dependencies are important in turn to identify other aspects when creating the management process. Thereby, we are working on explicitly defining semantic data dependencies between inputs, outputs and properties which can include other service properties relationships such as mutuality and exclusivity. Hence, as part of our short term perspective, we foresee to detail more the service properties relationships in the upper management ontology. In addition, at this level, our approach involves only getters and setters as managing operations. Thus, we plan to specify a composition for managing operations given by the service provider.

References

1. Boukhebouze, M., Amghar, Y., Benharkat, A.-N., Maamar, Z.: A rule-based modeling for the description of flexible and self-healing business processes. In: Grundspenkis, J., Morzy, T., Vossen, G. (eds.) ADBIS 2009. LNCS, vol. 5739, pp. 15–27. Springer, Heidelberg (2009)
2. Gottschalk, F., van der Aalst, W.M.P., Jansen-Vullers, M.H., Rosa, M.L.: Configurable workflow models. Int. J. Cooperative Inf. Syst. 17(2), 177–221 (2008)
3. Ouyang, B., Zhong, F., Liu, H.: An eca-based control-rule formalism for the bpel process modularization. Procedia Environmental Sciences 11(1), 511–517 (2011)
4. Gong, Y., Janssen, M.: Creating dynamic business processes using semantic web services and business rules. In: ICEGOV, pp. 249–258 (2011)
5. Weigand, H., van den Heuvel, W.J., Hiel, M.: Business policy compliance in service-oriented systems. Inf. Syst. 36(4), 791–807 (2011)
6. Boukhebouze, M., Amghar, Y., Benharkat, A.N., Maamar, Z.: Towards an approach for estimating impact of changes on business processes. In: CEC (2009)
7. Business process model and notation 2.0, `http://www.omg.org/spec/BPMN/2.0/`
8. Ferrante, J., Ottenstein, K.J., Warren, J.D.: The program dependence graph and its use in optimization. ACM Trans. Program. Lang. Syst. 9(3), 319–349 (1987)
9. Mao, C.: Slicing web service-based software. In: SOCA, pp. 1–8 (2009)
10. Koning, M., Ai Sun, C., Sinnema, M., Avgeriou, P.: Vxbpel: Supporting variability for web services in bpel. Information & Software Technology 51(2), 258–269 (2009)
11. Charfi, A., Dinkelaker, T., Mezini, M.: A plug-in architecture for self-adaptive web service compositions. In: ICWS, pp. 35–42 (2009)

Discovering Workflow-Aware Virtual Knowledge Flows for Knowledge Dissemination

Minxin Shen and Duen-Ren Liu

Institute of Information Management, National Chiao-Tung University
1001 Ta Hsueh Road, Hsinchu 300, Taiwan
{shen,dliu}@iim.nctu.edu.tw

Abstract. In order to effectively disseminate task-relevant and process-scope knowledge, knowledge-intensive enterprises adopt knowledge flows to explicitly represent workers' knowledge needs and referencing behavior of codified knowledge during the execution of business tasks. However, due to differences in expertise and experience, individual workers impose varied knowledge needs on the knowledge flows directed by the workflows they participate in. This study proposes a model of *workflow-aware knowledge-flow views*, i.e. virtual knowledge flows abstracted from workflow-driven knowledge flows, to provide adaptable knowledge granularity. Moreover, a text mining approach is developed to derive knowledge-flow views from codified knowledge objects of knowledge flows, such as documents. Both task knowledge semantics and task execution sequences are utilized to evaluate the degrees of workers' knowledge demands in workflow contexts. Knowledge management systems can thus present different abstracted knowledge flows to diverse workflow participants, and facilitate knowledge sharing and collaboration.

Keywords: knowledge flow, workflow, knowledge management, text mining.

1 Introduction

In knowledge-intensive work environments, workers require task-relevant knowledge and documents to support their execution of tasks. Thus, effectively fulfilling workers' knowledge-needs by preserving, sharing and reusing task-relevant knowledge is essential for realizing knowledge management and promoting business intelligence. Organizations can provide task-relevant knowledge through knowledge flows (KF), which represent the flow of an individual or group's knowledge-needs and referencing behavior of codified knowledge during task execution.

Numerous recent studies have focused on KF models and applications in business and academic contexts. One major research theme focuses on knowledge sharing among knowledge workers. For example, researchers cite prior studies and propose new ideas through publishing papers, thereby creating KFs in the realm of science [1]; and in the business domain, KFs facilitate knowledge sharing during the execution of tasks [2]. By analyzing workers' knowledge-needs, KFs can be discovered, and used to recommend appropriate codified knowledge [3].

C. Huemer and P. Lops (Eds.): EC-Web 2013, LNBIP 152, pp. 80–87, 2013.

When a task involves teamwork, knowledge workers have different roles and task functions, so they usually have diverse knowledge-needs. However, conventional KF models do not provide different KF perspectives to fulfill team members' diverse needs. Although several KF models have been proposed, they do not consider the concept of virtual KFs. Our previous work [4] proposed a KF view model for the construction of virtual KFs to serve workers' knowledge-needs. Virtual KFs are derived from a KF, and provide abstracted knowledge for different roles.

However, our prior work is generally a manual, expert-based method. Moreover, the links between KF views and codified knowledge objects are missing, and workers will not know where to access concrete knowledge documents. Hence, we revise the KF view model, and present a text mining approach to deriving KF views. Generally, codified knowledge objects, such as documents that include semantic content, are exploited. Text similarity measures are employed to estimate knowledge demands for different roles. Then, concept distributions in different tasks are used to identify descriptive topics for representing virtual knowledge nodes. This work contributes to a comprehensive KF view model and data-driven algorithms for generating KF views.

2 Related Work

Knowledge flow (KF) research focuses on how KFs transmit, share and accumulate knowledge in a team. KFs reflect the level of knowledge cooperation between workers or processes, and influence the effectiveness of teamwork or workflow [2]. Sarnikar and Zhao [5] developed a knowledge workflow framework to automate KFs across an organization by integrating workflow and knowledge discovery techniques. Luo et al. [6] designed a textual KF model for a semantic link network. They can recommend appropriate browsing paths to users after evaluating their interests and inputs. KFs also express the sequence of information-needs and knowledge reference patterns when workers perform tasks. Lai and Liu [3] constructed time-ordered KFs from document access logs for modeling workers' knowledge referencing behavior and recommending task-relevant knowledge to workers.

Workflow technology supports the management of organizational processes. Due to the increasing complexity of workflows and the variety of participants, there is a growing demand for flexible workflow models capable of providing appropriate process abstractions [7-9]. Our previous works [7] generated process-views, virtual processes, by an order-preserving approach to preserve the original order of tasks in a base process. A role-based method [10] was also proposed to discover role-relevant process-views for different workers. We further applied the process-view model for KFs to construct KF views [4]. However, our prior studies required expert involvement. Flow designers had to select seed nodes to be concealed to derive virtual nodes. Some profiles and parameters had to be manually specified to evaluate role-task relevance. Moreover, maintaining a specific ontology for the generalization of knowledge nodes is labor-intensive and unfeasible in the rapidly changing business environment.

3 Modeling Virtual Knowledge Flows

3.1 Knowledge Flow and Knowledge-Flow Views

A KF that may have multiple KF views is referred to herein as a *base* KF. A KF view is generated from either base KFs or other KF views, and is considered a virtual KF. Fig. 1 illustrates knowledge sharing based on KF views. Assume that the base KF shown in Fig. 1 is the KF of a software development workflow. Marketers do not need to know every concept in the KF, although they must know software quality topics in order to better serve customers. An appropriate KF view can be derived for the sales representatives as follows: kn_1 to kn_3 are mapped into vkn_1; kn_4 and kn_5 are mapped into vkn_2; kn_6 and kn_7 are mapped into vkn_3. KF views present codified knowledge at suitable granularity; thus, different participants can have their own KF views serving their individual needs.

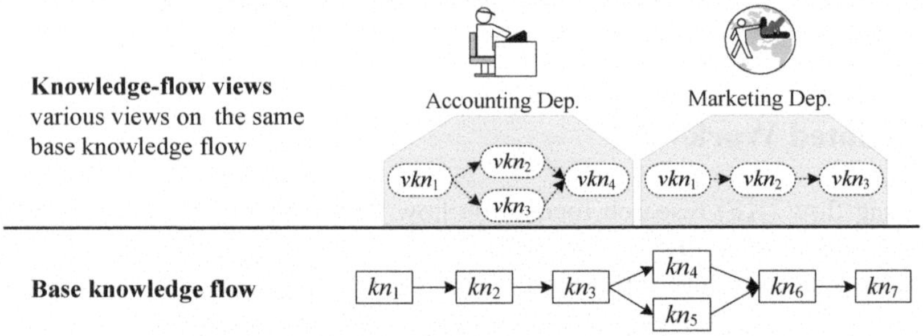

Fig. 1. Illustrative examples of knowledge-flow views

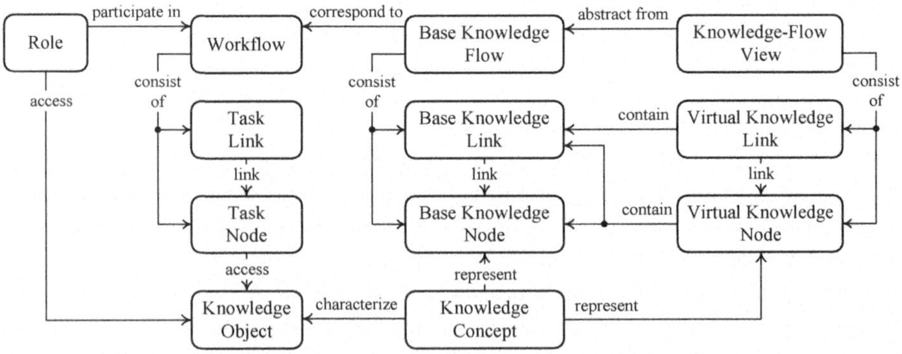

Fig. 2. Knowledge-flow view model

Fig. 2 illustrates how the components of our model are related. To reflect the progress of knowledge needs from the workflow aspect, a KF/knowledge node/knowledge link corresponds to a workflow/task node/task link. *Knowledge concepts*, i.e., key features that characterize codified knowledge objects, included in a knowledge node are the knowledge required by workers to fulfill the corresponding task (node). For example, a document about usability study may be accessed by task node "Web testing", thus the corresponding knowledge node may include a concept "user experience", a representative topic of the document. Furthermore, a KF view has a corresponding base KF from which it is derived. Generally, a virtual knowledge node is an abstraction of a set of base knowledge nodes and links.

3.2 Formal Definitions

Definition 1 (workflow): A *workflow WF* is a 2-tuple ⟨*TN*, *TL*⟩, where

1. *TN* is a set of *task nodes*. Each task node may access a set of knowledge objects.
2. *TL* is a set of *task links*. A task link is denoted by $t\text{-}link(tn_x, tn_y)$ to indicate that the routing can proceed from task node tn_x to tn_y. Links $t\text{-}link(tn_x,\varnothing)$ and $t\text{-}link(\varnothing, tn_y)$ denote that tn_x and tn_y are start and end nodes, respectively.
3. *Path*, *adjacent*, and *ordering relation*: A *path* is a sequence of task links. Two distinct task nodes tn_x and tn_y are *adjacent* if $t\text{-}link(tn_x, tn_y)$ or $t\text{-}link(tn_y, tn_x)$ exists. For tn_x, $tn_y \in TN$: (a) If there is a path from tn_x to tn_y, then the ordering of tn_x is higher than y, i.e., tn_x precedes tn_y. Their ordering relation is denoted by $tn_x > tn_y$ or $tn_y < tn_x$. (b) If no path exists from tn_x to tn_y or from tn_y to tn_x, then tn_x and tn_y are ordering independent, denoted by $tn_x \infty tn_y$, i.e., tn_x and tn_y proceed independently.
4. Knowledge objects represent organizational codified knowledge such as documents and databases. Knowledge concepts signify topics or keywords that characterize their corresponding knowledge objects. That is, a set of knowledge objects $KO_x=\{ko_1, \ldots, ko_m\}$ accessed by task node tn_x are characterized by a set of knowledge concepts $KC_x=\{kc_1, \ldots, kc_n\}$.
5. An organizational *role*, i.e., an abstraction of workers, is represented by a set of knowledge objects to indicate its required background knowledge or experience.

Definition 2 (knowledge flow): A *knowledge flow KF* is a 2-tuple ⟨*KN*, *KL*⟩, where

1. *KN* is a set of *knowledge nodes*. A knowledge node kn_x contains a set of knowledge concepts extracted from their corresponding knowledge objects, i.e., $kn_x = \{$knowledge concept $kc_i \mid kc_i \in KC_x'$, $KC_x' \subseteq KC_x$, and KC_x is the set of concepts extracted from the knowledge objects (KO_x) accessed by task node $tn_x\}$.
2. *KL* is a set of *knowledge links*. A knowledge link, denoted by $k\text{-}link(kn_x, kn_y)$, indicates that knowledge access proceeds from knowledge node kn_x to kn_y. The definitions of path, adjacent, and ordering relation in the knowledge flow are similar to those in workflow, and are omitted for brevity.

Definition 3 (knowledge-flow view). A *knowledge-flow view KFV* is a 2-tuple ⟨*VKN*, *VKL*⟩, where *VKN* is a set of *virtual knowledge nodes* and *VKL* is a set of *virtual knowledge links*.

According to the different properties of a KF, various methods can be developed to derive a KF view. Since task execution sequence (i.e. sequence of knowledge access) is a crucial property for business applications and analysis, our previous work, an *order-preserving* abstraction approach [7], is adopted to generate KF views. Intuitively, a virtual knowledge node/link is an aggregation of a set of base knowledge nodes/links. The approach ensures that the original knowledge access order revealed in a base KF is preserved. Namely, the ordering relation between two virtual knowledge nodes held in a KF view infers that the ordering relations between the respective members of these virtual activities hold in the base KF. The formal definition is described below. The proof of KF view order preservation is similar to that for process-view [7], and is omitted. Cyclic cases are also referred to [7]. In addition, task boundaries are utilized while the derivation of knowledge concepts for KF views (cf. Section 4.3). Therefore, the derived knowledge-flow view is *workflow-aware*, since task boundary and execution sequence are considered during the abstraction process.

Definition 4 (order-preserving knowledge-flow view): Given a knowledge flow *KF* = ⟨*KN*, *KL*⟩, a *knowledge-flow view KFV* is a 2-tuple ⟨*VKN*, *VKL*⟩, where

1. *VKN* is a set of *virtual knowledge nodes*. A virtual knowledge node vkn_x is a 3-tuple $\langle KN_x, KL_x, KC_x \rangle$, where
   (a) Members of KN_x are knowledge nodes or previously defined virtual knowledge nodes. For any $kn_i \in KN$, $kn_i \notin KN_x$, ordering relation $\Re \in \{<, >, \infty\}$: if $\exists\, kn_j \in KN_x$ such that $kn_i \Re kn_j$ holds in KF, then $kn_i \Re kn_k$ holds in KF for all $kn_k \in KN_x$. This means that the ordering relations between kn_i and all members (base knowledge nodes) of KN_x are identical in *KF*.
   (b) $KL_x = \{k\text{-}link(kn_i, kn_j) \mid kn_i, kn_j \in KN_x$ and $k\text{-}link(kn_i, kn_j) \in KL\}$.
   (c) $KC_x = \{$knowledge concept $c_j \mid c_j \in \cup KC_i', \forall kn_i \in KN_x, KC_i' \subseteq KC_i$, and KC_i is the set of concepts associated with knowledge node $kn_i\}$.
2. *VKL* is a set of *virtual knowledge links*. A virtual knowledge link from vkn_x to vkn_y, denoted by $vk\text{-}link(vkn_x, vkn_y)$, exists if $k\text{-}link(kn_i, kn_j)$ exists, where kn_i is a member of vkn_x, and kn_j is a member of vkn_y.

4 Discovering Virtual Knowledge Flows

Based on the above definitions, this section describes the procedure and algorithms for discovering KF views.

4.1 Estimating Knowledge Demands

Knowledge needs are subjective, and can be obtained from explicit user profiles or from implicit search and browsing logs. As an exploratory study, we simply utilize text similarity as the base for estimating knowledge demands. The basic idea is inspired by novelty-based recommendation. As shown in Fig. 2 and Definition 1, each role is associated with a set of knowledge objects as background knowledge or experience. Thus, a role is signified by its associated knowledge objects. Knowledge objects of knowledge nodes are less *understandable* to a role if they are less similar to the role profile, and vice versa. The more unfamiliar knowledge nodes must be abstracted to provide more general concepts in order to enhance knowledge comprehensibility and sharing. Without loss of generality, we may use documents to represent knowledge objects.

The vector space model has been applied in many content-based recommendation systems and information retrieval applications. Features (terms) of knowledge objects are extracted after stop-word removal, stemming and term weighting. Each codified knowledge object is described by a term vector comprised of representative terms and their term weights. We employ the well-known *tf-idf* approach to calculate term weights. The weight of term t_i in document d_j is $w_{ij} = tf_{ij} \times \log(F_D/f_{Di})$, where tf_{ij} denotes the term frequency of term t_i in document d_j; f_{Di} is the number of documents that contain the specific term t_i; and F_D is the total number of documents. The similarity between documents is usually measured by the cosine similarity measure. Two documents are considered similar if the cosine similarity score is high. The cosine similarity of two documents, d_1 and d_2, is $sim(d_1, d_2) = \vec{d}_1 \bullet \vec{d}_2 / |\vec{d}_1| \bullet |\vec{d}_2|$, where $\vec{d}_1$ and $\vec{d}_2$ are the feature vectors of d_1 and d_2, respectively.

The understandability degree of a knowledge node with regard to a role is estimated according to the text similarity of knowledge objects. We use the average similarity between knowledge nodes and roles as the understandability value. That is, $und(kn_x, r) = avg(sim(d_m^{kn_x}, d_n^r))$, $\forall d_m^{kn_x} \in kn_x, \forall d_n^r \in r$.

4.2 Generating the Knowledge-Flow View Structure

Based on the degrees of understandability, roles' KF views can be derived. Algorithm 1 determines the set of virtual knowledge nodes of a KF view from a base KF. The process begins with the *highest ordering* nodes in the base KF (line 8). When the *total understandability degree* of a set of base nodes approximates the *granular threshold TH*, a virtual node is found (line 9). Total understandability degree is the sum of understandability degrees of a set of base nodes. Namely, $und(KN, r) = \sum und(kn_x, r)$ $\forall kn_x \in KN$. Granular threshold *TH* determines the granularity of generated KF views. When the sum of the understandability degrees of some base nodes approximates the threshold value, these nodes can form a virtual node, which is deemed to be sufficiently understandable to the role. A larger *TH* corresponds to the generation of fewer virtual nodes (and more base nodes included in a virtual node). The above steps are repeated against residual base nodes until virtual nodes cover all the base nodes of the base KF. Thus, the virtual knowledge node set of the target KF view is found.

Algorithm 1 (The generation of virtual knowledge node set)

1: **input:** a base knowledge flow $BKF = \langle BKN, BKL \rangle$; $und(kn_x) \leq TH, \forall kn_x \in BKN$
2: **output:** the set of virtual knowledge node (VKN) of a KF view $VKF = \langle VKN, VKL \rangle$
3: **begin**
4: $i \leftarrow 1$, $VKN \leftarrow \emptyset$
5: **repeat**
6: $vkn_i = \langle KN_i, KL_i \rangle \leftarrow \langle \emptyset, \emptyset \rangle$
7: residual knowledge node set $RKN \leftarrow BKN - \{kn_x \mid \exists\, vkn_i$ s.t. $kn_x \in vkn_i\}$
8: select a highest ordering node kn_x from RKN
9: $vkn_i \leftarrow$ **getVirtualNode**(kn_x, RKN, BKF)
10: $VKN \leftarrow VKN \cup \{vkn_i\}$, $i \leftarrow i + 1$
11: **until** $\forall kn_x \in BKN, \exists\, vkn_i$ s.t. $kn_x \in vkn_i$
12: **return** VKN
13: **end**

Algorithm 2 (genVirtualNode) discovers a virtual knowledge node. Initially, *KN* contains only the given base node kn_x (line 3). *KN* is updated during the *while* loop (lines 7~15) by adding the adjacent nodes that cause *KN* to satisfy three conditions: the order-preserving property (line 10, cf. [7]); the threshold of total understandability degree; and that it does not overlap with previously derived virtual activities. The *repeat-until* loop (lines 4~16) continues until no other adjacent nodes are added to *KN*.

Algorithm 2 (The generation of a virtual node)

1: **getVirtualNode**(seed node kn_s, residual knowledge node set *RKN*, $BKF=\langle BKN,BKL\rangle$)
2: **begin**
3: $vkn = \langle KN, KL\rangle \leftarrow \langle\{kn_s\}, \varnothing\rangle$
4: **repeat**
5: temp knowledge node set $TKN \leftarrow KN$
6: adjacent node set $AKN \leftarrow \{kn_x | \, kn_x, kn_y \in RKN, kn_x \notin KN, kn_y \in KN, k\text{-}link(kn_x,kn_y)$ or $k\text{-}link(kn_y, kn_x) \in BKL\}$
7: **while** AKN is not empty **do**
8: select an base node kn_x from AKN
9: remove kn_x from AKN
10: $KN_{tmp} \leftarrow$ **getOrderPreserVN**($KN \cup \{kn_x\}, BKF$) //generate order-preserving virtual node
11: **if** $(und(KN_{tmp}) \leq TH)$ and $(KN_{tmp} \subseteq RKN)$ **then** //check threshold
12: $KN \leftarrow KN_{tmp}$
13: $AKN \leftarrow AKN - \{kn_y | kn_y \in AKN \cap KN\}$
14: **end if**
15: **end while**
16: **until** $KN = TKN$
17: link set $KL \leftarrow \{ k\text{-}link(kn_x, kn_y) \,|\, kn_x, kn_y \in KN$, and $k\text{-}link(kn_x, kn_y) \in BKL\}$
18: **return** $vkn = \langle KN, KL\rangle$
19: **end**

4.3 Generating Knowledge-Flow View Content

Finally, knowledge concepts are derived to represent (virtual) knowledge nodes. As described in Section 3.1, a knowledge node corresponds to a collection of knowledge objects that are accessed by the corresponding task node. Knowledge concepts of a knowledge node are the representative topical words generated from the corresponding knowledge objects.

Whether a word/phrase is an appropriate topic for a knowledge node is determined from a single knowledge node and the whole KF aspects. For example, "JUnit" is better than "test case" to represent "unit testing" in a software testing KF. That is, task (knowledge node) boundaries are the curtail factor for selecting suitable keywords from knowledge objects. Therefore, term statistics of inter- and intra-knowledge nodes are used to identify representative knowledge concepts.

First, in order to increase the comprehensibility of KFs and views, documents are mapped to Wikipedia concepts. That is, only Wikipedia terms in the text are recognized as candidates. Wikipedia dumps are utilized for the term extraction.

Next, term distributions of intra-knowledge nodes are measured by *term frequency* (*tf*). Moreover, term statistics of inter-knowledge nodes are measured by *inverse node frequency* (*inf*). Term t_i's $inf = \log(F_N/f_{Ni})$, where F_N is the number of knowledge nodes, and f_{Ni} is the number of knowledge nodes that contain term t_i. Finally, candidate terms are ranked according to *tf-inf*: *tf-inf* of term t_i in node n_j is $w_{ij} = tf_{ij} \times \log(F_N/f_{Ni})$, where tf_{ij} is the frequency of term w_i in node n_j. The main difference between base and virtual knowledge nodes is the boundary of nodes, and thus the knowledge concept generation process is the same for KF and KF views.

5 Conclusions

This work presents a KF view model for knowledge sharing and navigation. Knowledge granularity of KFs is adapted to the needs of workflow participants. Workers can thus obtain helpful views of a large and complex KF. To support the discovery of role-relevant KF views, this work utilizes text similarity of knowledge objects to measure the degrees of understandability between roles and knowledge nodes. Task execution sequence and knowledge access order are preserved while generating abstracted KFs. Moreover, task boundaries are employed to derive representative knowledge concepts for knowledge nodes. Therefore, role-relevant KF views are automatically generated using the proposed algorithms. Accordingly, knowledge management systems can disseminate KFs at suitable granularities for various organizational roles.

Acknowledgements. This research was supported by the National Science Council of the Taiwan under Grant No. NSC 99-2410-H-009-034-MY3 and NSC 102-2811-H-009-002.

References

1. Zhuge, H.: Discovery of Knowledge Flow in Science. Communications of the ACM 49, 101–107 (2006)
2. Zhuge, H., Guo, W.: Virtual Knowledge Service Market - for Effective Knowledge Flow within Knowledge Grid. Journal of Systems and Software 80, 1833–1842 (2007)
3. Lai, C.-H., Liu, D.-R.: Integrating Knowledge Flow Mining and Collaborative Filtering to Support Document Recommendation. Journal of Systems and Software 82, 2023–2037 (2009)
4. Liu, D.-R., Lin, C.-W., Chen, H.-F.: Discovering Role-Based Virtual Knowledge Flows for Organizational Knowledge Support. Decision Support Systems 55, 12–30 (2013)
5. Sarnikar, S., Zhao, J.: Pattern-Based Knowledge Workflow Automation: Concepts and Issues. Information Systems and E-Business Management 6, 385–402 (2008)
6. Luo, X., Hu, Q., Xu, W., Yu, Z.: Discovery of Textual Knowledge Flow Based on the Management of Knowledge Maps. Concurrency and Computation: Practice and Experience 20, 1791–1806 (2008)
7. Liu, D.-R., Shen, M.: Workflow Modeling for Virtual Processes: An Order-Preserving Process-View Approach. Information Systems 28, 505–532 (2003)
8. Weidlich, M., Smirnov, S., Wiggert, C., Weske, M.: Flexab - Flexible Business Process Model Abstraction. In: The Forum of the 23rd Intl. Conf. on Advanced Information Systems Engineering (CAiSE Forum 2011), pp. 17–24. CEUR-WS.org (2011)
9. Jagadeesh Chandra Bose, R.P., van der Aalst, W.M.P.: Abstractions in Process Mining: A Taxonomy of Patterns. In: Dayal, U., Eder, J., Koehler, J., Reijers, H.A. (eds.) BPM 2009. LNCS, vol. 5701, pp. 159–175. Springer, Heidelberg (2009)
10. Shen, M., Liu, D.-R.: Discovering Role-Relevant Process-Views for Disseminating Process Knowledge. Expert Systems with Applications 26, 301–310 (2004)

An Emotion Dimensional Model Based on Social Tags: Crossing Folksonomies and Enhancing Recommendations

Ignacio Fernández-Tobías, Iván Cantador, and Laura Plaza

Universidad Autónoma de Madrid, 28049 Madrid, Spain
{i.fernandez,ivan.cantador,laura.plaza}@uam.es

Abstract. In this paper we present an emotion computational model based on social tags. The model is built upon an automatically generated lexicon that describes emotions by means of synonym and antonym terms, and that is linked to multiple domain-specific emotion folksonomies extracted from entertainment social tagging systems. Using these cross-domain folksonomies, we develop a number of methods that automatically transform tag-based item profiles into emotion-oriented item profiles. To validate our model we report results from a user study that show a high precision of our methods to infer the emotions evoked by items in the movie and music domains, and results from an offline evaluation that show accuracy improvements on model-based recommender systems that incorporate the extracted item emotional information.

Keywords: emotions, folksonomies, cross domains, recommender systems.

1 Introduction

Emotions are intense feelings that are directed at someone or something. For instance, a person may be glad when she comes across an old friend, and may be excited when she receives a gift. Moods, in contrast, are feelings that tend to be less intense than emotions, and often – though not always – lack a contextual stimulus [8]. Moreover, emotions are more transitory than moods. Quoting the example given in [11], a person may feel angry when someone has been rude to her. This intense feeling of anger probably comes and goes quickly, maybe in a matter of seconds. In contrast, when a person is in a bad mood, she could feel bad for several hours.

Emotions and moods can be comprised in the generic concept of *affect* [11]. Emotions can turn into moods when there is a loss of focus on the contextual stimuli (people, objects or events) that started the feelings. In the opposite direction, moods can elicit more emotional responses to contextual stimuli. In this paper, since we aim to model the mostly ephemeral feelings caused by entertainment items – such as movies and music –, we use the term *emotions* to refer to both emotions and moods.

In adaptive and personalized systems, emotions are usually considered as contextual signals that can lead to enhanced approaches in a wide array of applications, such as constructing user behavior models [10], tailoring search results [13], and filtering and recommending items [18], to name a few. Hence, modeling, capturing and exploiting emotions present challenging problems that are addressed in distinct Computer Science

C. Huemer and P. Lops (Eds.): EC-Web 2013, LNBIP 152, pp. 88–100, 2013.

research areas that intersect with Psychology and Social Sciences, such as Human Computer Interaction [7], Artificial Intelligence and Robotics [3], Opinion Mining and Sentiment Analysis [6], and Information Access and Retrieval [16]. Here we focus on the **emotion modeling** task, and restrict our attention to situations where emotions are expressed in (and can be extracted from) **text contents** – such as reviews in blogs, and annotations in social tagging systems –, differently to e.g. situations where emotions are recognized in either the visual or auditory modalities [7][19].

Computational models of emotion can be categorized according to the emotional theories they adopt, namely the *categorical emotion theory* – which characterizes emotions as discrete units –, the *emotional dimension theory* – which conceive emotions as points in a continuous space –, and the *appraisal theory* – which represents emotions as outcomes of events and situations. Our model adopts the **emotional dimension theory** by representing an emotion as a vector, whose components correspond to terms in an emotion lexicon, and have assigned positive or negative weights depending on whether their terms are synonyms or antonyms of labels that describe the emotion. As we shall show in this paper, the projections of our emotion vectors into a two-dimension space are in accordance with the psychological **circumplex model of affect** [15].

The input data used for capturing and modeling emotions can also be used to categorize the existing computational models of emotion. Hence, we can distinguish linguistic approaches that extract emotions from *text*, image processing approaches that recognize emotions in facial expressions from *images* and *videos*, and speech recognition approaches that identify emotions on *audio* data. The linguistic approaches usually create or make use of text corpora and resources – such as lexicons, thesauri and ontologies – that provide specific vocabularies for describing emotions. In this paper we propose an approach that generates a **lexicon** and **folksonomies** to represent generic emotions and domain-specific emotional categories. These resources are automatically generated from a generic thesaurus and social tagging systems in entertainment domains, namely the movie, music and book domains.

Using the generated emotion lexicon and cross-domain folksonomies, we develop a number of methods that transform tag-based item profiles into **emotion-oriented item profiles**. We evaluated the quality of such profiles by conducting a user study, whose results show a high precision of our methods to infer the emotions evoked by items in the movie and music domains. Moreover, we performed an offline evaluation, whose results show that exploiting the extracted emotional information improves the accuracy of various **model-based recommender systems** on the above domains.

2 Related Work

The study and development of computational systems aimed to recognize, interpret and process human feelings is usually referred to as Affective Computing. This discipline involves a number of research fields and applications. In Artificial Intelligence, for instance, endowing robots with emotions for improving human-robot interaction has been largely studied [3].

Emotion recognition in natural language is becoming increasingly important as well. One of the most outstanding applications concerns discovering the affective relevance of user online reviews of products and services [6]. Other works have focused on annotating texts (e.g. news items and tweets) with emotions [14].

The use of emotions in User Modeling and Recommender Systems is mainly concerned with detecting and modeling the user's mood, and suggesting items according to such mood [18]. Kaminskas and Ricci [12] present an approach to recommend music compositions for places of interest by means of social tags that represent the user's emotional state when listening to music and visiting places. To attach emotional tags to music, they use the Geneva Emotional Music Scale (GEMS) model [19]. Others have studied how to describe music in terms of the emotions it evokes. Feng et al. [9] map two dimensions of tempo and articulation into mood categories, such as *happiness*, *sadness* and *fear*. Shi et al. [16] propose a mood-specific movie similarity, which is exploited in a joint matrix factorization model for enhanced context-aware (mood-specific) recommendations.

As done by Baldoni et al. [2], we propose to extract emotional information from item annotations in social tagging systems. However, while they use ontologies and lexicons to assist the identification of emotions, we automatically derive emotions based on simple domain-specific emotional categories existing in specialized systems, such as the Jinni[1]'s movie categories and GEMS' music categories. Moreover, to make our approach generic and ensure cross-domain interoperability, the domain-specific emotional categories are mapped to the general and well accepted emotions of Russell's circumplex model [15].

3 A Core Emotion Lexicon

Among the existing dimensional models of emotion, the circumplex model is a dominant one. It suggests that emotions are distributed in a two-dimensional circular space formed by two independent dimensions: *arousal* and *pleasure*. Figure 1a shows such distribution. Arousal represents the vertical axis and reflects the intensity of an emotion; and pleasure represents the horizontal axis and reflects if an emotion is positive or negative. The center of the circle represents medium levels of arousal and pleasure. Any emotion can be represented at any level of arousal and pleasure, including a neutral level of one or both of such factors. Hence, for instance, *happiness* and *sadness* can be considered as emotions with the highest and lowest levels of pleasure, respectively, but with neutral arousal levels, with respect to other emotions such as *tension* (with high arousal) and *calmness* (with low arousal). The figure shows the distribution of 16 core emotions. Our model also considers this set of emotions.

The dimensional model we propose is built upon an automatically generated lexicon $\mathcal{L} = \{\mathtt{t}_1, \dots, \mathtt{t}_K\}$ composed of synonym and antonym terms $\mathtt{t}_k$ of the core emotions' names – which are adjectives (e.g. *happy*, *sad*), as shown in Figure 1a. The synonym and antonym terms of each emotion are obtained from the online thesaurus provided by Dictionary.com[2]. Specifically, the lexicon is composed of the synonyms

[1] Jinni movie search and recommendation engine, `http://www.jinni.com`
[2] Dictionary.com thesaurus, `http://thesaurus.com`

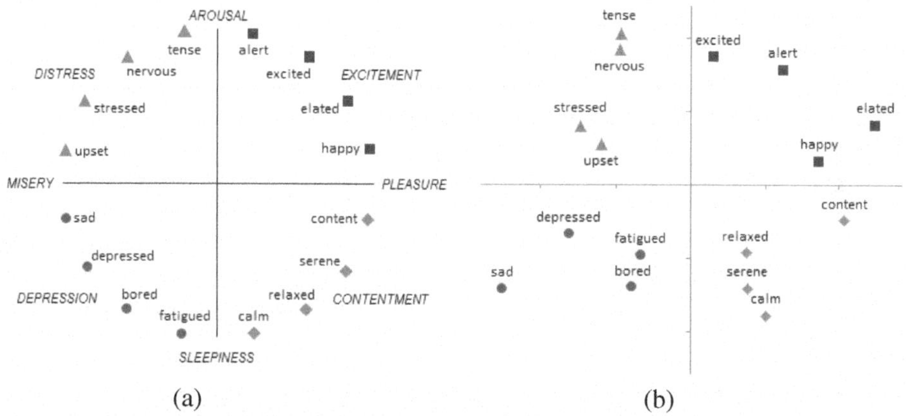

Fig. 1. Two-dimensional distributions of core emotions established in the circumplex model (1a) and automatically obtained in our tag-based model (1b)

Table 1. Considered core emotions and some of their synonym terms

Emotion	Synonym terms	Emotion	Synonym terms
alert	alert, active, animated, lively, sprightly	***fatigued***	fatigued, tired, fatigued, drained, exhausted
excited	excited, stimulated, agitated, moved	***bored***	bored, apathetic, exasperated, indifferent
elated	elated, jubilant, overjoyed, exhilarated	***depressed***	depressed, dejected, despondent, disconsolate
happy	happy, merry, cheerful, joyful, bright	***sad***	sad, sorrowful, doleful, downcast, gloomy
content	content, satisfied, gratified, pleased, enjoyed	***upset***	upset, bother, disturbed, troubled, distressed
serene	serene, quiet, placid, tranquil, peaceful	***stressed***	stressed, tormented, harassed, vexed, irked
relaxed	relaxed, moderated, mitigated, loose, free	***nervous***	nervous, apprehensive, uneasy, disturbed
calm	calm, mild, appeased, smooth, soften	***tense***	tense, restless, uptight, jittery, restive

and antonyms of all noun, adjective and verb entries in the above thesaurus for the emotions' names. Table 1 shows some of the gathered synonyms for each emotion.

Once the lexicon $\mathcal{L}$ is generated, a core emotion $e_i \in \mathcal{E}$ is represented as a vector $\mathbf{e}_i = (e_{i,1}, \ldots, e_{i,K}) \in \mathbb{R}^K$, in which the component $e_{i,k}$ corresponds to the term $t_k \in \mathcal{L}$ (that can describe various emotions), and is a numeric value defined as:

$$e_{i,k} = \begin{cases} tfidf(t_k, e_i) & \text{if } t_k \in synonyms(e_i) \\ -tfidf(t_k, e_i) & \text{if } t_k \in antonyms(e_i) \\ 0 & \text{otherwise} \end{cases} \quad (1)$$

The component $e_{i,k}$ is greater than 0 if the term t_k is a synonym of the emotion e_i, lower than 0 if t_k is an antonym of e_i, and 0 otherwise. Its absolute value corresponds to the TF-IDF weight of t_k computed by considering the lexicon $\mathcal{L}$ as the *collection vocabulary*, and the set $\mathcal{E}$ of emotions (described as sets of synonym and antonym terms) as the *collection documents*. Formally,

$$tfidf(\mathrm{t_k}, \mathrm{e_i}) = tf(\mathrm{t_k}, \mathrm{e_i}) \cdot idf(\mathrm{t_k}, \mathcal{E})$$

where $tf(\mathrm{t_k}, \mathrm{e_i})$ is the normalized term frequency of $\mathrm{t_k}$ for $\mathrm{e_i}$, which measures how relevant the term is to describe the emotion, and which is defined as:

$$tf(\mathrm{t_k}, \mathrm{e_i}) = \frac{f(\mathrm{t_k}, \mathrm{e_i})}{\max\{f(\mathrm{t}, \mathrm{e_i}) : t \in synonyms(\mathrm{e_i}) \cup antonyms(\mathrm{e_i})\}}$$

being $f(\mathrm{t_k}, \mathrm{e_i})$ the number of times that term $\mathrm{t_k}$ appears in the sets of synonyms and antonyms of $\mathrm{e_i}$'s thesaurus entries; and where $idf(\mathrm{t_k}, \mathcal{E})$ is the inverse document frequency of $\mathrm{t_k}$ in $\mathcal{E}$, which measures how rare (and thus informative) is the term across all the emotions' descriptions, and which is defined as:

$$idf(\mathrm{t_k}, \mathcal{E}) = \log \frac{|\mathcal{E}|}{|\{\mathrm{e} \in \mathcal{E} : \mathrm{t_k} \in synonyms(\mathrm{e}) \cup antonyms(\mathrm{e})\}|}$$

With the proposed vector representation, we can measure (dis)similarities between emotions. Specifically, we can use the cosine similarity $sim(\mathrm{e_i}, \mathrm{e_j}) = \cos(\mathbf{e}_i, \mathbf{e}_j)$.

To validate the correspondences between our computational model and the theoretic circumplex model, Figure 1b shows the projections of the emotion vectors into a two-dimensional space by applying Principal Component Analysis. We can see that our model locates all the 16 basic emotions in their corresponding quadrants. More interestingly, in our model the axes defined by the two most informative components are related to the *arousal* and *pleasure* factors of the circumplex model. Thus, positive emotions (e.g. *happy*, *calm*) are in the right quadrants, while negative emotions (e.g. *sad*, *upset*) are in the left ones, for the horizontal (pleasure) axis; and more intense emotions (e.g. *tense*, *alert*) are in the upper quadrants, while less intense emotions (e.g. *relaxed*, *bored*) are in the lower quadrants, for the vertical (arousal) axis.

We note that, as done in [4], we tested other term weighting methods – such as the BM25 probabilistic model – and emotion similarity functions – such as the Jaccard similarity. We finally used the TF-IDF weighting method and cosine similarity since they let generate the two-dimensional distribution of emotions closest to the circumplex model's. We also note that we did not perform any cleaning and filtering process on the original sets of synonyms and antonyms obtained from the online thesaurus. Such process may increase the quality of the representations (e.g. by discarding ambiguous terms), and thus may let generate a better emotion distribution.

4 A Cross-Domain Emotion Folksonomy

In a social tagging system users create or upload items, annotate them with freely chosen tags, and share them with other users. The whole set of tags constitutes an unstructured knowledge classification scheme that is known as *folksonomy*. This implicit classification is then used to search and recommend items. The purpose for tagging is manifold: describing the content of the items, providing contextual information about the items, expressing qualities and opinions about the items, or even stating self-references and personal tasks related to the items.

Within the set of tags that express qualities and opinions about the items, there are tags that refer to emotions caused by the annotated items. In most cases, however, such emotions are not the core emotions presented in Section 3, but domain-specific emotional categories – such as *suspense* in the movie domain, and *nostalgia* in the music domain –, which indeed may be related to one or more core emotions.

In this section we extend our emotion model by linking the core emotions with domain-specific emotional categories described by tags in different folksonomies. Specifically, we focus on the movie and music entertainment domains by exploiting the MovieLens and Last.fm folksonomies provided in the HetRec'11 workshop [5] (Sections 4.1 and 4.2). With the extended model we propose to build emotion-oriented item profiles (Section 4.3) and cross-domain folksonomies (Section 4.4).We make all the generated data – lexicon, folksonomies, and item profiles – publicly available[3].

4.1 An Emotion Folksonomy for Movies

To build an emotion folksonomy in the movie domain, we first select a total of 15 emotional categories listed under the *mood* topic in Jinni movie search and recommendation system. We describe each category by 4 to 6 associated feeling terms, and use them as seed terms (see Table 2). Next, we extend the seed terms with their synonyms and antonyms in Thesaurus.com, but restricted to those existing as social tags in the MovieLens dataset. Finally, we repeat the process explained in Section 3 to represent an emotional category as a vector of weighted terms. In this vector, positive components represent synonyms while negative components represent antonyms. In this way, each emotional category is represented as a set of tags that lets establish (dis)similarities with other categories.

Table 2. Considered movie emotional categories and seed terms

Category	Seed terms	Category	Seed terms
clever	clever, cerebral, reflective	***sexy***	sexy, erotic, sensual
offbeat	offbeat, quirky, surreal, witty	***sexual***	sexual, lascive, horny
exciting	exciting, energetic, frantic, forceful	***uplifting***	uplifting, inspirational, hope
suspenseful	suspenseful, tense	***bleak***	bleak, grim, depressing, hopeless
captivating	captivating, rousing, poignant	***gloomy***	gloomy, sad, melancholic, nostalgic
emotional	emotional, passionate, romantic	***rough***	rough, brutal, lurid, macabre, wry
feel good	cute, merry, happy	***scary***	scary, creepy, menacing, eerie
humorous	humorous, funny, comical		

Figure 2a depicts the cosine similarity values between each pair of emotional categories (green/red cells correspond to positive/negative values). It can be observed

[3] Emotion lexicon, folksonomies, profiles, and online evaluation tool, `http://ir.ii.uam.es/emotions`

that close emotional categories, such as *gloomy* and *bleak*, present high similarity, while very distinct categories, such as *gloomy* and *feel good*, present low similarity.

4.2 An Emotion Folksonomy for Music

To generate an emotion folksonomy in the music domain, we select as emotional categories the 9 emotions proposed in the GEMS model (see Table 3). As initial seed terms we use the category names and their associated feeling terms given in [19]. Next, we extend these terms with their synonyms and antonyms in Thesaurus.com, but restricted to those existing as social tags in the Last.fm dataset. The emotional category vectors are then created as for the movie domain. Table 3 shows some of the most informative tags for each emotional category.

Figure 2b shows the similarity values between each pair of emotional categories. Again, close categories, such as *tenderness* and *nostalgia*, present high similarity, while very distinct categories, such as *sadness* and *joy*, present low similarity.

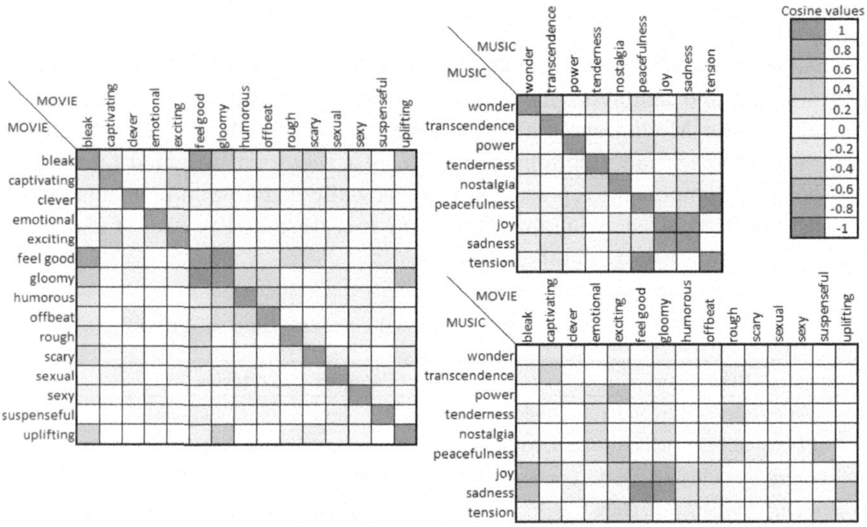

Fig. 2. Cosine similarity values between movie and music emotional categories

Table 3. Considered music emotional categories and seed terms

Category	Main tags	Category	Main tags
joy	funny, happy, amusing, jolly	***tenderness***	tender, gentle, mellow, romantic
nostalgia	nostalgic, melancholic, sentimental	***tension***	tense, edgy, angry, fierce
peacefulness	peaceful, quiet, calm, gentle	***transcendence***	transcendent, fascinating, enchanting
power	powerful, strong, energetic, intense	***wonder***	wonderful, strange, fantastic
sadness	sad, sorrowful, unhappy, dismal, tearful		

4.3 Emotion-Oriented Tag-Based Profiles

The proposed representation of emotions lets transform tag-based item profiles (i.e., the items' annotation sets) into emotion-oriented profiles. In particular, we propose to perform such transformation in two stages. First, tag-based profiles are transformed into domain emotion-oriented profiles. Next, the obtained domain emotion-oriented profiles are transformed into core emotion-oriented profiles. Formally, let a core emotion $\mathrm{e}_i^C \in \mathcal{E}$ and a domain-specific emotional category $\mathrm{e}_j^D \in \mathcal{E}_D$ be defined as in formula (1). That is, they are vectors whose components represent lexicon terms and folksonomy tags that are synonyms and antonyms of the considered emotions. For an item (object) o_n, let $\mathbf{o}_n^T = (o_{n,1}, \dots, o_{n,|\mathcal{T}|}) \in \mathbb{R}^{|\mathcal{T}|}$ be the item's **tag-based profile**, where $o_{n,i}$ corresponds to the tag $\mathrm{t}_i \in \mathcal{T}$ of the item's folksonomy. Then, from such profile, we define:

- the item's **domain emotion-oriented profile** as $\mathbf{p}_n^D = (p_{n,1}, \dots, p_{n,|\mathcal{E}_D|}) \in [-1,1]^{|\mathcal{E}_D|}$, where the i-th component corresponds to the domain emotional category $\mathrm{e}_i^D \in \mathcal{E}_D$, and its weight is computed as $p_{n,i} = cos(\mathbf{o}_n^T, \mathbf{e}_i^D)$, and
- the item's **core emotion-oriented profile** as $\mathbf{q}_n^C = (q_{n,1}, \dots, q_{n,|\mathcal{E}|}) \in [-1,1]^{|\mathcal{E}|}$, where the i-th component corresponds to the core emotion $\mathrm{e}_i^C \in \mathcal{E}$, and its weight is computed as $q_{n,i} = \sum_{k=1}^{|\mathcal{E}_D|} p_{n,k} \cdot cos(\mathbf{e}_i^C, \mathbf{e}_k^D)$.

Moreover, for each of these types of emotion-oriented profiles, we consider two alternatives for defining the (core and domain) emotion vectors $\mathbf{e}_i^C$ and $\mathbf{e}_j^D$: **basic vectors**, whose components correspond to terms of the lexicon, as defined in formula (1), and **extended_N vectors**, whose components correspond to the N folksonomy tags that cooccur most frequently (in the tag-based item profiles) with the terms of the basic vectors. These tags are not necessarily synonyms/antonyms of the seed terms, and it is not clear whether they can be valuable to effectively assign emotions to items.

4.4 Crossing Emotion Folksonomies

In our model it is possible to relate core emotions and domain-specific emotional categories by computing the cosine similarity between their vector representations. Figure 3 shows the relation between some domain-specific emotional categories and the different core emotions for both the movie and music domains. It can be observed that, for instance, the emotional category *suspenseful* in the movie domain strongly overlaps with the *tense* and *nervous* core emotions, while the *peacefulness* category in the music domain intersects tightly with the *calm*, *relaxed* and *serene* core emotions.

Moreover, the intersection between cross domain-specific emotional categories could be computed to obtain a measure of similarity between them. Figure 2c shows the cosine similarity between pairs of cross-domain emotional categories. It can be seen that emotional categories such as *feel good-joy* and *gloomy-sadness*, which are very close in both valence and arousal, present very high similarity, while very distinct pairs of emotional categories, such *joy-gloomy* and *sadness-uplifting*, present very low similarity. Other interesting pairs of very similar cross-domain emotional categories are *tension-suspenseful, power-exciting* and *nostalgia-emotional.*

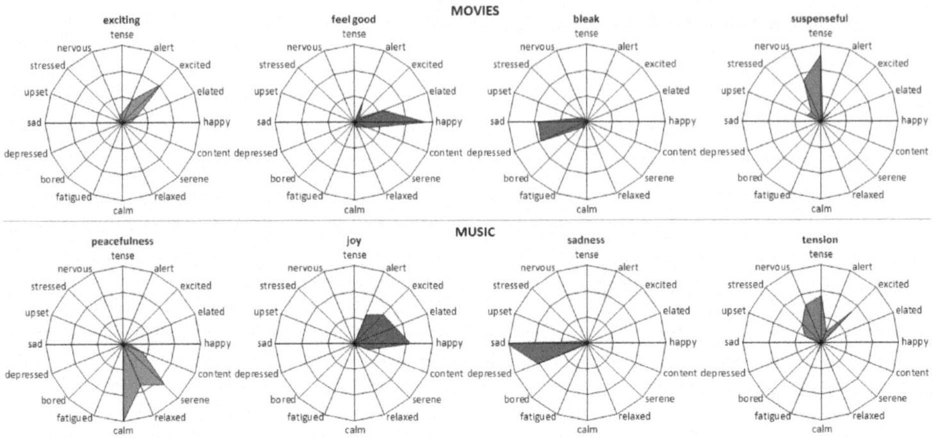

Fig. 3. Relations between core emotions and domain-specific emotional categories

5 Experiments

5.1 User Study

To evaluate our methods that assign emotions to tagged items (see Section 4.3), we conducted a user study in which participants, recruited via social networking sites, were presented with sets of movies or musicians (no combinations of both), and were requested to freely select one or more core and domain-specific emotions for each item. A total of 72 users participated, evaluating 178 movies and 132 musicians. They generated 713 evaluation cases, assigning an average of 4.08 and 3.38 domain-specific emotional categories, and 3.30 and 4.18 core emotions, to items in the movie and music domains, respectively. To facilitate the evaluation, the users could select preferred movie and music genres and the language – English or Spanish – of the online evaluation tool (http://ir.ii.uam.es/emotions), and skip any item they did not want to evaluate.

We note that, as expressed by some of the participants, there are cases in which it is difficult to assign certain emotions to an item. Opposite emotions (e.g. *happiness* and *sadness*) can be evoked in different parts of a particular movie, and by different compositions of the same musician. This fact should be taken into account carefully in the future, and may have caused an underestimation of the precision of our methods; several participants decided not to assign certain emotions, which could have been retrieved by our methods, but were not considered as relevant.

Table 4 shows the top emotional categories assigned by the users to items belonging to some of the 26 genres considered from the Jinni and Last.fm systems, in the movie and music domains, respectively. Table 5 shows cooccurrence values of some core emotions in movie and music item profiles created by the users. These tables show coherent correspondences between domain emotions and genres (e.g. *exciting* for action movies, and *peacefulness* for ambient music), and between core emotions within the quadrants of Russell's circumplex model (e.g. *happy* and *content*). It is interesting to note that there are emotions that barely relate with others (e.g. *bored* and *sad*).

Table 4. Top emotional categories implicitly assigned to some movie and music genres

Movie genre	Top emotional categories	Music genre	Top emotional categories
action	exciting, suspenseful, offbeat	***ambient***	peacefulness, nostalgia, transcendence
comedy	humorous, feel good, offbeat	***classical***	nostalgia, peacefulness, joy
crime	suspenseful, clever, bleak	***jazz***	nostalgia, peacefulness, power
drama	emotional, captivating, gloomy	***rock***	power, tension, joy
horror	scary, rough, exciting	***pop***	joy, power, tenderness
war	emotional, captivating, rough	***world***	wonder, transcendence, power

Table 5. Cooccurrence values of some core emotions in movie and music profiles

	movies								music							
	excited	***happy***	***content***	***serene***	***bored***	***sad***	***nervous***	***tense***	***excited***	***happy***	***content***	***serene***	***bored***	***sad***	***nervous***	***tense***
excited	55	11	9			3	12	25	38	15	10	2			5	8
happy	11	108	89	12			2	3	15	54	26	8			1	3
content	9	89	113	12			1	1	10	26	53	12				1
serene		12	12	17					2	8	12	37		2		
bored					7		1						1			
sad	3					11	3	6				2		7		
nervous	12	2	1		1	4	24	18	5	1					7	6
tense	25	3	1			3	18	44	8	3	1				6	10

5.2 Evaluating Emotion-Oriented Tag-Based Profiles

In the user study, participants stated which core and domain-specific emotions they consider as relevant for each item (movie or musician), thus manually (and collectively) creating emotion-oriented item profiles, which we consider as ground truth.

To evaluate the quality of the emotion-oriented profiles generated by our methods (Section 4.3) with respect to the ground truth profiles, we compared them with precision metrics. Specifically, we computed Precision at position k, P@k, which, for a particular item, is defined as the percentage of the top k emotions returned by a method that are relevant for the item, as stated by the users of our study. We also computed R-precision, which is defined as the precision of the top R emotions returned by a method for an item, being R the number of emotions that are relevant, as stated by the users of our study. Under a reasonable set of assumptions, R-precision approximates the area under the precision-recall curve [1]. Table 6 shows average precision values of the different methods (and a random emotion ranking method) on the movie and music domains.

The **basic method** was the best performing approach in both domains (with highest P@1 values around 70%), only outperformed by the extended_10 method in the movie domain for the core emotion-oriented profiles. In general, the methods performed in the **music domain** better than in the movie domain, and were able to identify **domain emotional categories** more effectively than core emotions in both domains.

Table 6. P@k and *R*-precision values of the considered emotion-oriented profiles

Profile type	Emotion vector model	movies					music				
		#evals	P@1	P@2	P@3	R-Prec	#evals	P@1	P@2	P@3	R-Prec
core emotion-oriented	*random*	165	0.297	0.305	0.302	0.300	129	0.327	0.339	0.345	0.348
	basic	107	0.598	0.528	0.514	0.481	109	0.606	**0.670**	**0.636**	**0.547**
	extended_10	77	**0.675**	**0.643**	**0.589**	**0.519**	11	**0.636**	0.636	0.546	0.497
	extended_50	142	0.373	0.324	0.406	0.365	44	0.546	0.625	0.568	0.502
domain emotion-oriented	*random*	165	0.379	0.382	0.377	0.380	129	0.418	0.416	0.414	0.414
	basic	108	**0.722**	0.625	**0.571**	**0.579**	109	**0.743**	**0.587**	**0.532**	**0.546**
	extended_10	77	0.675	**0.656**	0.554	0.399	11	0.727	0.546	0.455	0.503
	extended_50	144	0.507	0.490	0.463	0.412	44	0.682	0.443	0.394	0.428

5.3 Evaluating Emotion-Oriented Recommendations

In the user study, participants initially stated which movie and music genres they were interested in, and, in addition to emotions, they assigned to movies and musicians numeric ratings in the range [1, 10] according to their tastes.

In a second part of our experiment, we evaluated **whether emotional information of items can be used to increase the accuracy of recommendation based on the users' past ratings**. For such purpose, and due to the limited number of ratings in the study, we addressed the recommendation problem as a (binary) classification task instead of as a rating prediction task, in which collaborative filtering strategies could be applied. For each user, we considered as *relevant* those items to which she assigned a rating over her average rating value, and as *non-relevant* to the reminder items she rated. We then built patterns datasets in which each pattern was associated to an evaluation case [*user u, item i, rating r, core emotions* $\{e_1^C, \dots, e_{|\mathcal{E}|}^C\}$, *domain-specific emotions* $\{e_1^D, \dots, e_{|\mathcal{E}_D|}^D\}$]. A pattern's class was 0 or 1, *relevant* or *non-relevant*, based on *r* and what was explained above. Its attributes were binary values associated to *u*'s genres of interest, binary values associated to *i*'s core emotions, and binary values associated to *i*'s domain-specific emotions. To assess the impact of emotions in recommendation, we separately evaluated classification cases with/without the consideration of the emotion attributes. We used such cases (patterns) to build and evaluate several well known classifiers, namely Naïve Bayes, Random forest, Multilayer Perceptron (MLP), and Support Vector Machine (SVM), which we used as model-based recommender systems.

Table 7 shows the best average (10-fold cross validation) performance values of the classifiers for the distinct pattern attribute configurations and domains. In addition to accuracy values, we also report $g = \sqrt{acc^+ \cdot acc^-}$ and AUC values to take the class balance levels into account. Classifiers incorporating emotion attributes outperformed those built with only the users' genres of interest. For movies, **core emotions** were more valuable, whereas for musicians, **domain-specific emotions** were better. **Random forest** (for movies) and **SVM** (for music) were the best performing classifiers.

Table 7. Performance values obtained by the model-based recommender systems built with the different profile types (attribute configurations). Global top values are in bold, and best values for each profile type are underlined.

Profile type	Classifier	movies					music				
		acc	acc+	acc-	g	AUC	acc	acc+	acc-	g	AUC
-	*Majority class*	56.009	100.000	0.000	0.000	0.402	57.273	100.000	0.000	0.000	0.417
emotion-unaware	*Naïve Bayes*	53.648	77.011	23.902	42.904	0.502	49.545	53.175	44.681	48.743	0.497
	Random forest	<u>59.442</u>	56.322	63.415	<u>59.763</u>	<u>0.596</u>	<u>55.909</u>	65.079	43.617	<u>53.278</u>	<u>0.556</u>
	MLP	59.227	64.751	52.195	58.135	0.592	50.909	53.968	46.809	50.261	0.511
	SVM	57.296	61.303	52.195	56.566	0.573	50.455	56.349	42.553	48.968	0.505
core emotion-aware	*Naïve Bayes*	58.798	73.946	39.512	54.054	0.575	52.727	61.111	41.489	50.353	0.525
	Random forest	61.588	55.556	**69.268**	**<u>62.034</u>**	0.616	<u>54.091</u>	61.111	44.681	<u>52.254</u>	<u>0.540</u>
	MLP	**<u>62.876</u>**	69.732	54.146	61.447	**<u>0.627</u>**	48.636	55.556	39.362	46.763	0.486
	SVM	59.871	63.602	55.122	59.210	0.599	50.000	50.794	48.936	49.856	0.503
domain emotion-aware	*Naïve Bayes*	57.940	**80.077**	29.756	48.814	0.550	52.727	62.698	39.362	49.678	0.523
	Random forest	<u>60.515</u>	55.939	66.341	<u>60.918</u>	<u>0.606</u>	58.182	**65.079**	48.936	56.433	0.581
	MLP	59.657	66.667	50.732	58.156	0.595	55.455	60.317	48.936	54.330	0.555
	SVM	57.511	63.218	50.244	56.359	0.574	**<u>59.091</u>**	62.698	**54.255**	**<u>58.324</u>**	**<u>0.592</u>**

6 Future Work

The next step in our research is to exploit the generated emotion-oriented profiles for developing mood-based and cross-domain recommendation strategies. We are interested in determining which items (according to the emotions they evoke) should be suggested to a user based on her current mood, and which items in a (target) domain should be suggested to a user whose preferences in a distinct (source) domain are available. We believe our emotion model and its cross-domain folksonomies could help address such problems independently or in combination with existing approaches [2][17].

Acknowledgements. This work was supported by the Spanish Government (TIN2011-28538-C02) and the Regional Government of Madrid (S2009TIC-1542).

References

1. Aslam, J.A., Yilmaz, E.: A Geometric Interpretation and Analysis of R-precision. In: 14th ACM Conference on Information and Knowledge Management, pp. 664–671 (2005)
2. Baldoni, M., Baroglio, C., Patti, V., Rena, P.: From Tags to Emotions: Ontology-driven Sentiment Analysis in the Social Semantic Web. Intell. Artificiale 6(1), 41–54 (2012)
3. Breazeal, C.: Emotion and Sociable Humanoid Robots. International Journal of Human-Computer Studies 59, 119–155 (2003)
4. Cantador, I., Bellogín, A., Fernández-Tobías, I., López-Hernández, S.: Semantic Contextualisation of Social Tag-Based Profiles and Item Recommendations. In: Huemer, C., Setzer, T. (eds.) EC-Web 2011. LNBIP, vol. 85, pp. 101–113. Springer, Heidelberg (2011)

5. Cantador, I., Brusilovsky, P., Kuflik, T.: Second Workshop on Information Heterogeneity and Fusion in Recommender Systems. In: 5th ACM Conference on Recommender Systems, pp. 387–388 (2011)
6. Carrillo de Albornoz, J., Plaza, L., Gervás, P.: A Hybrid Approach to Emotional Sentence Polarity and Intensity Classification. In: 14th Intl. Conference on Computational Natural Language Learning, pp. 153–161 (2010)
7. Cassell, J.: Nudge Nudge Wink Wink: Elements of Face-to-Face Conversation for Embodied Conversational Agents. In: Embodied Conversational Agents, pp. 1–27 (2003)
8. Ekman, P., Davidson, R.J. (eds.): The Nature of Emotions: Fundamental Questions. Oxford University Press (1994)
9. Feng, Y., Zhuang, Y., Pan, Y.: Popular Music Retrieval by Detecting Mood. In: 6th ACM SIGIR Conf. on Research and Development in Information Retrieval, pp. 375–376 (2003)
10. Hastings, J., Ceusters, W., Smith, B., Mulligan, K.: The Emotion Ontology: Enabling Interdisciplinary Research in the Affective Sciences. In: Beigl, M., Christiansen, H., Roth-Berghofer, T.R., Kofod-Petersen, A., Coventry, K.R., Schmidtke, H.R. (eds.) CONTEXT 2011. LNCS, vol. 6967, pp. 119–123. Springer, Heidelberg (2011)
11. Hume, D.: Emotions and Moods. In: Robbins, S.P., Judge, T.A. (eds.) Organizational Behavior, pp. 258–297
12. Kaminskas, M., Ricci, F.: Location-Adapted Music Recommendation Using Tags. In: Konstan, J.A., Conejo, R., Marzo, J.L., Oliver, N. (eds.) UMAP 2011. LNCS, vol. 6787, pp. 183–194. Springer, Heidelberg (2011)
13. Meyers, O.C.: A Mood-based Music Classification and Exploration System. MSc Thesis. School of Architecture and Planning, MIT (2007)
14. Roberts, K., Roach, M.A., Johnson, J., Guthrie, J., Harabagiu, S.M.: EmpaTweet: Annotating and Detecting Emotions on Twitter. In: 8th International Conference on Language Resources and Evaluation, pp. 3806–3813 (2012)
15. Russell, J.A.: A Circumplex Model of Affect. Journal of Personality and Social Psychology 39(6), 1161–1178 (1980)
16. Shi, Y., Larson, M., Hanjalic, A.: Mining Mood-specific Movie Similarity with Matrix Factorization for Context-aware Recommendation. In: Workshop on Context-Aware Movie Recommendation, pp. 34–40 (2010)
17. Shi, Y., Larson, M., Hanjalic, A.: Tags as Bridges between Domains: Improving Recommendation with Tag-Induced Cross-Domain Collaborative Filtering. In: Konstan, J.A., Conejo, R., Marzo, J.L., Oliver, N. (eds.) UMAP 2011. LNCS, vol. 6787, pp. 305–316. Springer, Heidelberg (2011)
18. Winoto, P., Ya Tang, T.: The Role of User Mood in Movie Recommendations. Expert Systems with Applications 37(8), 6086–6092 (2010)
19. Zentner, M., Grandjean, D., Scherer, K.: Emotions Evoked by the Sound of Music: Characterization, Classification, and Measurement. Emotion 8, 494–521 (2008)

Cold-Start Management with Cross-Domain Collaborative Filtering and Tags

Manuel Enrich, Matthias Braunhofer, and Francesco Ricci

Free University of Bozen - Bolzano,
Piazza Domenicani 3, 39100 Bolzano, Italy
{menrich,mbraunhofer,fricci}@unibz.it

Abstract. Recommender systems suffer from the new user problem, i.e., the difficulty to make accurate predictions for users that have rated only few items. Moreover, they usually compute recommendations for items just in one domain, such as movies, music, or books. In this paper we deal with such a cold-start situation exploiting cross-domain recommendation techniques, i.e., we suggest items to a user in one target domain by using ratings of other users in a, completely disjoint, auxiliary domain. We present three rating prediction models that make use of information about how users tag items in an auxiliary domain, and how these tags correlate with the ratings to improve the rating prediction task in a different target domain. We show that the proposed techniques can effectively deal with the considered cold-start situation, given that the tags used in the two domains overlap.

Keywords: Collaborative filtering, cross-domain recommendation, matrix factorization, tags.

1 Introduction

Recommender systems (RSs) are software tools that address the information overload problem by retrieving and suggesting items that are estimated as relevant for a user, based on her user profile. However, most of the available RSs [1] suffer from the data sparseness problem caused by the fact that users usually rate only a few items. This is especially true for users that have just joined the system and have not provided yet many ratings. To address this problem, researchers have considered cross-domain scenarios, i.e., have attempted to reuse users' knowledge in an auxiliary and better known domain in order to improve the accuracy of recommendations in another, less known, target domain [2]. The key challenge in cross-domain recommendation is to discover useful relationships among items or users in different domains, e.g., using similarities between items, or (as we will show in this paper) using the similarities of the conditions under which the items in the different domains are rated. Usually, the considered domains are heterogeneous (e.g., music vs. places of interest), making it difficult to find relationships or links between them.

In this research, we leverage user-assigned tags as a "bridge" between different domains. Tags have been shown in previous research to be useful for matching

C. Huemer and P. Lops (Eds.): EC-Web 2013, LNBIP 152, pp. 101–112, 2013.

items in one domain with those in others [3,4,5]. Our proposed technique relies on the usual overlap between the tag vocabularies used in different domains. For instance, the tag "romantic" could be used to describe a movie, a place of interest or a song. Hence, if for instance a RS targeted to a particular domain is able to learn, in an auxiliary domain, that a tag has a positive effect on the ratings, i.e., that when the tag is present the ratings are generally higher, then it could be possible to transfer this dependency from the auxiliary domain to the target one.

In this paper, we present three novel cross-domain rating prediction models, named as UserItemTags, UserItemRelTags and ItemRelTags, that are able to use tagging and rating data in an auxiliary domain to support rating prediction in a target domain for a completely new set of users. UserItemTags and UserItemRelTags predict a target user rating by considering the tags this user has assigned to the target item. While, ItemRelTags exploits the tags in a more general way, i.e., it considers all tags assigned by any user on the target item to compute rating predictions. Hence, this last algorithm does not use the knowledge of how the target user has tagged the target item to generate a rating prediction.

We have formulated the following hypothesis: the information about how users tag items in a particular domain can be exploited to improve the rating prediction accuracy in a completely different domain. To evaluate this hypothesis, we have carried out a series of tests using the MovieLens and the LibraryThing datasets, and have compared the results to those obtained by a state-of-the-art single domain recommendation algorithms based on matrix factorization [6].

The rest of the paper is structured as follows: in section 2 we position our work with respect to the state of the art. Section 3 presents our proposed cross-domain rating prediction models. Section 4 describes the experiments that we have performed in order to evaluate our models, and discusses the obtained results. Finally, conclusions and directions for future work of the presented approach are pointed out in section 5.

2 Related Work

As shown by [7], cross-domain recommendation techniques can tackle cold-start problems in collaborative filtering. Four methods for cross-domain collaborative filtering are there identified: centralized prediction, distributed peer identification, distributed neighborhood formation, and distributed prediction. However, differently from our work, they consider scenarios where the cross-domain recommenders do share some users, i.e., there are users that have rated items in several domains. Producing cross-domain recommendations for a new user in a target domain, without having any user ratings in auxiliary domains (as in our case) is more challenging since only item relationships across domains can be exploited.

Another example of a cross-domain recommender system developed to overcome cold-start problems is Tag-induced Cross-Domain Collaborative Filtering

(TagCDCF) [5]. TagCDCF exploits shared tags to link different domains through an extended matrix factorization framework. In TagCDCF, first the user-item matrices of different domains are factorized into domain-specific latent user and item features. Then, the latent features are linked across domains using tag-induced cross-domain similarities. The cross-domain scenario considered in [5] in similar to the one we have studied (there are not common users or items across domains), however, their approach requires the target user to have tagged several items in order to obtain accurate similarities between the target user in one domain and other users in the auxiliary domain.

Without relying on cross-domain techniques, one can tackle cold-start problems by exploiting, in addition to the ratings, other kinds of data relating users and items. For instance, SVD++ [6] extends the popular SVD matrix factorization model by exploiting implicit feedback. In SVD++ the factor-based profile of a user is additionally affected by the items that the user simply bought or browsed. This is achieved by introducing a second set of item-related factors' vectors that are learned on the base of the set of items that the users browsed or purchased.

A similar extension to SVD is presented in [8]; it exploits contextual factors (e.g., budget, time of the day, weather) in order to alter the rating prediction in a places of interest RS. Here the system learns to which extent the presence of a contextual condition influences the ratings, and this knowledge is used when a new recommendation is to be made. Our models generalize their idea: instead of using pre-defined contextual parameters, our proposed models can use any kind of user-generated textual information assigned to items to improve the recommendation.

In conclusion, the two aforementioned approaches [6,8] are similar to the one described in this paper: they both extend SVD considering additional item and user knowledge in order to deal with cold-start problems. However, to learn the prediction models, they require an extensive set of training data (i.e., browsing / purchase history, ratings in context) that is specific to the application's target domain, whereas our proposed models can improve the rating prediction task in a target domain by just re-using knowledge about tags usage acquired in the target domain as well as in a totally different domain, provided that there is an overlap between the set of tags used in the two domains.

3 Tag-Based Rating Prediction Models

This section describes the tag-based rating prediction models that we have developed to provide cross-domain recommendations. The underlying intuition is that tags could be used to improve the item model computed in matrix factorisation models. In fact, the tags assigned by users to items provide additional information about that item's rating. In our models we rely on tag applications for modelling the item's profile, i.e., how much a item loads the factors' model. Once the information about the impact of a tag is captured in one domain, we conjecture that it can be re-used to support rating prediction in a totally new domain (e.g., composed by totally different items and users), as long as there is an overlap of the tag vocabularies in the two domains. In other words, we conjecture that the effect of tags on the factor model of items is cross-domains.

3.1 UserItemTags

The first model is based on the idea that the user ratings for an item may be dependent on the specific tags the user attached to the item. This means that the model, when generating a rating prediction, is considering the tags used by the target user requesting the recommendation. To exploit this model we assume therefore that the user tagged an item, without providing a rating, and we exploit these tags to better predict her rating. This happens in many situations: a common example is the Delicious[1] social bookmarking website, in which users can apply tags to their bookmarks, but are not asked to rate the bookmarked website.

Given a user u, an item i and the set of tags $T_u(i)$ assigned by u to i, UserItemTags predicts a rating using the following rule:

$$\hat{r}_{ui} = p_u \cdot (q_i + \frac{1}{|T_u(i)|} \sum_{t \in T_u(i)} y_t), \tag{1}$$

where p_u, q_i and y_t are the latent factor vectors associated with the user u, the item i and the tag t, respectively. The model parameters are learned, as it is common in matrix factorization [6], by minimising the associated regularised squared error function through stochastic gradient descent. This is done by looping over all known ratings in K, computing:

- $p_u \leftarrow p_u + \gamma \cdot [(q_i + \frac{1}{|T_u(i)|} \cdot \sum_{t \in T_u(i)} y_t) \cdot e_{ui} - \lambda \cdot p_u]$
- $q_i \leftarrow q_i + \gamma \cdot (p_u \cdot e_{ui} - \lambda \cdot q_i)$
- $\forall t \in T_u(i) : y_t \leftarrow y_t + \gamma \cdot (p_u \cdot \frac{1}{|T_u(i)|} \cdot e_{ui} - \lambda \cdot y_t)$

3.2 UserItemRelTags

UserItemRelTags is a variant of the previous model: UserItemTags. Its definition is based on the intuition that tags have different relevances when performing rating prediction. For example, a tag assigned to a movie could be the name of the main actor(s), the year of production or a textual label that is only meaningful to the user applying that tag (e.g., the occasion when the user watched that movie). This introduces a huge variety of tags, and only part of them can be useful (i.e., relevant) when predicting users' ratings. UserItemRelTags considers only a set of relevant tags, minimising the "noise" introduced by irrelevant tags. To assess whether a tag is relevant or not, we used the Wilcoxon rank-sum test (95% confidence) and compared, for each tag, the distribution of the ratings assigned with or without the presence of the tag. Hence, a tag is judged statistically relevant if the average of all the users' ratings where the tag is present is

[1] Delicious: `https://delicious.com/`

significantly different from the average of all the users' ratings where the tag is not used. We chose the Wilcoxon rank-sum test over the more commonly used two-samples t-test because we can not make any assumption about the normality of the distributions of the ratings. We observe that more sophisticated techniques for filtering out irrelevant tags can be implemented; for instance, as shown in [9], one can categorize tags in different semantic groups and then treat them as having different relevance weights.

Denoting with $TR_u(i)$ the set of relevant tags assigned by user u on item i, UserItemRelTags predicts user ratings as follows:

$$\hat{r}_{ui} = p_u \cdot (q_i + \frac{1}{|TR_u(i)|} \sum_{t \in TR_u(i)} y_t). \quad (2)$$

Model parameters are determined in the same way as for UserItemTags.

3.3 ItemRelTags

The last model, ItemRelTags, does not rely on the tags assigned by the target user to the target item but it considers all the tags applied to the target item by any user. This allows to overcome the main limitation of the two previous models, which is the inability to provide a rating prediction for an item that was not tagged by the target user. In fact, ItemRelTags requires only the knowledge of $TR(i)$, which is the set of relevant tags applied to item i by any user. The relevance of a tag is estimated using a Wilcoxon rank-sum test as in UserItemRelTags. The intuition motivating this model is that the ratings of an item are affected by all the relevant tags applied to it. Moreover, we assume that tags have a common influence for any user (i.e., they are used in a non-personalized way). This assumption is clearly imprecise, but in the absence of the information about how the target user has tagged the target item, it is all one can do. We will test experimentally whether there is a dependence of a user rating on the full set of the tags given to the target item by the users population.

Since this model uses all the relevant tags assigned by any user to the target item, the same tag can appear multiple times. We may imagine that if a tag has been assigned several times to a single item, then it better characterizes the item. Therefore, we have also exploited the tag usage frequency into the model. Let us call TRo_i the relevant tag occurrences for item i, i.e., all the relevant tags applied to the item, duplicates included, and $TRo_i(t)$ representing the relevant tag occurrences of tag t in item i. Then, the prediction rule for ItemRelTags is as follows:

$$\hat{r}_{ui} = p_u \cdot (q_i + \frac{1}{|TRo_i|} \sum_{t \in TR(i)} TRo_i(t) y_t). \quad (3)$$

Even in this case, the model parameters are learned by stochastic gradient descent optimization of the associated squared error function.

4 Experimental Evaluation

In order to evaluate the proposed rating prediction models, we performed two experiments. The goal of the first experiment was to measure the rating prediction accuracy of the models in a cross-domain scenario. In the second experiment, we assessed the quality of rating prediction using only rating and tagging data in a single domain and compared it with the previous results (exploiting cross-domain data).

4.1 Cross-Domain Recommendations

In this section, we present the results of the evaluation study of our models in the cross-domain scenario. We first describe the datasets used in the evaluation, then the experimental design, and finally we present the performance of our rating prediction models compared with SVD.

Datasets. We have evaluated the proposed models using two freely available datasets: MovieLens[2], containing 10 million ratings, and LibraryThing[3], containing over 700 thousand ratings. In both datasets, the ratings are expressed on a scale from 1 to 5, with steps of 0.5. Moreover, MovieLens contains 100,000 tag assignments applied by 72,000 users on 10,000 movies, and LibraryThing contains 2 million tag assignments applied by over 7,000 users on 37,000 books.

Many ratings contained in MovieLens do not contain tag assignments, i.e., the user only rated the item. When computing a prediction without exploiting any tagging information our models behaves exactly as SVD. Since in the tests we wanted to investigate the benefit produced by the tagging data in cross-domain predictions, we therefore considered only the ratings in which at least one tag was used. In this way we obtained a total of 24,565 ratings. In order to limit the effect produced by the variation in the quantity of the ratings we considered in the LibraryThing domain only its first 24,564 ratings, exactly the same number of ratings with tags found in MovieLens. In this subset of the available ratings, the tags in MovieLens covered 29.31% of the tags used in LibraryThing, and the tags from LibraryThing covered 14.54% of the tags used in MovieLens. In LibraryThing there are less distinct tags and they are also used more than in MovieLens. We conjecture that these differences are important to estimate how useful an auxiliary domain can be in the prediction of the ratings in the target domain. More details about the datasets are provided in table 1.

Evaluation Design. For each tested model we have obtained two results: one using MovieLens as target and LibraryThing as auxiliary domain, and another using LibraryThing as target and MovieLens as auxiliary domain. In order to ensure the reliability of our results, we cross validated them. For the cross validation process, we shuffled the target domain rating data and then split it in

[2] MovieLens dataset: `http://www.grouplens.org/node/73`

[3] LibraryThing dataset: `http://www.librarything.com/`

Table 1. Features of the MovieLens and LibraryThing datasets used to test the models

	MovieLens	LibraryThing
Total number of ratings	24,564	24,564
Unique users	2,026	283
Unique items	5,088	12,554
Unique tags	9,486	4,708
Tag assignments	44,805	78,239
Average ratings per user	12.12	86.80
Average tags per rating	1.82	3.18
% of tags overlapping with LibraryThing / MovieLens	14.54	29.31

ten parts (ten-folds cross validation). In each validation iteration, we used one of the obtained splits as test and the remaining data as training set. In order to test the behaviour of the developed models with different amounts of data in the target domain (representing therefore a recommender system in which users and ratings are incrementally introduced), we split the training candidates data again into ten parts. Each of the obtained parts contains therefore a set of non overlapping ratings (each containing 10% of the total training data), that we have used incrementally in our tests. Hence, for estimating the system performance with small knowledge of the target domain we have used 10% of the training data, i.e., 24,564 * 9/100 = 2210 ratings. For simulating a situation where some more knowledge of the target domain is available, we used 20% of the training data, i.e., the first two parts of the training set, etc. The selected amount of target domain data is then extended with the full set of the auxiliary data to obtain the actual training data of the predictive models. This process was repeated ten times, allowing to test our models with each of the original ten target splits as testing data.

We have compared our models with SVD. SVD cannot exploit additional information coming from the auxiliary domain because the set of users are disjoint. This is peculiar to the cross-domain situation that we consider in this paper. Hence, SVD is only able to use the training data in the target domain.

The model parameters (i.e., dimensionality f, learning rate γ and regularization λ) that yielded the best prediction results were obtained by the Nelder-Mead simplex algorithm [10] using the union of the MovieLens and LibraryThing datasets, and were as shown in Table 2.

Table 2. Model parameters obtained using the Nelder-Mead algorithm (cross-domain)

	γ	λ	f
SVD	0.037	0.012	18
UserItemTags	0.018	0.013	10
UserItemRelTags	0.015	0.02	10
ItemRelTags	0.031	0.022	10

Evaluation Results. The obtained average mean absolute errors (MAEs) show that the proposed models, which are based on tagging information from an auxiliary domain, outperform SVD in terms of prediction accuracy (see Figure 1 and Figure 2). In these figures, we marked with a black (grey) circle when we obtained a significant better (worse) result than the baseline SVD (using a t-test at 95%), and no circle when there is no statistical difference. As can be seen, in most of the cases the usage of rating and tagging data in the auxiliary domain reduces the prediction error in the target domain. However, when the target is MovieLens the tagging data from LibraryThing was not able to improve the prediction accuracy in the very cold start situation, i.e., when only 10% or 20% of the ratings in MovieLens were user. We believe that this result is explained by the fact that the tags from the auxiliary domain (i.e., LibraryThing) only cover a small part of the tags used in the target domain (i.e., MovieLens). This makes the knowledge transfer more difficult, since only a small part of the dependency between ratings and tags learned in the auxiliary domain can be successfully exploited. Moreover, when only 10% of the rating in the target domain are used, the predictive model is much more influenced by the relationships between tags and ratings that are present in the auxiliary domain.

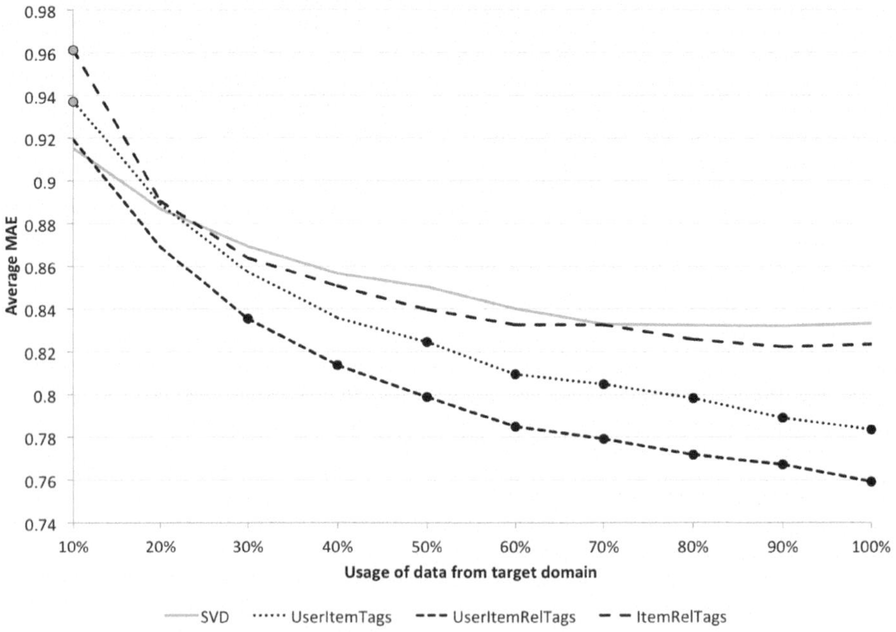

Fig. 1. Average MAEs using MovieLens as target domain and LibraryThing as auxiliary domain

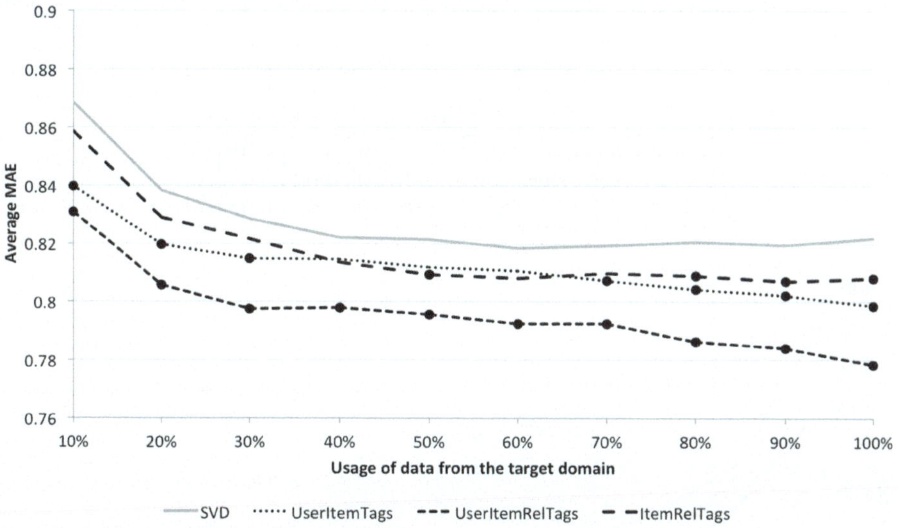

Fig. 2. Average MAEs using LibraryThing as target domain and MovieLens as auxiliary domain

4.2 Single-Domain Recommendations

This section describes the experimental design and the results of the evaluation of the proposed tag-based rating prediction models in a single-domain scenario. We aimed at verifying whether the proposed models can provide good predictions using only rating and tagging data in the target domain. Moreover, since we have observed that UserItemRelTags always performs better than ItemUserTags we do not show here the results for UserItemTags.

Evaluation Design. In order to ensure the reliability of our results, we cross validated them as we did in the cross-domain experiment: we shuffled the data in the target domain and then split it in ten parts (ten-folds validation). In each validation iteration, we used one of the obtained split as test, and the remaining data as training set. We split the training data into ten further parts, to obtain a set of non overlapping incremental data segments to be used as training. This process was repeated ten times, allowing to test our models with each of the original ten target splits as testing data.

We used again SVD as baseline model. Moreover, we have compared the accuracies of the prediction models in the single domain with those previously obtained in the cross-domain scenario. The goal was to understand whether the improvement with respect to SVD is due to the knowledge transferred across domains, or by the additional tagging information in the target domain.

Table 3. Model parameters obtained using the Nelder-Mead algorithm (single domain)

	MovieLens			LibraryThing		
	γ	λ	f	γ	λ	f
SVD	0.014	0.016	17	0.016	0.016	16
UserItemTags	0.02	0.015	10	0.02	0.01	15
UserItemRelTags	0.023	0.018	10	0.02	0.01	15
ItemRelTags	0.015	0.02	10	0.02	0.02	16

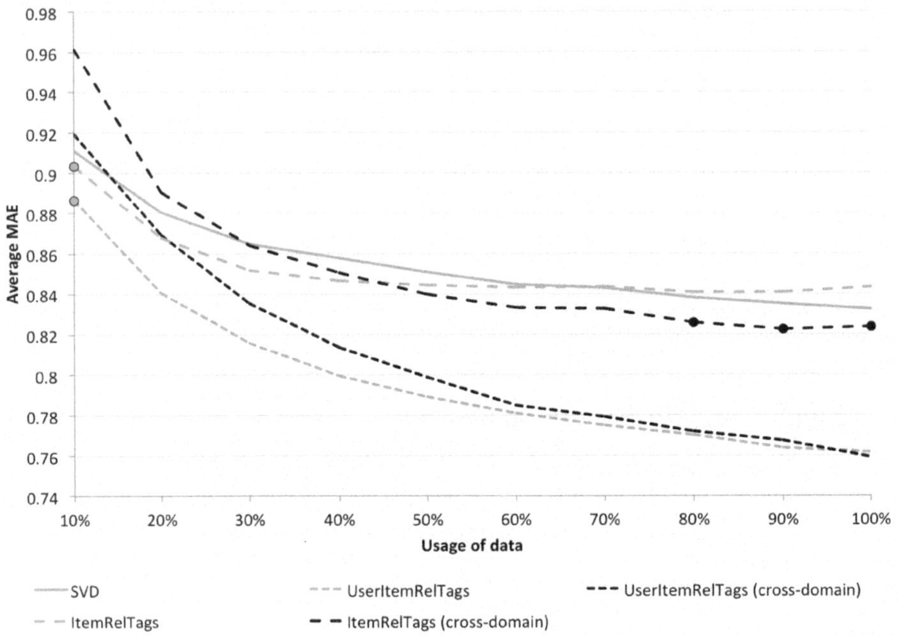

Fig. 3. Comparison of models' MAEs - single vs. cross domain (MovieLens target)

Like in the cross-domain case, also here the model parameters have been obtained using the Nelder-Mead approach [10] but separately for each data set (see Table 3).

Evaluation Results. The obtained results are shown in Figure 3 and 4. In these figures, a black (grey) circle is used to indicate that the results obtained in the cross domain situation are significantly better (worse) than the ones obtained by the same model in the single domain situation. For better visibility, as mentioned above, we omit the curves of UserItemTags which always performed worse than UserItemRelTags. It can be noted that the tagging information always yields a benefit compared with SVD. Comparing single domain vs. cross domain tagging usage the situation is again different in the two data sets. When the target is MovieLens the single domain approach is normally better.

While in LibraryThing the auxiliary domain tagging data are useful, especially in the cold start situation, i.e., when a small quantity of training data from the target domain is provided. It is quite surprising to note that in MovieLens ItemRelTags is better in the cross-domain application than in the single domain one only when the largest portion of the ratings in MovieLens are used. A possible explanation to this is given by the fact that the auxiliary domain only covers part of the tags used in the target domain, and therefore when only a small amount of data from the target domain is used in the training phase the models are not able to successfully exploit the knowledge acquired from the auxiliary domain. However, this is only a conjecture that deserves a more extensive evaluation.

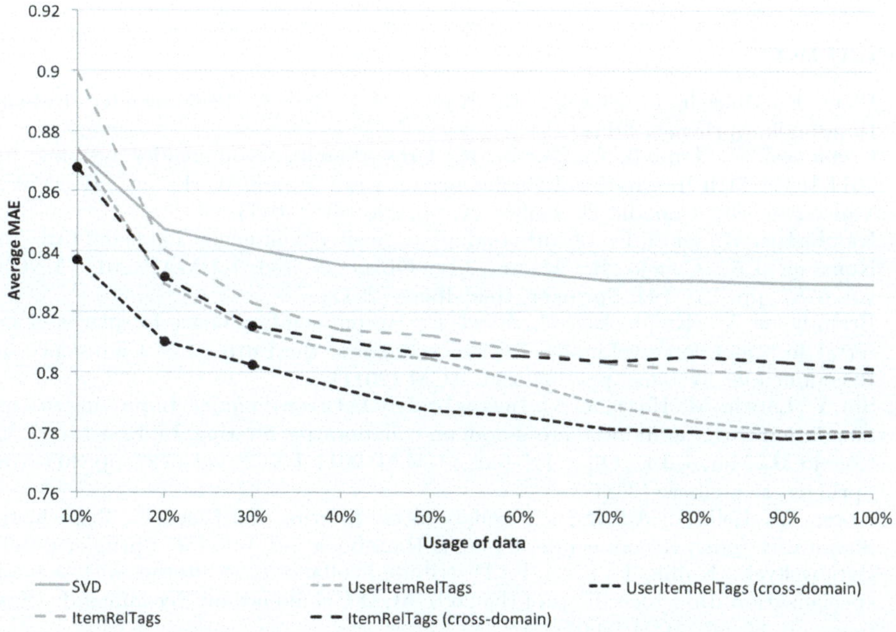

Fig. 4. Comparison of models' MAEs - single vs. cross domain (LibraryThing target)

5 Conclusions and Future Work

In this paper we have presented a set of novel cross-domain recommender system models, called UserItemTags, UserItemRelTags and ItemRelTags. They are shown to be able to improve the accuracy of the rating prediction on a target domain using rating and a tagging data coming from an auxiliary domain, even if the users in the two domains are disjoint. In these models, the knowledge transfer across domains is performed using information about which items have been annotated with certain tags. We have formulated the following experimental hypothesis: the information about how users tag items in a domain can be exploited in order to improve the rating prediction accuracy in a totally different domain. Results obtained from a series of tests conducted on the MovieLens and LibraryThing datasets confirmed this hypothesis.

The proposed cross-domain recommendation techniques are new, and there is a number of research questions left unaddressed. First of all, we should better correlate algorithm performance to the characteristics of the data sets (sparsity, distribution of tags, overlap of tags between domains). Secondly, the performance of our proposed models on other datasets should be assessed and a comparison with other cross-domain recommenders is in order [11,12,5]. Moreover, we are interested in better understanding the conditions when the tag-based models can be exploited, e.g., in context-aware recommender systems, and if these techniques could be used to generate more diverse recommendations.

References

1. Ricci, F., Rokach, L., Shapira, B., Kantor, P.B. (eds.): Recommender Systems Handbook. Springer (2011)
2. Cremonesi, P., Tripodi, A., Turrin, R.: Cross-domain recommender systems. In: 2011 IEEE 11th International Conference on Data Mining Workshops (ICDMW), Vancouver, BC, Canada, December 11, pp. 496–503 (2011)
3. Kaminskas, M., Ricci, F.: Location-adapted music recommendation using tags. In: Konstan, J.A., Conejo, R., Marzo, J.L., Oliver, N. (eds.) UMAP 2011. LNCS, vol. 6787, pp. 183–194. Springer, Heidelberg (2011)
4. Braunhofer, M., Kaminskas, M., Ricci, F.: Recommending music for places of interest in a mobile travel guide. In: Proceedings of the Fifth ACM Conference on Recommender Systems, pp. 253–256. ACM (2011)
5. Shi, Y., Larson, M., Hanjalic, A.: Tags as bridges between domains: Improving recommendation with tag-induced cross-domain collaborative filtering. In: Konstan, J.A., Conejo, R., Marzo, J.L., Oliver, N. (eds.) UMAP 2011. LNCS, vol. 6787, pp. 305–316. Springer, Heidelberg (2011)
6. Koren, Y., Bell, R.: Advances in collaborative filtering. In: Ricci, F., Rokach, L., Shapira, B. (eds.) Recommender Systems Handbook, pp. 145–186. Springer (2011)
7. Berkovsky, S., Kuflik, T., Ricci, F.: Distributed collaborative filtering with domain specialization. In: Proceedings of the 2007 ACM Conference on Recommender Systems, pp. 33–40. ACM (2007)
8. Baltrunas, L., Ludwig, B., Peer, S., Ricci, F.: Context relevance assessment and exploitation in mobile recommender systems. Personal and Ubiquitous Computing 16(5), 507–526 (2012)
9. Cantador, I., Konstas, I., Jose, J.M.: Categorising social tags to improve folksonomy-based recommendations. Web Semantics: Science, Services and Agents on the World Wide Web 9(1), 1–15 (2011)
10. Nelder, J.A., Mead, R.: A simplex method for function minimization. The Computer Journal 7(4), 308–313 (1965)
11. Abel, F., Herder, E., Houben, G.J., Henze, N., Krause, D.: Cross-system user modeling and personalization on the social web. User Modeling and User-Adapted Interaction 23(2-3), 169–209 (2013)
12. Wang, W., Chen, Z., Liu, J., Qi, Q., Zhao, Z.: User-based collaborative filtering on cross domain by tag transfer learning. In: Proceedings of the 1st International Workshop on Cross Domain Knowledge Discovery in Web and Social Network Mining, pp. 10–17. ACM (2012)

UtilSim: Iteratively Helping Users Discover Their Preferences

Saurabh Gupta and Sutanu Chakraborti

Department of Computer Science and Engineering,
Indian Institute of Technology Madras, Chennai, India - 600036
{sgupta,sutanuc}@cse.iitm.ac.in

Abstract. Conversational Recommender Systems belong to a class of knowledge based systems which simulate a customer's interaction with a shopkeeper with the help of repeated user feedback till the user settles on a product. One of the modes for getting user feedback is *Preference Based Feedback*, which is especially suited for novice users(having little domain knowledge), who find it easy to express preferences across products as a whole, rather than specific product features. Such kind of novice users might not be aware of the specific characteristics of the items that they may be interested in, hence, the shopkeeper/system should show them a set of products during each interaction, which can constructively stimulate their preferences, leading them to a desirable product in subsequent interactions. We propose a novel approach to conversational recommendation, UtilSim, where utilities corresponding to products get continually updated as a user iteratively interacts with the system, helping her discover her hidden preferences in the process. We show that UtilSim, which combines domain-specific "dominance" knowledge with SimRank based similarity, significantly outperforms the existing conversational approaches using *Preference Based Feedback* in terms of recommendation efficiency.

Keywords: Knowledge based Recommendation, Preference Based Feedback, Utility estimation, Case Based Recommendation.

1 Introduction

Imagine a prospective camera buyer who actually has very little domain knowledge about cameras. Due to lack of information about product characteristics, it becomes difficult for her to express her preferences adequately/fluently at the start of her interaction with the system[1]. She might not be aware of the product features/attributes that she may be interested in (due to lack of domain knowledge). Therefore, the recommender system should show her appropriate products spread across multiple interactions, which can help stimulate her preferences and lead her to an acceptable product. Typically, knowledge based recommendation systems estimate utility of a product with respect to a given query(or a reference product) by using a weighted linear combination of the local similarities(usually defined by experts) between the features of the query(or the reference product) and the product concerned[2]. We refer to this model as the *weighted similarity model* . Among the knowledge based approaches, *single shot retrieval* approaches assume that there is a fixed set of weights(importances) for each attribute and

C. Huemer and P. Lops (Eds.): EC-Web 2013, LNBIP 152, pp. 113–124, 2013.

use these weights to compute the utility of each product for each type of user. *Single shot retrieval* is of limited use for novice or non expert users who find it difficult to express their preferences beforehand in the form of a query, as described earlier in this section. If the user is not satisfied with what she is served by the system, then she has to revise the initial query and start from scratch again. Also, even involving domain experts to get a handle on the weights used by these systems cannot be foolproof, because the weights are user specific. As an alternative to *single shot retrieval*, *conversational recommender systems* try to simulate the kind of interaction which usually happens between a user and a shopkeeper with the goal of minimizing the cognitive load experienced by the user. Cognitive load can be defined as the effort on the part of the user while interacting with the recommender system. Conversational systems provide a way to capture user feedback at varying levels of granularity which can iteratively help the recommendation system to get a handle on the hidden needs/preferences of the user. Different user feedback mechanisms based on the decreasing order of cognitive load experienced by the user as summarized by [3] are: *Asking questions directly from the user*[4], *Ratings based user feedback*[5], *Critique based feedback*(user puts constraints on features) [6,7,8,9,10] and *Preference based feedback*(user selects one product over the others).

Case Based Recommender systems generally use the *weighted similarity model* to estimate utilities of products. One drawback associated with range normalized local similarity measures commonly used in the *weighted similarity model* was pointed by [11] who argue that in view of the different types of range normalization(narrow or wide) used for computing local similarities, it is not correct to assume that the way these local similarity measures estimate similarity is equivalent. Another problem with defining local similarity measures is the knowledge engineering effort involved.

In this paper, we propose a new conversational recommendation approach, **UtilSim**, which dynamically updates product utilities while interacting with users. UtilSim integrates two kinds of knowledge to provide effective recommendations - a) domain specific "dominance" knowledge across attributes, which is user invariant and easy to acquire. For example - $Price = 20$ "dominates" (is better than) $Price = 40$. b) SimRank[12] based similarity, which keeps getting robust with more data and does not involve some of the drawbacks associated with traditional similarity measures as discussed earlier.

2 Related Work

Several knowledge based recommendation techniques rely on some notion of *weighted similarity* to calculate the utility of a product for a user. *Compromise driven retrieval(CDR)*[13], a single shot retrieval scheme, uses a notion of compromise to better reflect the user's needs. Compromises may be defined as the ways in which the retrieved products differ from the user's requirements(specified query). Since it does single shot retrieval, *CDR* would work well in scenarios when the user is well informed about the domain and has her preferences clearly defined in her head. In contrast, our algorithm is incremental and adaptive in nature and is able to help non expert users as well (who do not have their preferences defined clearly in their head) to reach an acceptable product.

More Like This(MLT)[14] is a commonly used strategy using *Preference Based Feedback*(user prefers one item over the others), with the user selecting a product P during every interaction cycle. In the next iteration, the user is shown those products that are most similar(according to *weighted similarity model*) to P. *False-leads* is a problem which plagues the MLT approach. Using all features of the selected product as the next query might be a bad idea if some of the features of the selected product were irrelevant for the user[15]. *wMLT* [14] dynamically weighs *attribute values* while interacting with the user, based on the difference of the *attribute value* of the selected product to those of the rejected products. UtilSim differs from *wMLT* in that it uses a SimRank based notion of similarity as opposed to the *weighted similarity model* . Also, it uses domain-specific "dominance" knowledge coupled with PageRank[16] to compute utility of a particular **attribute value**. *Adaptive Selection(MLT-AS)*[15], another conversational strategy based on *Preference Based Feedback* uses *weighted similarity model* along with a diversity component and ***preference carrying*** mechanism to effectively focus the recommender system in an appropriate region of the product space. On the other hand, in addition to not using *weighted similarity model*, UtilSim does not include an explicit diversity metric in its utility computation and the utility associated with *attribute values* is dynamic. While ItemRank[17] uses collaborative data to establish links between different movies, UtilSim uses "dominance" knowledge across attributes to establish links between different *attribute values*. The notion of "dominance" has earlier been used to define *Simple Dominance Model*[18] which tries to identify and explain such decision phenomena as Asymmetric Dominance Effect[19] and Compromise Effect[20]. Our approach, on the other hand, uses "dominance" knowledge to implicitly infer the individual feature-value utilities during user interaction.

3 Our Approach

Numerous feedback mechanisms have been used to capture user preferences in conversational recommender systems. It was shown in [21] that expert users were more satisfied with attribute based feedback elicitation methods whereas novice users considered it more useful to express their preferences on products as a whole, from which attribute preferences can then be implicitly computed. In scenarios where the users are not well versed with the domain, they might find it difficult to put constraints at the level of specific attributes as required by *critiquing*. With a view towards improving recommendation quality in these scenarios, our approach, UtilSim, uses a *Preference based feedback* strategy where the user just expresses a preference for one product over the others. After receiving feedback from the user, the system now has to construct a revised model of the user's preferences to account for the dynamic changes in user preferences.

SimRank Based Similarity: To compute product-product as well as *attribute-value - attribute-value* similarities, we construct a bipartite graph consisting of products and their particular *attribute values* as shown in Figure 1. If an *attribute value* is present in a particular product, then a link is created from that *attribute value* node to the product node. The nodes A, B and C in Figure 1 refer to three cameras in our database. The other nodes represent *attribute values* with M denoting $Memory$, R denoting $Resolution$

and P denoting *Price*. The numbers that follow M,R and P are the values of the respective attributes. For e.g.- R6 means that *Resolution* equals 6. To infer similarities from the product data, we use the main idea in SimRank - two objects are similar if they are related to similar objects[12]. Hence, we can say that products are similar if they have similar attribute values and attribute values are similar if they are present in similar products. This kind of circularity leads to a recursive definition for similarity computation which is defined for bipartite graphs in [12] as:

$$sim(A,B) = \frac{C}{|I(A)||I(B)|} \sum_{i=1}^{|I(A)|} \sum_{j=1}^{|I(B)|} sim(I_i(A), I_j(B)) \quad (1)$$

$$sim(a,b) = \frac{C}{|O(a)||O(b)|} \sum_{i=1}^{|O(a)|} \sum_{j=1}^{|O(b)|} sim(O_i(a), O_j(b)) \quad (2)$$

where C is a constant and $I_i(A)$ represents the ith in-neighbour of A and $I_j(B)$ represents the jth in-neighbour of B. $O_i(A)$ represents the ith out-neighbour of A and $O_j(B)$ represents the jth out-neighbour of B. In Figure 1, $P300$ is an in-neighbour of A and A is the out-neighbour of $P300$. Figure 2 shows how the flow of similarity takes

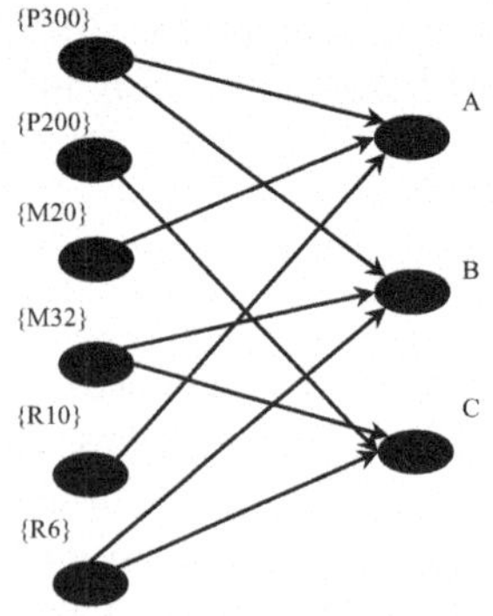

Fig. 1. Graph G having links from attribute values to products

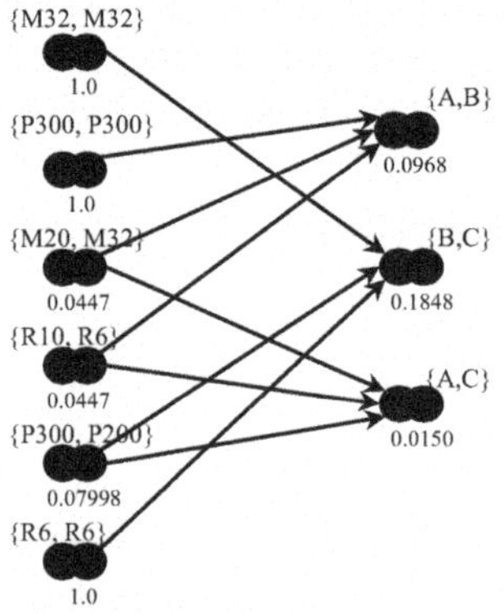

Fig. 2. Node pair graph G^2 with SimRank scores for C=0.8

place between the product-product nodes and the *attribute value - attribute value* nodes. This representation allows us to calculate similarities between *Price* = 200 and *Price* = 300 as well as product *A* and product *B* simultaneously.

Dominance Criteria across Attributes: We adopt the criteria used by [13] and divide the numerical attributes into two sets - *more is better* (MIB) and *less is better* (LIB). For the Camera dataset, we classify attributes *Price* and *Weight* as LIB attributes which implies that a lesser value of these attributes dominates a greater value. All the other attributes - *Optical Zoom, Digital Zoom, Resolution, Memory Included* are considered as

MIB attributes which implies that a greater value of these attributes dominates a lesser value. The idea of using MIB and LIB as the criteria for dominance can be motivated through the following example: A camera with *lower Price* and *higher Resolution* will always be preferred to a camera with *higher Price* and *lower Resolution*, all else being equal. Similarly, for the PC dataset, we classify *Processor Speed*, *Monitor*, *Memory*, *Capacity* as MIB attributes and *Price* as an LIB attribute. For example : $Price = 200$ dominates $Price = 500$. We make an assumption about the rationality of the user that if she selects product A, it must have at least one attribute a_i, which "dominates" the corresponding attribute b_i of at least one of the rejected products B. Note that in principle, not every product attribute would be monotonic. There might be attributes whose middle values are preferred to the extreme values. But, we think that those attributes can also be handled in a similar manner by transforming them through a function so that they reduce to being monotonic. For example, let us assume that an attribute X has values in the range 0 to 24, with the value of 12 being the most preferred. Therefore, we can transform X into

$$Y = 1 - \frac{|12 - X|}{12} \tag{3}$$

with Y being treated as an MIB attribute.

Dominance across nominal attributes is calculated as follows: Suppose, the user is currently at the Rth iteration in her interaction with the system. Considering a nominal attribute like $Manufacturer$ for a camera, let S denote the list of all the values corresponding to the $Manufacturer$ attribute for all the $R - 1$ selected products till the current iteration. In the list S, the latest(last) value corresponds to the $Manufacturer$ value of the product selected in the $(R-1)^{th}$ iteration, in that order. For any two products a and b in the current recommendation set, we say that a_M dominates b_M, where a_M and b_M denote the $Manufacturer$ value of product a and b respectively if:

$$\Big[\Big(\sum_{k \in S} \alpha \cdot sim(a_M, k)\Big) - \Big(\sum_{k \in S} \beta \cdot sim(b_M, k)\Big)\Big] \geq 0 \tag{4}$$

where sim corresponds to the SimRank based similarity. The values of α and β keep on changing based on the position of k in S. If the position of k is towards the end of S, the values of α and β are high as compared to the scenario in which k is near the front of the list. These values are so kept to give higher weights to values which were selected more recently than to those which were selected during the initial part of the interaction.

3.1 UtilSim

We now explain how UtilSim computes revised product utilities after each user interaction through the following example. Assuming that products 1, 2 and 3 from Table 1 are the most similar(according to the weighted similarity model) products to the user query, the recommender system shows to the user these three products during the initial interaction. Notice that the use of weighted similarity model is a one time affair at the start of each dialogue after which it is never used in our approach. In principle, even for the first recommendation cycle we can generate recommendations using only SimRank

Table 1. Camera Models in a Shop

Product	Price	Resolution	Memory
1	300	10.0 MP	20
2	400	6.0 MP	32
3	200	8.0 MP	18
4	500	12.0 MP	32
5	600	12.1 MP	48

based similarity, but for all purposes in this paper, we used weighted similarity to start off the interaction process. Assuming that the user chooses product 3, we start off by giving high importance to all the *attribute values* of product 3 by creating links from *Price* value of product 1 to *Price* value of product 3 and from *Price* value of product 2 to *Price* value of product 3, repeating the same procedure for attributes *Resolution* and *Memory* as shown in Figure 3.

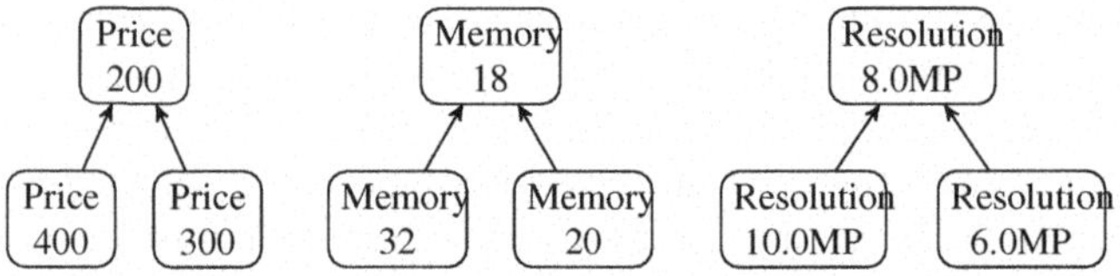

Fig. 3. Links formed due to the global dominance of selected product

But it may not be the case that the user liked all the *attribute values* of product 3 vis a vis the other products.

Therefore in the second step, we create links from all the dominated *attribute values* to the dominating *attribute values*, where domination is based on the criteria discussed earlier. For example - we observe that the *Resolution* value of the selected product 3, is dominated by the *Resolution* value of product 1. So, a link going out from the *Resolution* value node of product 3 to the *Resolution* value node of product 1 is drawn. Similar process is followed for all the other *attribute values*, with the newly formed links shown in dashed lines in Figure 4. A node should have high utility if it is pointed to by large number of high utility nodes; this circularity has a parallel with the observation that a

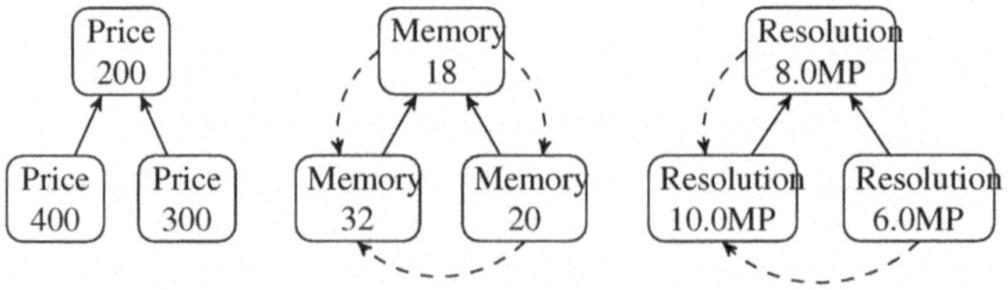

Fig. 4. Links formed due to the local dominance of *attribute values*

web page is important if it is pointed to by several important pages, and is hence resolved using PageRank[16] over the graph in Figure 4. Applying Pagerank on the graph shown in Figure 4 gives us utilities of individual ***attribute values***.

The final step involves recalculating the utility values of all the products in the catalog. Let the *Price*, *Resolution* and *Memory* values of an arbitrary product c be denoted by P_c, R_c and M_c respectively. Similarly, $Price$, *Resolution* and *Memory* values of the selected product(product 3) are denoted by P_3, R_3 and M_3 respectively. Now, the revised utility of a product *c* is calculated as

$$U(c)=sim(P_3, P_c)\cdot util(P_3)+sim(R_3, R_c)\cdot util(R_3) + sim(M_3, M_c)\cdot util(M_3) \quad (5)$$

where $util(P_3)$ is the utility of $Price = 200$ (product 3's $Price$), calculated by running PageRank[16] on the graph shown in Figure 4. The system then presents to the user, the top k products according to the revised utilities as obtained from Eq. 5. The user can either terminate the interaction if she is satisfied by a product in the current recommendation set or can issue a preference for any one of the shown products and the system re-estimates the utilities of the products through the same process outlined above. The *sim* function used in Eq. 5 is the SimRank based similarity measure between attribute value pairs, calculated according to Equations 1 and 2 applied to a bipartite graph, similar to the one shown in Figure 1. The *util* function used in Eq. 5 is not a predefined weight value for a particular attribute. Instead, it is a dynamic measure of importance of a particular *attribute value*. Individual feature value utility estimation is made efficient in the case of UtilSim by the use of PageRank(applied on a relatively small graph like the one shown in Figure 4), during every recommendation cycle. UtilSim can scale with increasing number of products since SimRank based similarity estimation between products is done offline. Although large number of attributes might lead to efficiency issues, theoretically, we can encode dominance knowledge into the system as a one time effort. However, in practical recommendation settings, it may not always be cognitively appealing to expose users to a system that requires specification of large number of features.

4 Experimental Results

We compare UtilSim with well known preference based approaches - MLT[14], wMLT[14] and MLT-AS[15]. We use two standard datasets in our experiments - **Camera**[1] and **PC**[14]. The **Camera** dataset contains 210 cameras with 10 attributes and the **PC** dataset contains 120 PC's with 8 attributes. We use a leave one out methodology similar to the one used in [15], where each product is removed from the products database and used to generate a particular query of interest. For each query, that product is considered as target, which is most similar to the product from which the query is generated. The target corresponding to a particular query is computed using the weighted similarity model(used by MLT, WMLT and MLT-AS approach) and not the SimRank based notion of similarity on which UtilSim based. Hence, UtilSim starts off with a bit of a disadvantage. We report the average number of cycles and unique products presented to a user en route a target product during a recommendation dialogue, as reported

[1] `http://josquin.cs.depaul.edu/~rburke/research/downloads/camera.zip`

in [15,10]. For both the datasets, we generated queries of length 1, 3 and 5 to distinguish between ***difficult***, ***moderate*** and ***easy*** queries respectively[22]. We refer to queries of length 1, 3 and 5 as Q-1, Q-3 and Q-5 respectively. Q-1 corresponds to a non expert user having limited domain knowledge who finds it difficult to express her preferences clearly at the start whereas Q-5 corresponds to a user close to being an expert, who is able to specify her preferences clearly. A total of 3938 and 2382 queries were generated for the Camera and PC dataset respectively. In all our experiments, 4 products are presented in every recommendation cycle. Also, all the algorithms are made to select that product in every cycle which is most similar to the target. The only difference is that while all other algorithms use the weighted similarity model, UtilSim uses a similarity measure based on SimRank.

Highly Focused Recommendation Framework

For a highly focused recommendation framework, we simulate an artificial user who is relatively sure of her preferences and who, during each cycle, chooses a product which is maximally similar to the target product. As can be seen from Figure 5a through Figure 5d, UtilSim outperforms all the other algorithms, in terms of cycles and unique items. Specifically for the Q-1 case on the PC dataset, while MLT, MLT-AS and wMLT take 11.705 cycles(and 22.14 items), 7.82 cycles(and 16.85 items) and 6.66 cycles(and 19.26 items) to reach the target respectively, UtilSim takes 5.07 cycles(and 15.45 items) to reach the target, a 56% reduction in terms of cycles and 30% reduction in terms of unique items over MLT. A similar trend is observed for the Camera dataset.

Preference Noise

We simulate an agent which does not act optimally during each recommendation cycle by making it choose a product that might not be the most similar to the target. Noise is introduced into the process by disturbing the similarities of the products in the recommendation set to the target product by some random amount within a threshold. We have used a noise level of 5% in our experiments. As explained in [15], preference noise of 5% implies that the similarities of each of the individual products to the target might be changed by up to +/-5% of its actual value. As can be seen from Figure 5e through Figure 5h, UtilSim outperforms the other algorithms on both the datasets. For the Q-1 case on the PC dataset, while MLT, MLT-AS and wMLT take on an average 12.085 cycles(22.72 items), 7.66 cycles(16.55 items) and 8.52 cycles(22.69 items) respectively to reach the target, UtilSim takes 5.25 cycles(16.17 items) to reach the target, a reduction of 56% in terms of cycles and 28% in terms of unique items over MLT. It is interesting to note that wMLT which performs better than MLT-AS in a highly focused framework of recommendation(in terms of number of cycles), does not perform better than MLT-AS in the presence of preference noise(especially for the Camera dataset). This might be due to the fact that in the presence of noise, the recommendation dialogues associated with wMLT include a lot of false leads, whereas MLT-AS is able to neutralize their effect due to its diversity component. For reasons of brevity, it is worth noting that UtilSim's performance is superior to all the other approaches, even at higher levels of noise.

Finding All "good" Items

Finding all "good" items is also important for users who only have some vague idea about their preferences, because they can be sure that the recommender system will recommend all the "interesting" products efficiently. Given a predefined target product for a particular query, chosen as described earlier, we also treat as target for that query, those products which are "better" than the target product according to some criterion. For the Camera dataset, a camera which has a ***higher*** *Resolution*, *Optical Zoom*, *Digital Zoom*, *Memory* and ***lower*** *Weight* and *Price* than the target product is also added to the list of target products. For the PC dataset, a PC having ***higher*** *Speed*, *Memory*, *Capacity* and ***lower*** *Price* than the target product is also considered as a target product. Let the set of target products for a query be defined as T. During every recommendation cycle, the simulated agent selects that product from the recommendation set which has the highest average similarity to all the elements in T. If an element from T is part of the recommendation set in a particular cycle, then that element is removed from T and a similar process is followed until T becomes empty. As shown in Figure 5i and Figure 5j, for the Q-1 case on the PC dataset, while MLT, MLT-AS and wMLT take on an average 23.83 cycles(40.87 items), 18.30 cycles(31.28 items) and 15.19 cycles(35.94 items) respectively, UtilSim takes 12.02 cycles(30.73 items) to reach the target product, a reduction of 49% in terms of cycles and 24% in terms of unique items over MLT. For the Camera dataset, Figure 5k and Figure 5l present an interesting case study where UtiSim significantly outperforms MLT-AS in terms of number of cycles but under performs MLT-AS in terms of number of unique items shown. For the Q-1 case on the Camera dataset, MLT-AS shows 36.26 unique items(reduction of 37.66% as compared to MLT), whereas UtilSim shows 38.77 items(reduction of 33.35% as compared to MLT). The marginal increase in the number of unique items notwithstanding, we think that UtilSim is of value in this scenario as well because of the huge reduction it is able to offer in terms of the number of cycles. For Q-1 on Camera dataset, UtilSim takes 14.71 cycles(reduction of 61.79% compared to MLT) as compared to MLT-AS which takes 24.26 cycles(reduction of 36.98% compared to MLT).

Why UtilSim Works

We considered reduced samples of the original PC dataset - the size of the smaller datasets ranging from 30 to 120 products. The number of cycles taken by different algorithms to reach the target are reported in Figure 6. We devised an algorithm, MLT-sRank, which works exactly like the MLT approach, except that it uses a SimRank based similarity measure to estimate utility instead of the weighted similarity model which is used by MLT. As we can see from Figure 6, when the dataset size is between 30 and 90 products, MLT-sRank, which uses SimRank based similarity as a substitute for utility, under-performs MLT. This is because SimRank does not get sufficient data to model similarities in the domain effectively. But once it finds sufficient data(120 products), it, on its own outperforms MLT. More interestingly, we see that for any sample size, UtilSim, with its additional layer of "dominance" knowledge over SimRank based similarity, is able to perform better than MLT-sRank. Moreover, starting from dataset size of 60 onwards, UtilSim starts outperforming even MLT, even though MLT-sRank, based on the same SimRank based similarity as UtilSim, cannot match up to MLT.

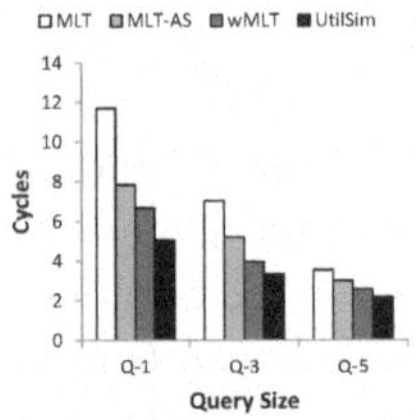

(a) PC Data

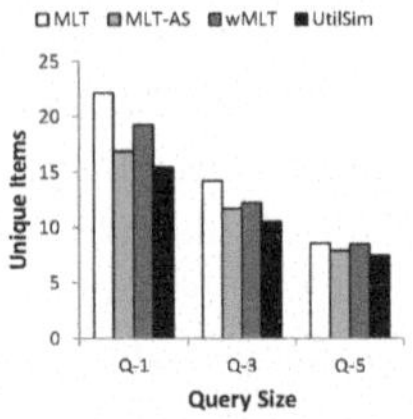

(b) PC Data

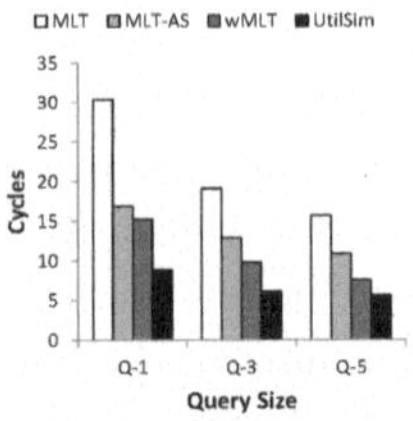

(c) Camera Data

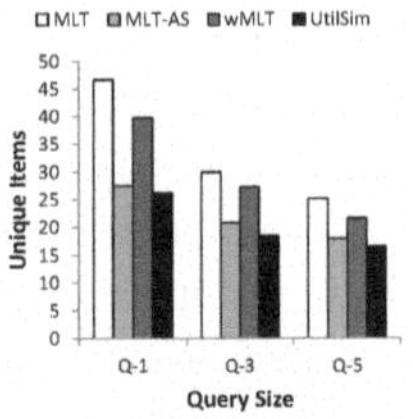

(d) Camera Data

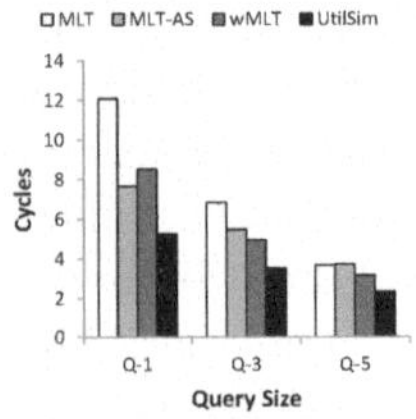

(e) PC Data

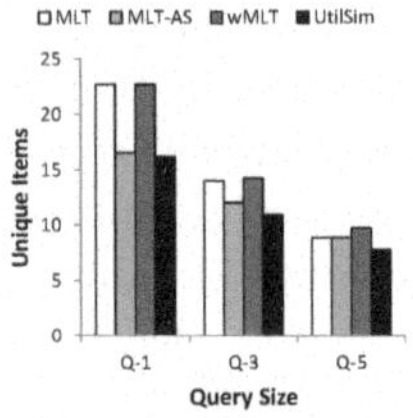

(f) PC Data

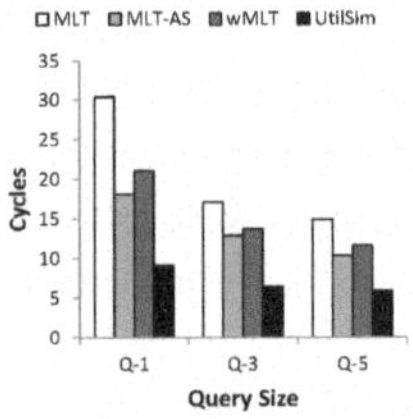

(g) Camera Data

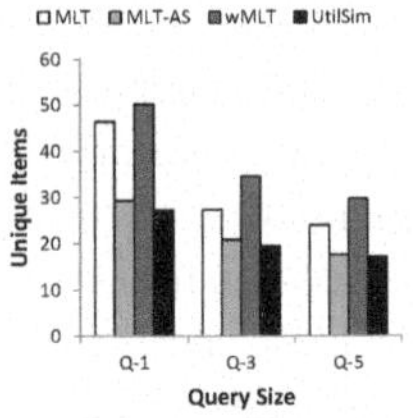

(h) Camera Data

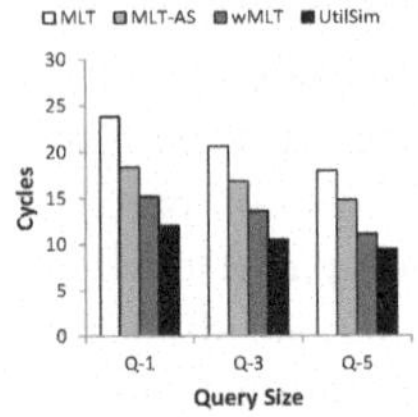

(i) PC Data

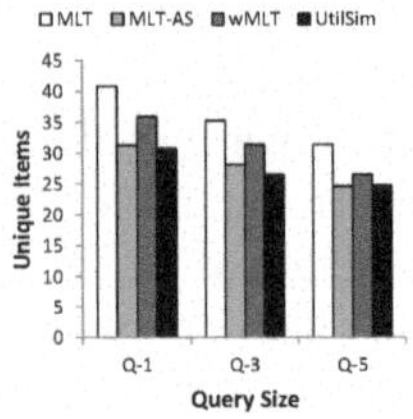

(j) PC Data

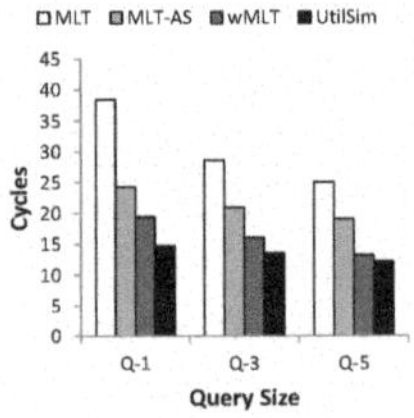

(k) Camera Data

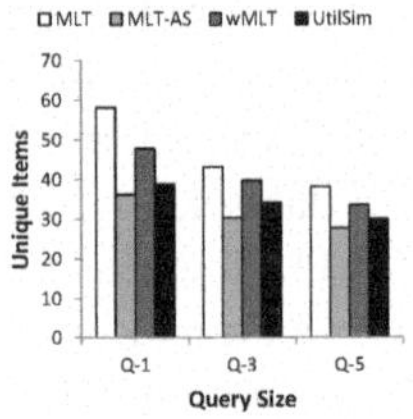

(l) Camera Data

Fig. 5. Performance Analysis for (a) Highly focussed scenario (Row 1) (b) Preference Noise (Row 2) (c) "All Good Items task" (Row 3)

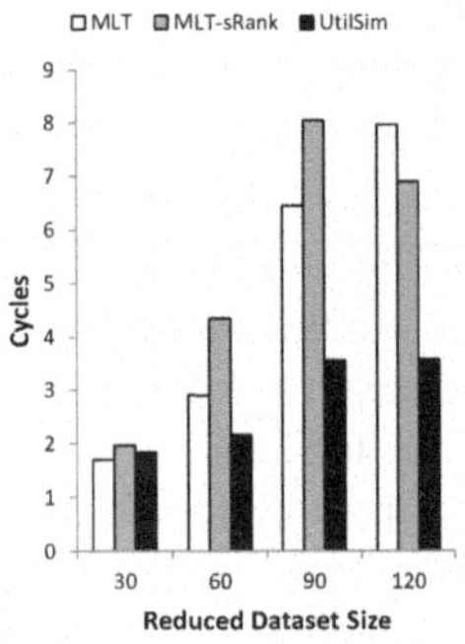

Fig. 6. Cycles for variable number of products

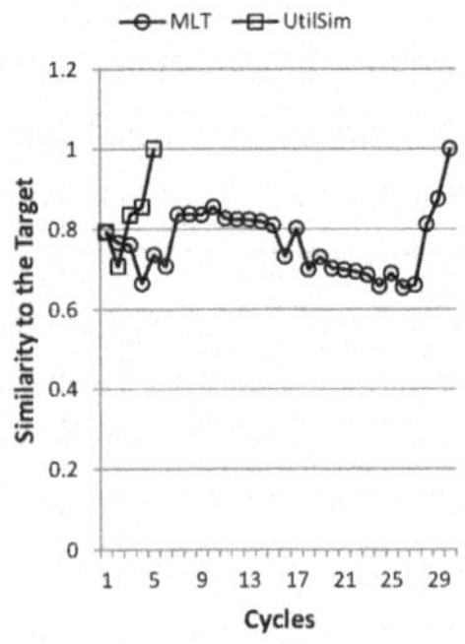

Fig. 7. Selected products' similarity to target in a session

In Figure 7, we have plotted the similarity(corresponding to weighted similarity model) of the preferred product in every cycle, to the target product during a typical recommendation dialogue. Generally, we would expect the similarity of selected products to the target, to increase over a period of a few cycles, instead, for MLT, we observe that it encounters similarity troughs from cycles 1-4 and from 8-27, during which the similarity to the target changes a little or falls down. We quantify this ability of each algorithm to lead to the target by aggregating the slopes of all the lines joining the successively preferred products divided by the number of cycles taken by the algorithm for a typical recommendation dialogue like the one shown in Figure 7. We then calculate the average of such scores obtained across all the recommendation dialogues for the PC dataset. The scores achieved by UtilSim across Q-1, Q-3, Q-5 are 0.045, 0.029, 0.016 respectively. The scores achieved by MLT for Q-1, Q-3, Q-5 are 0.026, 0.020, 0.011 respectively. The higher scores achieved by UtilSim across dialogues associated with all query sizes show that it has a better ability to lead the user to the target.

5 Conclusions

In this paper, we proposed a novel algorithm, UtilSim, which helps non-expert/novice users (who have limited knowledge about product features and have difficulty in expressing their preferences clearly) discover their preferences in an iterative and adaptive fashion. UtilSim leads to efficient recommendations by combining domain-specific "dominance" knowledge with SimRank based similarity as opposed to weighted similarity which is generally used in case based recommender systems. The promising results obtained by the use of SimRank based similarity has positive implications for domains where it might be difficult to define local similarity measures across attributes. We observe that the utility function used in UtilSim can get richer by taking into account feature interactions. Most Preference-Based Feedback algorithms do not model feature interactions and we would like to pursue this line of research in the future.

References

1. Pu, P., Chen, L.: User-Involved Preference Elicitation for Product Search and Recommender Systems. Ai Magazine 29, 93–103 (2008)
2. Ricci, F., Rokach, L., Shapira, B.: Introduction to recommender systems handbook. In: Recommender Systems Handbook, pp. 1–35 (2011)
3. Smyth, B.: Case-Based Recommendation. In: Brusilovsky, P., Kobsa, A., Nejdl, W. (eds.) Adaptive Web 2007. LNCS, vol. 4321, pp. 342–376. Springer, Heidelberg (2007)
4. Shimazu, H.: Expertclerk: navigating shoppers' buying process with the combination of asking and proposing. In: Proceedings of the 17th International Joint Conference on Artificial Intelligence, IJCAI 2001, vol. 2, pp. 1443–1448. Morgan Kaufmann Publishers Inc., San Francisco (2001)
5. Smyth, B., Cotter, P.: A Personalized TV Listings Service for the Digital TV Age. Knowledge-Based Systems 13(2-3), 53–59 (2000)
6. Burke, R., Hammond, K., Yound, B.: The findme approach to assisted browsing. IEEE Expert 12(4), 32–40 (1997)

7. McCarthy, K., Reilly, J., McGinty, L., Smyth, B.: Experiments in dynamic critiquing. In: Proceedings of the 10th International Conference on Intelligent User Interfaces, IUI 2005, pp. 175–182. ACM, New York (2005)
8. Reilly, J., Zhang, J., McGinty, L., Pu, P., Smyth, B.: A comparison of two compound critiquing systems. In: Proceedings of the 12th International Conference on Intelligent user Interfaces, IUI 2007, pp. 317–320. ACM, New York (2007)
9. Zhang, J., Jones, N., Pu, P.: A visual interface for critiquing-based recommender systems. In: Proceedings of the 9th ACM Conference on Electronic Commerce, EC 2008, pp. 230–239. ACM, New York (2008)
10. Llorente, M.S., Guerrero, S.E.: Increasing retrieval quality in conversational recommenders. IEEE Trans. Knowl. Data Eng. 24(10), 1876–1888 (2012)
11. Bridge, D., Ferguson, A.: An expressive query language for product recommender systems. Artif. Intell. Rev. 18(3-4), 269–307 (2002)
12. Jeh, G., Widom, J.: Simrank: a measure of structural-context similarity. In: KDD 2002: Proceedings of the Eighth ACM SIGKDD International Conference on Knowledge Discovery and Data Mining, pp. 538–543. ACM Press, New York (2002)
13. Mcsherry, D.: Similarity and compromise. In: Ashley, K.D., Bridge, D.G. (eds.) ICCBR 2003. LNCS (LNAI), vol. 2689, pp. 291–305. Springer, Heidelberg (2003)
14. McGinty, L., Smyth, B.: Comparison-based recommendation. In: Craw, S., Preece, A.D. (eds.) ECCBR 2002. LNCS (LNAI), vol. 2416, pp. 575–589. Springer, Heidelberg (2002)
15. Smyth, B., Mcginty, L.: The power of suggestion. In: IJCAI, pp. 127–132. Morgan Kauffman (2003)
16. Lawrence, P., Sergey, B., Motwani, R., Winograd, T.: The pagerank citation ranking: Bringing order to the web. Technical report, Stanford University (1998)
17. Gori, M., Pucci, A.: Itemrank: a random-walk based scoring algorithm for recommender engines. In: Proceedings of the 20th International Joint Conference on Artifical Intelligence, IJCAI 2007, pp. 2766–2771. Morgan Kaufmann Publishers Inc., San Francisco (2007)
18. Teppan, E.C., Felfernig, A.: Calculating decoy items in utility-based recommendation. In: Chien, B.-C., Hong, T.-P., Chen, S.-M., Ali, M. (eds.) IEA/AIE 2009. LNCS (LNAI), vol. 5579, pp. 183–192. Springer, Heidelberg (2009)
19. Dan, A., Thomas, W.: Seeking Subjective Dominance in Multidimensional Space: An Explanation of the Asymmetric Dominance Effect. Organizational Behavior and Human Decision Processes 63(3), 223–232 (1995)
20. Simonson, I.: Choice Based on Reasons: The Case of Attraction and Compromise Effects. Journal of Consumer Research 16(2), 158–174 (1989)
21. Knijnenburg, B.P., Willemsen, M.C.: Understanding the effect of adaptive preference elicitation methods on user satisfaction of a recommender system. In: Proceedings of the Third ACM Conference on Recommender Systems, RecSys 2009, pp. 381–384. ACM, New York (2009)
22. Salamó, M., Reilly, J., McGinty, L., Smyth, B.: Knowledge discovery from user preferences in conversational recommendation. In: Jorge, A.M., Torgo, L., Brazdil, P.B., Camacho, R., Gama, J. (eds.) PKDD 2005. LNCS (LNAI), vol. 3721, pp. 228–239. Springer, Heidelberg (2005)

Contextual eVSM: A Content-Based Context-Aware Recommendation Framework Based on Distributional Semantics

Cataldo Musto, Giovanni Semeraro, Pasquale Lops, and Marco de Gemmis

Department of Computer Science
University of Bari Aldo Moro, Italy
{cataldo.musto,giovanni.semeraro,pasquale.lops,marco.degemmis}@uniba.it

Abstract. In several domains contextual information plays a key role in the recommendation task, since factors such as user location, time of the day, user mood, weather, etc., clearly affect user perception for a particular item. However, traditional recommendation approaches do not take into account contextual information, and this can limit the goodness of the suggestions. In this paper we extend the enhanced Vector Space Model (eVSM) framework in order to model contextual information as well. Specifically, we propose two different context-aware approaches: in the first one we adapt the *microprofiling* technique, already evaluated in collaborative filtering, to content-based recommendations. Next, we define a contextual modeling technique based on distributional semantics: it builds a context-aware user profile that merges user preferences with a semantic vector space representation of the context itself. In the experimental evaluation we carried out an extensive series of tests in order to determine the best-performing configuration among the proposed ones. We also evaluated Contextual eVSM against a state of the art dataset, and it emerged that our framework overcomes all the baselines in most of the experimental settings.

Keywords: Context-aware Recommendations, Filtering, User Modeling, Content-based Recommenders.

1 Introduction

Recommender Systems (RSs) are tools that can help users in *'making order'* in the plethora of information today available on the Web, by providing them with personalized suggestions about items that are supposed to be of interest according to their preferences or their information needs [12].

The process RSs deal with is very natural and common, since people get advice all the time, especially when they have to choose among several alternatives and the knowledge to critically discern them is not enough: *what music should I listen to? what movie should I watch? what restaurant should I choose?* A list of examples could be infinite. However, in all the abovementioned scenarios there is an aspect that plays a key role in order to determine which one is the best suggestion to provide: *the context.*

C. Huemer and P. Lops (Eds.): EC-Web 2013, LNBIP 152, pp. 125–136, 2013.

Do you need music to better concentrate or to play during a party? Do you want a movie for a funny night or for a romantic one? It is clear that, in most of the cases, the context actually influences the process of generating the recommendations. As a consequence, an effective recommendation algorithm should take into account as much contextual information as possible: location, time of the day, companion, task to be carried out, user mood, etc However, traditional recommendation approaches do not model any contextual information: collaborative filtering [14] produces recommendations by just exploiting similarities among user behavioral patterns (e.g. buying, clicking, rating, etc.). In the same way, content-based filtering [15] typically generates the recommendations by comparing the textual features describing the items with those stored in a user profile built upon the items the user enjoyed in the past. The need for recommendation approaches able to manage contextual information is taken for granted. Consequently, several context-aware recommendation algorithm recently emerged [1]. Techniques for generating context-aware recommendations can be broadly split into three categories: *pre-filtering, post-filtering and contextual modeling.* The basic idea behind pre-filtering is to generate context-aware recommendations by exploiting only the subset of the information (e.g. ratings) expressed by the users under some specific context. For example, if a user needs suggestions on the best music for a party, the algorithm builds the recommendation set by filtering out all the preferences expressed in contexts different from the target one. On the other side, post-filtering generates the recommendations by exploiting all the available data, next it uses contextual information to filter out the items that do not match some contextual constraints. For example, a post-filtering recommendation algorithm could filter the restaurants too far from the current location of the user. Finally, contextual modeling implants information about the context in the algorithm itselft, thus influencing the step of building user profiles as well as that of generating recommendations.

The main contribution of this paper is CONTEXTUAL eVSM, a framework for content-based context-aware recommendations. The main building block of the framework is the enhanced Vector Space Model (eVSM) [17], an adapation of the vector space model to the requirements of content-based recommender systems (CBRS), boosted by distributional semantics [24] and quantum negation [25]. In this work the eVSM has been further extended to make it context-aware: this has been done by introducing a pre-filtering approach as well as a novel contextual modeling technique. As pre-filtering approach we adapted to CBRS the well-known *microprofiling* [5] technique. Specifically, we split user ratings according to the contextual situation the preference is expressed in, and we exploited this information to build several context-aware *(micro)* profiles that are used to generate context-aware recommendations. As contextual modeling approach, we introduced a novel technique that exploits distributional semantics to represent the context as a vector and merges it with a vector space representation of user preferences, thus building a context-aware user profile able to provide users with context-aware recommendations.

The paper is organized as follows. In Section 2 the most relevant work in the area of context-aware recommendation are sketched. Next, in Section 3, we focus the attention on Contextual eVSM: we describe the main building blocks of the eVSM, then we show how the framework is made context-aware by introducing pre-filtering and contextual modeling techniques. Details about the experimental settings are provided in Section 4: we exploit a state-of-the-art dataset to evaluate the goodness of our framework against other relevant work in the area. Finally, Section 5 contains conclusions and future directions of this research.

2 Related Work

Even if there exists a very vast literature on RSs [21], the research about context-aware RSs (CARS) is relatively new. One of the first attempts towards the construction of recommendation algorithms able to manage contextual information has been carried out by Herlocker and Kostan, that proposed in [11] a technique that adapted the recommendation list to the specific task of the user. This work represents one of the first evidences towards the goodness of the insights behind CARS, since 88% of the users involved in the user study designed by the authors preferred the context-aware version of the system. Almost in parallel, Adomavicius and Tuzhlin proposed in [3] a *multi-dimensional model* able to extend the classical user-item matrix in order to store additional contextual information. This research line has been further extended in [2], where the authors applied a *reduction-based* approach that reduces the dimensionality of the original matrix. In our experimental evaluation we exploited the same dataset and the same experimental settings used in that work, in order to guarantee comparable experimental results. The insight of reducing the complexity of the recommendation task by building a smaller matrix has been followed by Karatzoglou et al. [13], that proposed a framework for *multiverse recommendations* based on the tensor factorization. The most recent trends in the area of CARS have been discussed in the recent series of CARS[1] and CAMRa[2] workshopsas well as in a recent survey [1]. The abovementioned classification between *pre-filtering, post-filtering and contextual modeling* has been proposed by Adomavicius and Tuzhilin [4]. As stated above, pre-filtering algorithms filter the set of available data in order to exploit only those that are relevant for a certain contextual scenario. A typical approach is the micro-profiling, discussed in [5]. Similarly, Baltrunas and Ricci introduced the technique of *item splitting*, where each item is split into several fictitious items based on the different contexts in which these items can be consumed. However, pre-filtering is very prone to suffer of the sparsity problem, since it is likely that only a little subset of data is available for a certain context. In order to handle this issue, in [26] the authors introduced the concept of context relaxation for pre-filtering algorithms. In the experimental evaluation

---

[1] `http://cars-workshop.org/`

[2] `http://camrachallenge.com/`

they showed an improvement of the performance of their CARS. A broad comparison between pre and post-filtering techniques is provided by Panniello et al. [20]. The empirical results showed that post-filtering generally performs better than pre-filtering. However, the authors stated that it is not possible to clearly determine the best performing technique and the choice really depends on the application domain. Our contextual modeling approach got inspiration from the *weighted post-filtering* proposed by Panniello, since we used the vector space representation of the context as a weighting factor that is merged with a vector space representation of user preferences. According to the presented literature, the novelty of our work lies in the following aspects:

- Most of the proposed techniques focus on the enrichment of collaborative filtering approaches to model and store information about context. Differently, in this paper we propose an extension of a content-based recommendation framework. Up to our knowledge, this is one of the first attempts towards this direction. In [19] the authors exploited the data stored in DbPedia[3], the RDF mapping of Wikipedia, to provide context-aware movie recommendation for a mobile application, while in [8] the authors use contextual information to improve the performances of a content-based news recommender systems. Beyond these attempts, the area of context-aware content-based recommender sysems has not been properly investigated, yet;
- Our approach exploits distributional models (DMs) [24] to build a semantic vector space representation of the context. DMs state that the meaning of the terms can be inferred in a totally unsupervised way by just analyzing their usage patterns in a specific language, with the insight that terms that are usually used together (e.g. beer, wine, etc.) are supposed to share a similar meaning. According to this insight, we decided to exploit distributional models to build a semantic vector space representation of the contextas well. Specifically, we assumed that the context could be represented as a vector obtained by combining the semantic representation of the terms used to describe items labeled as relevant in that context. Similarly, in [9] the authors exploit the distributional hypothesis to calculate similarities between different contexts and use this information to relax contextual pre-filtering constraints. However, differently from this work, we used the distributional semantics as a *weighting factor* of a contextual modeling technique.

3 Contextual eVSM

The eVSM [17] is a content-based recommendation framework based on vector space model (VSM) [23].

3.1 Basis of eVSM

The whole framework is built upon the following building blocks:

[3] `http://dbpedia.org/`

- The VSM is the core of the framework. *Items* as well as *user profiles* are represented as vectors in a vector space. However, since VSM does not provide any semantic modeling of the information, distributional models are exploited to build a lightweight *semantic* representation, according to the co-occurrences of the terms within the corpus;
- Techniques based on distributional models are not scalable (e.g. LSA [10]). In order to guarantee the scalability required by CBRS, distributional semantics has been coupled with an incremental and effective dimensionality reduction technique called Random Indexing [22], that has been used to reduce the dimension of the vector space;
- Since VSM cannot model any negative evidence, a quantum negation operator, proposed by Widdows [25], has been integrated in the framework.

Thanks to the combination of distributional models, Random Indexing and quantum negation, it is possible to represent items as points in a (semantic) vector space built in a incremental and scalable way. Similarly, a semantic user profile, able to model also negative evidences (e.g. information about items the user disliked), can be learned. Specifically, let I a set of items split into I_u^+ and I_u^- (items the user liked and items the user disliked, respectively), let $d_1..d_n \in I$ be a set of already rated items, let $r(u, d_i)$ $(i = 1..n)$ the rating given by the user u to the item d_i, it is possible to define two different user profiling approaches.

In the first one, denoted as Weighted Random Indexing (WRI), the user profile is a vector that combines in a weighted way the vector space representation of the items the user liked in the past.

$$\boldsymbol{WRI(u)} = \sum_{i=1}^{|I_u^+|} \boldsymbol{d_i} * \frac{\boldsymbol{r(u, d_i)}}{\boldsymbol{MAX}} \tag{1}$$

Where MAX is the maximum rating. Next, the Weighted Quantum Negation (WQN) profile models into a single vector $\boldsymbol{WQN(u)}$ the information coming from $\boldsymbol{WRI(u)}$ with that coming from $\boldsymbol{WRI_{neg}(u)}$, a vector space representation of the items the user disliked:

$$\boldsymbol{WRI_{neg}(u)} = \sum_{i=1}^{|I_u^-|} \boldsymbol{d_i} * \frac{\boldsymbol{MAX - r(u, d_i)}}{\boldsymbol{MAX}} \tag{2}$$

Under a geometrical point of view, the user profile $\boldsymbol{WQN(u)}$ represents the projection of $\boldsymbol{WRI(u)}$ on the subspace orthogonal to those generated by $\boldsymbol{WRI_{neg}(u)}$ [7].

Finally, given a vector space representation of user preferences (WRI or WQN), the recommendation set is built by exploiting cosine similarity: specifically, the items with the highest cosine similarity are returned as recommendations. Even if a complete description of the eVSM framework is out of the scope of this paper, it is worth to note that the framework has been already evaluated in several experimental settings [17,18], where the effectiveness of the approach was always confirmed. In the next section we will evaluate the framework in the task of providing users with contextual recommendations.

3.2 Introducing Context into eVSM

The concept of *context* has been studied in multiple disciplines, and each one tends to take its own view of it. As stated by Bazire et Batillon [6], it is not possible to provide a unique universally shared definition: in the area of personalization and recommender systems, for example, a rich overview of the definitions as well as the scope of this multifaceted concept is contained in [1]. However, the definition of the concept of *context* is out of the scope of this paper. For the sake of simplicity we can consider the context *as a set of (external) factors able to influence user perception of the utility of a certain item.* Several aspects fall into this definition: the task to be accomplished, the company, the location, the mood, the weather and so on. Formally, we can define the *context* as a set of contextual variables $C = \{c_1, c_2 \ldots c_n\}$. Each contextual variable c_i has its own domain $dom(c_i)$. Typically, $dom(c_i)$ is categorical. Formally, $dom(c_i) = \{v_1, v_2 \ldots v_m\}$, where v_j is one of the m values allowed for the variable c_i. For example, if we consider as contextual variable the task to be accomplished, $dom(task) = \{studying, running, dancing \ldots\}$. Clearly, many variables are not categorical: user location, for example, can be defined through GPS coordinates. However, in this work we just focused on those variables that can be modeled through a set of categorical values.

Pre-filtering: as pre-filtering approach, we adapted to CBRS the microprofiling technique proposed by Baltrunas and Amatriain [5]. The insight behind microprofiling is that the complete user profile, containing all the information about the preferences of the target user, can be split in several (micro) profiles containing only the information that the user expressed under a specific contextual situation. Intuitively, if the target user needs to receive suggestions about music to play during a party, it makes sense to build the recommendation set by taking into account only the preferences she expressed in that context. Formally, given a set of n contextual variables, each of which can assume m different values, the user profile (WRI or WQN) is split into at most $m \times n$ smaller microprofiles, according to the available ratings. The rating function is split as well, since user preferences can change in different contextual situations. Let $r(u, d_i, c_i, v_j)$ a contextual rating function that models the rating of user u on item d_i under the context v_j, where $v_j \in dom(c_i)$. We can define the set $I_u^+(c_i, v_j)$ as the set of the items the user likes in a specific context. Given these definition, we can define a contextual WRI profile for user U in the context v_j as:

$$\boldsymbol{preWRI}(\boldsymbol{u}, \boldsymbol{c_i}, \boldsymbol{v_j}) = \sum_{i=1}^{|I_u^+(c_i, v_j)|} \boldsymbol{d_i} * r(u, d_i, c_i, v_j) \quad (3)$$

Due to space limitations the formula for building the negative counterpart $\boldsymbol{preWRI_{neg}(u, c_i, v_j)}$ is not provided, but it can be easily obtained from the previous one. Identically, $\boldsymbol{preWQN(u, c_i, v_j)}$ is obtained by combining both positive and negative microprofiles through quantum negation. As for uncontextual recommendations, given the vector representing a microprofile of the target user, the recommendation set is built by just calculating the cosine similarity between the profile and all the avaiable items. Since the profile is context-aware, the recommendations become context-awareas well.

Contextual Modeling: the insight behind microprofiling is very intuitive and easy to implement. However, it suffers from a clear issue: by splitting the whole user profile into several smaller profiles, it is likely that the available data are not enough to properly model user preferences. It's not by chance that several work in the state of the art [9,26] already tried to make the exact pre-filtering much more flexible and able to exploit data coming from other (similar) contextual situations. As a consequence, we introduced a novel contextual modeling approach that considers the context as a *weighting factor* that just influences the recommendation score for a certain item. Our insight is to combine the uncontextual vector space representation of user preferences $\boldsymbol{WRI(u)}$ or $\boldsymbol{WQN(u)}$ with a vector space representation of the *context* itselft. As vector space representation of the context we used $\boldsymbol{preWRI(u, c_i, v_j)}$, since it models the information coming from the items the user like in that specific context. Next, the contextual user profile is a linear combination of both vectors:

$$\boldsymbol{contextWRI(u, c_i, v_j)} = \alpha * \boldsymbol{WRI(u)} + (1 - \alpha) * \boldsymbol{preWRI(u, c_i, v_j)} \quad (4)$$

Intuitively, if the user didn't express any preference in that specific context the right part of the formula will be 0, so she will receive uncontextual recommendations. That makes sense, since we can state that it is a good choice to provide uncontextual recommendations if we don't have any evidence about user preferences in that context. Otherwise, the formula gives a greater weight to those preferences expressed in the target context, according to the weight α. As for pre-filtering, the negative counterpart $\boldsymbol{contextWQN(u, c_i, v_j)}$ or can be easily obtained, so it is omitted. Finally, given a contextual profile, we use the cosine similarity to extract the context-aware recommendations.

4 Experimental Evaluation

The goal of the experimental session was to evaluate the performances of Contextual eVSM in terms of predictive accuracy. Specifically, we designed two different experiments: in the first one we compared the effectiveness of contextual approaches with respect to their uncontextual counterparts, next, we compared our framework with another relevant state of the art approach. In order to obtain comparable experimental results, we adopted the same dataset as well as the same experimental design proposed by Adomavicius et al. [2].

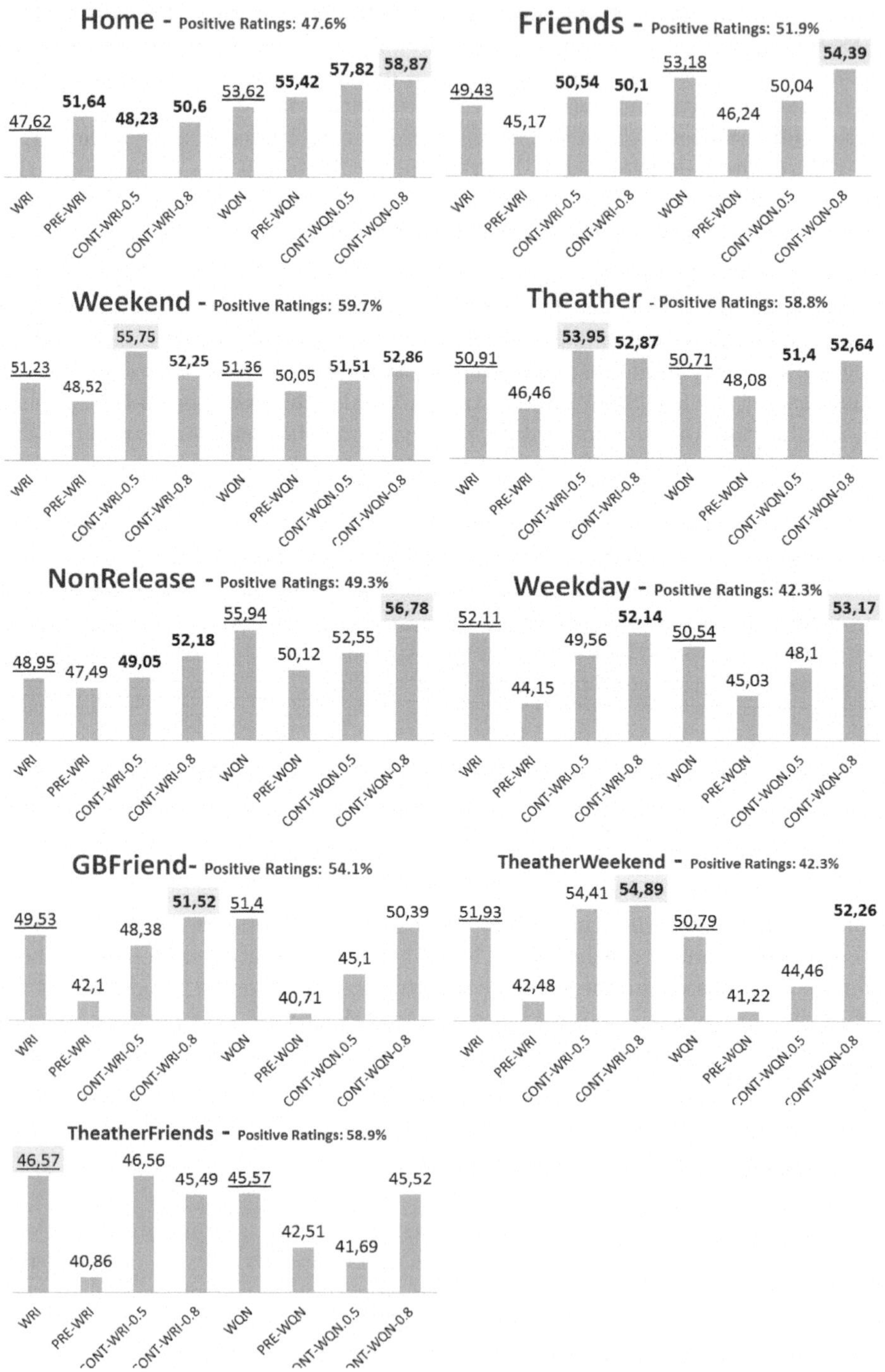

Fig. 1. Results of the experiments, split all over the contextual segments

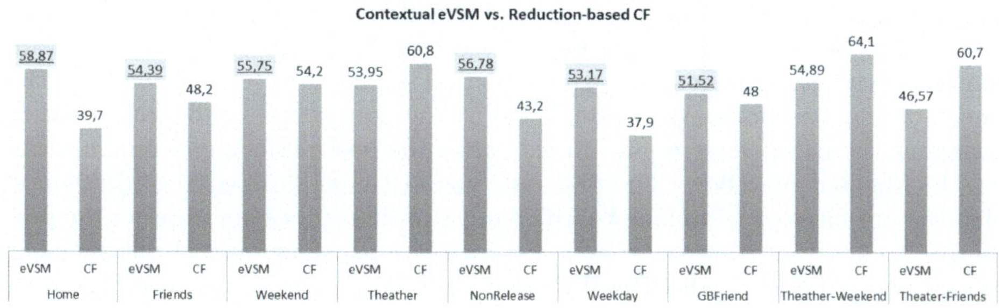

Fig. 2. Comparison with state of the art

In that papers the authors evaluated their context-aware recommender in the scenario of movie recommendation. They used a dataset crawled from IMDB[4], containing 1755 ratings coming from 117 users under different contextual situations. Specifically, four different categorical contextual variables were defined: TIME (weekday, weekend), PLACE (theather, home), COMPANION (alone, friends, boy/girlfriend, family) and MOVIE-RELATED (release week, non release week). The complete dataset has been further processed, as in [2], in order to filter all the ratings coming from users that didn't rated at least 10 movies. The final dataset contained 1457 ratings coming from 62 users on 202 movies. Since our contextual recommendation framework is a CBRS, we also gathered textual content from Wikipedia, by mapping the title of the movie with the title of the Wikipedia page. For each movie we extracted textual information about the plot, the abstract, the genre, the title, the director and the actors. According to the experimental protocol proposed by Adomavicius, the complete dataset was split into several overlapping subsets, called *contextual segments*. Each contextual segment modeled the ratings provided by the users under a specifical context, in order to evaluate the ability of the approach of providing users with good suggestions in specific contextual settings. The contextual segments containing less than 145 ratings (10% of the dataset) were filtered out. To sum up, our algorithms were evaluated against nine different contextual segments: HOME (727 ratings), FRIENDS (565 ratings), NON-RELEASE (551 ratings), WEEKEND (538 ratings), WEEKDAY (340 ratings), GBFRIEND (319 ratings), THEATHER-WEEKEND (301 ratings), THEATHER-FRIENDS (274 ratings). As experimental protocol we adopted the *bootstrapping* method [16]: for each contextual segment, 500 random re-samples were performed. In each sample 29/30th of the data were used as training and 1/30th as test. Each movie was rated on a 13-point discrete scale. All the ratings above 9 were considered as positive. Finally, we used Precision, Recall and F1-measure to evaluate the accuracy of the recommendation sets.We considered WRI and WQN as uncontextual baselines, and we compared them with both pre-filtering (PRE-WRI and PRE-WQN) and contextual modeling (CONTEXT-WRI and CONTEXT-WQN) configurations. In contextual modeling we also evaluated two different values of α, that is to say, 0.5 and 0.8.

[4] `http://www.imdb.com/`

To sum up, for each contextual segment 8 different configurations were evaluated. The results of the experimental sessions, in terms of F1 measure, are plotted in the next image. For each contextual segment, we underlined both the uncontextual baselines (WRI and WQN). The contextual configurations that overcame the baseline were put in bold, while the best-performing configuration was highlighted in yellow. The first outcome of the experimental evaluation is that the pre-filtering technique based on microprofiling does not improve the predictive accuracy of context-aware recommendations, since only in one segment out of nine (HOME), both PRE-WRI and PRE-WQN got an improvement with respect to WRI and WQN. On the other side, it clearly emerges that our novel contextual modeling technique based on distributional semantics overcomes the baseline in 8 out of 9 segments with at least one setting. This outcome confirms those emerged from Adomavicius' experiment, since their context-aware recommender improved the F1 measure in 8 out of 9 contextual segmentsas well. Furthermore, results show that the configurations with α set to 0.8 generally got an higher F1 measure with respect to those with α=0.5. This suggests that user profiles should be modeled by giving a greater weight to user preferences, and by using contextual information just to slightly influence the recommendation score calculated by eVSM. Generally speaking, configurations with α=0.8 got the best F1 in 6 out of 8 segments. Another interesting outcome emerged by analyzing the relationship between the best-performing setting and dataset balance in terms of positive and negative ratings. Indeed, if a lot of negative evidence is available, results show that the configurations exploiting quantum negation overcome those that model only positive preferences; when the amount of positive ratings is under 52% the setting that obtains the best results is always the CONT-WQN-0.8. In all the other cases, the configurations without negation overcome those that model negative preferences. The usefulness of modeling negative evidences through our quantum negation operator further confirms the outcomes already discussed in [17] for uncontextual recommendations. In our second experimental setting we compared our best-performing configurations with the best-performing configuration coming out from Adomavicius' experiments. For the sake of clarity, it is necessary to underline that the results are just *partially comparable*: even if our work shares the same dataset as well the same experimental protocol, it is not possible to ensure that the generated samples are actually the same. However, the bigger the number of iterations, the bigger the likelihood that the results can be considered as comparable.

The comparison between CONTEXTUAL EVSM and the reduction-based approach proposed by Adomavicius et al. is provided in Figure 2. A quick analysis of the plot provides other interesting outcomes, since the results show that our approach clearly overcomes the state of the art algorithm in 6 out of 9 contextual segments. Even if the experiment has not been completed with a statistical test, it is likely that the difference between the algorithms is significant for most of the settings, since in 3 segments the gaps is over 10% in terms of F1-measure. This important result further confirms the goodness of the insights behind the contextual modeling approach integrated into eVSM.

5 Conclusions and Future Work

In this paper we proposed the CONTEXTUAL eVSM, a context-aware content-based recommendation framework based on VSM. Specifically, we investigated two different techniques to incorporate contextual information into CBRS: in the first one we adapted the well-known microprofiling approach to the CBRS scenario, while in the second one we introduced a novel contextual modeling approach that exploits *distributional semantics* to build a vector space representation of the context that is combined with a vector representing the preferences of the target user, in order to make the recommendation process context-aware. In the experimental evaluation the proposed approaches were evaluated against a state of the art dataset in order to determinate the best performing configuration, and it emerged that the approach based on distributional semantics can overcome both a non-contextual baseline as well as a state of the art algorithm for context-aware collaborative recommendation. In the future, we will continue through this preliminary experimental session by evaluating more values for the parameter α and by designing a statistical test to validate the outcomes presented in this paper. Furthermore, since CBRS heavily rely on textual content, we will investigate the integration of the information coming from Open Knowledge Sources, such as Wikipedia or the Linked Open Data cloud. Finally, we are going to plan a user study in order to analyze the impact of our recommendation framework on real users, in terms of predictive accuracy as well as user-centered metrics, such as novelty, diversity, serendipity and so on.

Acknowledgments. This work fullfils the research objectives of the project PON 01 00850 ASK-Health (Advanced System for the interpretation and sharing of knowledge in health care) funded by the Italian Ministry of Universty and Research (MIUR)

References

1. Adomavicius, G., Mobasher, B., Ricci, F., Tuzhilin, A.: Context-aware recommender systems. AI Magazine 32(3), 67–80 (2011)
2. Adomavicius, G., Sankaranarayanan, R., Sen, S., Tuzhilin, A.: Incorporating contextual information in recommender systems using a multidimensional approach. ACM Trans. Inf. Syst. 23(1), 103–145 (2005)
3. Adomavicius, G., Tuzhilin, A.: Multidimensional recommender systems: A data warehousing approach. In: Fiege, L., Mühl, G., Wilhelm, U.G. (eds.) WELCOM 2001. LNCS, vol. 2232, pp. 180–192. Springer, Heidelberg (2001)
4. Adomavicius, G., Tuzhilin, A.: Context-aware recommender systems. In: Recommender Systems Handbook, pp. 217–253. Springer (2011)
5. Baltrunas, L., Amatriain, X.: Towards Time-Dependant Recommendation based on Implicit Feedback. In: Context-aware Recommender Systems (CAMRa) Workshop at ACM Recsys (2009)
6. Bazire, M., Brézillon, P.: Understanding context before using it. In: Dey, A.K., Kokinov, B., Leake, D.B., Turner, R. (eds.) CONTEXT 2005. LNCS (LNAI), vol. 3554, pp. 29–40. Springer, Heidelberg (2005)

7. Birkhoff, G., Von Neumann, J.: The logic of quantum mechanics. The Annals of Mathematics 37, 823–843 (1936)
8. Cantador, I., Bellogín, A., Castells, P.: News@hand: A Semantic Web Approach to Recommending News. In: Nejdl, W., Kay, J., Pu, P., Herder, E. (eds.) AH 2008. LNCS, vol. 5149, pp. 279–283. Springer, Heidelberg (2008)
9. Codina, V., Ricci, F., Ceccaroni, L.: Semantically-enhanced pre-filtering for context-aware recommender systems. In: Proceedings of the 3rd Workshop on Context-awareness in Retrieval and Recommendation, pp. 15–18 (2013)
10. Deerwester, S.C., Dumais, S.T., Landauer, T.K., Furnas, G.W., Harshman, R.A.: Indexing by latent semantic analysis. Journal of the American Society of Information Science 41, 391–407 (1990)
11. Herlocker, J.L., Konstan, J.A.: Content-independent task-focused recommendation. IEEE Internet Computing 5(6), 40–47 (2001)
12. Jannach, D., Zanker, M., Felfernig, A., Friedrich, G.: Recommender systems: an introduction. Cambridge University Press (2010)
13. Karatzoglou, A., Amatriain, X., Baltrunas, L., Oliver, N.: Multiverse recommendation: n-dimensional tensor factorization for context-aware collaborative filtering. In: Proceedings of ACM RecSys, pp. 79–86 (2010)
14. Linden, G., Smith, B., York, J.: Amazon.com Recommendations: Item-to-Item Collaborative Filtering. IEEE Internet Computing 7(1), 76–80 (2003)
15. Lops, P., de Gemmis, M., Semeraro, G.: Content-based recommender systems: State of the art and trends. In: Recommender Systems Handbook, pp. 73–105. Springer (2011)
16. Mitchell, T.M.: Machine Learning. McGraw-Hill Series in Computer Science. WCB/McGraw-Hill, Boston (1997)
17. Musto, C., Semeraro, G., Lops, P., de Gemmis, M.: Random indexing and negative user preferences for enhancing content-based recommender systems. In: Huemer, C., Setzer, T. (eds.) EC-Web 2011. LNBIP, vol. 85, pp. 270–281. Springer, Heidelberg (2011)
18. Musto, C., Semeraro, G., Lops, P., de Gemmis, M., Narducci, F.: Leveraging social media sources to generate personalized music playlists. In: Huemer, C., Lops, P. (eds.) EC-Web 2012. LNBIP, vol. 123, pp. 112–123. Springer, Heidelberg (2012)
19. Ostuni, V.C., Di Noia, T., Mirizzi, R., Romito, D., Di Sciascio, E.: Cinemappy: a context-aware mobile app for movie recommendations boosted by dbpedia. In: SeRSy. CEUR-WS, vol. 919, pp. 37–48 (2012)
20. Panniello, U., Gorgoglione, M.: Incorporating context into recommender systems: an empirical comparison of context-based approaches. Electronic Commerce Research 12(1), 1–30 (2012)
21. Ricci, F., Rokach, L., Shapira, B., Kantor, P.B. (eds.): Recommender Systems Handbook. Springer, New York (2011)
22. Sahlgren, M.: An introduction to random indexing. In: Methods and Applications of Semantic Indexing Workshop, TKE 2005 (2005)
23. Salton, G.M., Wong, A.K.C., Yang, C.-S.: A Vector Space Model for Automatic Indexing. Comm. of the ACM 18(11), 613–620 (1975)
24. Turney, P.D., Pantel, P.: From frequency to meaning: Vector space models of semantics. J. Artif. Intell. Res. (JAIR) 37, 141–188 (2010)
25. Widdows, D.: Orthogonal negation in vector spaces for modelling word-meanings and document retrieval. In: ACL, pp. 136–143 (2003)
26. Zheng, Y., Burke, R., Mobasher, B.: Differential context relaxation for context-aware travel recommendation. In: Huemer, C., Lops, P. (eds.) EC-Web 2012. LNBIP, vol. 123, pp. 88–99. Springer, Heidelberg (2012)

Context-Aware Movie Recommendations: An Empirical Comparison of Pre-filtering, Post-filtering and Contextual Modeling Approaches

Pedro G. Campos[1,2], Ignacio Fernández-Tobías[2], Iván Cantador[2], and Fernando Díez[2]

[1] Departamento de Sistemas de Información
Universidad del Bío-Bío 4081112 Concepción, Chile
[2] Escuela Politécnica Superior
Universidad Autónoma de Madrid 28049 Madrid, Spain
pgcampos@ubiobio.cl,
{pedro.campos,i.fernandez,ivan.cantador,fernando.diez}@uam.es

Abstract. Context-aware recommender systems have been proven to improve the performance of recommendations in a wide array of domains and applications. Despite individual improvements, little work has been done on comparing different approaches, in order to determine which of them outperform the others, and under what circumstances. In this paper we address this issue by conducting an empirical comparison of several pre-filtering, post-filtering and contextual modeling approaches on the movie recommendation domain. To acquire confident contextual information, we performed a user study where participants were asked to rate movies, stating the time and social companion with which they preferred to watch the rated movies. The results of our evaluation show that there is neither a clear superior contextualization approach nor an always best contextual signal, and that achieved improvements depend on the recommendation algorithm used together with each contextualization approach. Nonetheless, we conclude with a number of cues and advices about which particular combinations of contextualization approaches and recommendation algorithms could be better suited for the movie recommendation domain.

Keywords: Context-aware recommender systems, pre-filtering, post-filtering, contextual modeling, time context, social context.

1 Introduction

Recommender systems (RS) suggest items to users relying on preferences –usually expressed in the form of numeric ratings– of similar-minded people. Context-Aware Recommender Systems (CARS) additionally take into consideration contextual information (e.g. time, location, social companion, and mood) associated to the collected preferences. In this way, CARS can discriminate the interest a user may have in a particular item within different contexts and situations.

Several approaches have been proposed to properly deal with contextual information. Adomavicius et al. [1, 2] distinguish three main types of CARS: those

C. Huemer and P. Lops (Eds.): EC-Web 2013, LNBIP 152, pp. 137–149, 2013.

based on *contextual pre-filtering*, which prune the available user preference data according to the target recommendation context, prior to applying a recommendation algorithm; those based on *contextual post-filtering*, which apply a recommendation algorithm on the original preference data, and afterwards adjust the generated recommendations according to the target recommendation context; and those based on *contextual modeling*, which incorporate contextual information into the model used for generating recommendations.

In the literature, pre-filtering, post-filtering and contextual modeling have been proven to improve the performance of recommendations in a wide array of domains and applications. Despite individual improvements, little work has been done on comparing different approaches, in order to determine which of them outperform the others, and under what circumstances. In this paper we address this issue by conducting an empirical comparison of several pre-filtering, post-filtering and contextual modeling approaches on the movie recommendation domain. Specifically, we frame the problem as a multi-label classification task, where recommender systems are required to properly classify a given test pattern (composed of user preference, item attribute and/or contextual data) with a class label corresponding to certain rating value. This lets us to directly use well known Machine Learning algorithms for contextual modeling, and compare pre-/post-filtering with context modeling.

A major difficulty for evaluating CARS is the lack of availability of context-enriched datasets. Obtaining contextual information imposes an extra effort from the user to explicitly state or describe the current context, or system/device requirements to automatically infer the current context, e.g. by capturing time and location signals, or by analyzing the user's interactions with the system. This fact makes it difficult to gain access to contextual data really valuable for evaluation. Addressing this problem, in order to acquire confident contextual information, we performed a user study where participants were asked to rate movies, stating the time and social companion with which they preferred to watch the rated movies.

In the study we aimed to address the following research questions: **RQ1**, which CARS approaches –pre-filtering, post-filtering or contextual modeling– are able to better predict the rating a user would assign to a movie in a particular context? And **RQ2**, which contextual signal –time or social companion (or a combination of both)– provides more useful information for predicting the above rating?

The results of our evaluation show that there is neither a clear superior contextualization approach nor an always best contextual signal, and that achieved improvements depend on the underlying recommendation algorithm used together with each contextualization approach. Nonetheless, we conclude with a number of cues and advices about which particular combinations of contextualization approaches and recommendation algorithms could be better suited for the movie recommendation domain.

The reminder of the paper is organized as follows. In Section 2 we discuss related work. In Section 3 we describe the analyzed contexts, and the evaluated contextualization and recommendation approaches. In Section 4 we describe the experiments conducted, and report the results obtained. Finally, in Section 5 we provide some conclusions and future research directions of our work.

2 Related Work

Context is a multifaceted concept that has been studied in different research disciplines, and thus has been defined in multiple ways [2]. Quoting [3], "context is any information that can be used to characterize the situation of an entity." In the case of RS, an entity can be a user, an item, or an experience the user is evaluating [4]. Hence, any information signal –e.g. location, time, social companion, device, and mood– regarding the situation in which a user experiences an item can be considered as context.

Generally speaking, the recommendation problem relies on the notion of *rating* as a mechanism to capture user preferences for different items. Two common strategies to RS are *content-based* (CB) recommendations, which recommends items similar to those preferred by the user in the past, and *collaborative filtering* (CF), which recommends items preferred in the past by similar-minded people. *Hybrid* recommenders combine CB and CF in order to overcome particular limitations of each individual strategy. For any of the above strategies, recommendation approaches can be classified as *heuristic-based* or *model-based*. Heuristic-based approaches utilize explicit formulas that aggregate collected user preferences to compute item relevance predictions. Model-based approaches, in contrast, utilize collected user preferences to build (machine learning) models that, once built, provide item relevance predictions [5].

Traditional RS exploit only user and item profile data associated to past ratings in order to predict ratings of unseen items [1], and they do not take any contextual information into account. Extending the rating notion, Adomavicius et al. [1] incorporate additional dimensions assuming that the context can be represented as a set of contextual dimensions. By using this formulation, CARS can be classified as *contextual pre-filtering*, *contextual post-filtering*, and *contextual modeling* systems [1, 2]. In contextual pre-filtering the target recommendation context –i.e., the context in which the target user expects to consume the recommended items– is used to filter user profile data relevant to such context before rating prediction computation. In contextual post-filtering rating predictions are adjusted according to the target context after being computed (on entire user profiles). In both cases traditional non-contextualized recommendation algorithms can be utilized, as the contextualization involves independent pre- or post-processing computations. On the other hand, contextual modeling incorporates context information directly into the model used to estimate rating predictions.

Different pre-filtering, post-filtering and contextual modeling approaches can be found in the literature. For instance, Adomavicius and colleagues [1] propose a pre-filtering based on pruning all ratings irrelevant to the target context. Baltrunas and Amatriain [6] created contextual micro-profiles, each of them containing ratings in a particular context, as a pre-filtering strategy aimed to better detect the user's preferences for specific time contexts. Baltrunas and Ricci [7, 8] proposed a pre-filtering technique called *Item Splitting*. This technique divides (i.e., splits) preference data for items according to the context in which such data were generated, assuming that there exist significant differences in the user preferences received by items among contexts. Panniello and colleagues [9] present a post-filtering strategy that penalizes the recommendation of items with few ratings in the target context.

One of the first contextual modeling approaches is presented in [10], where several contextual dimensions including time, social companion, and weather were incorporated into a Support Vector Machine model for recommendation. In [11] Karatzoglou and colleagues used Tensor Factorization to model *n*-dimensional contextual information. They called their approach as multiverse recommendation because of its ability to bridge data pertaining to different contexts (universes of information) into a unified model. Another example is given in [12], where Factorization Machines were used to combine different types of contextual information.

Although different approaches and algorithms have been developed for exploiting contextual information, little work has been done on comparing them, in order to better understand the circumstances that affect their performance. As noted by [2], context-aware recommendation is a relatively unexplored area, and still needs a much better comprehension. The most notable work in comparing CARS approaches correspond to the series of studies from Panniello et al. [9, 13–15]. They compare CARS approaches using heuristic-based CF algorithms. Differently from that work, we evaluate CARS using model-based as well as heuristic based CF algorithms, and moreover we include a hybrid approach that exploits CB user preferences in a CF fashion, providing a more diverse set of configurations and enabling a broader analysis of existing CARS approaches.

3 Evaluating Context-Aware Recommendation

We compare several pre-filtering, post-filtering and contextual modeling RS, using different contextual signals. In this section we describe the analyzed contextual signals and acquired information, and detail the evaluated CARS.

3.1 Analyzed Contextual Signals

We focus on two types of contextual signals: Time context and social context (i.e., the user's current companion). Exploiting time context has been proved to be an effective approach to improve recommendation performance, as shown e.g. in the Netflix Prize competition. Additionally, social context has also been found as a source for improving CARS performance [1, 2].

Among the existing contextual dimensions, time context –i.e., contextual attributes related to time, such as *time of the day*, *day of the week*, and *current time/date*– can be considered as the most versatile one. Time can be represented both as continuum information (e.g. current date/time), and as periodic, discrete information (e.g. day of the week). This lets classify Time-aware Recommender Systems (TARS) according to the way they model time information: *continuous TARS* –which model time context information as a continuous variable– and *categorical TARS* –which model time as one or more categorical variables [16]. Interestingly, when timestamps are available, both continuous and categorical context information can be extracted and exploited.

In general, collecting time information of user interactions with a system does not require additional user effort nor impose strict system/device requirements. Moreover, it has been used as a key input for achieving significant improvements on recommendation accuracy [17]. Hence, the timestamps of collected user preferences are valuable, easy-to-collect data for improving recommendations. Due to these benefits, recent years have been prolific in the research and development of TARS. However, it is important to note that if a RS collects ratings instead of usage/consumption data, the collected timestamps do not necessarily correspond to item usage/consumption time, and thus may not be considered as the context in which the user prefers to use/consume the item.

Some other contextual signals can be inferred with appropriated devices, such as location or weather, by means e.g. of mobile devices with GPS. In contrast, for other contextual signals there may not exist devices to automatically infer them (or they may be unfeasible due to cost or physical constraints), such as mood or social (companion) context, but may represent important signals for determining user preferences. In particular, social context has been proved as a key factor for the users' actions [18, 19]. One way to obtain social context signals is to take advantage of online social networks such as Facebook[1] and Twitter[2], which have given raise to social network-based recommender systems [19]. However, the context information obtained in this way is used to find general preferences of related users (those connected in the social network), and generally does not correspond to the item usage/consumption context of the target user.

Thus, in order to count with confident context signals related to user preferences, we collected a movie ratings dataset, including time and social context information, as described in the next subsection.

3.2 Acquired Contextual Information

We collected a dataset of user preferences for movies. Since we were interested in the effect of time and social context on user interests, we built our own Web application, and asked users (recruited via social networks) for using it to provide personal ratings for movies they had watched. Specifically, participants rated a freely chosen set of movies by using a rating scale from 1 to 5 (1 representing no user interest, and 5 for a maximum user interest). The final dataset used in our study consisted of 481 ratings from 67 users given to 174 movies. The rating distribution of the dataset was 2.7%, 7.7%, 19.1%, 44.7%, and 25.8% for ratings values of 1, 2, 3, 4, and 5 respectively. This non-uniform distribution is important to take into account when analyzing the results reported in Section 4.

In addition to ratings, participants stated which time of the day (*morning*, *afternoon*, *night*, and *indifferent*), which period of the week (*working day*, *weekend*, and *indifferent*), and with whom (*alone*, *with my couple*, *with my family*, *with friends*, and *indifferent*) they would prefer to watch the rated movies.

In order to gain a first insight about the context influence on user preference, we analyze the differences in ratings between movie genres and contexts. Figure 1 shows the average movie rating value computed over the different contexts in our study,

---

[1] `http://www.facebook.com`
[2] `http://www.twitter.com`

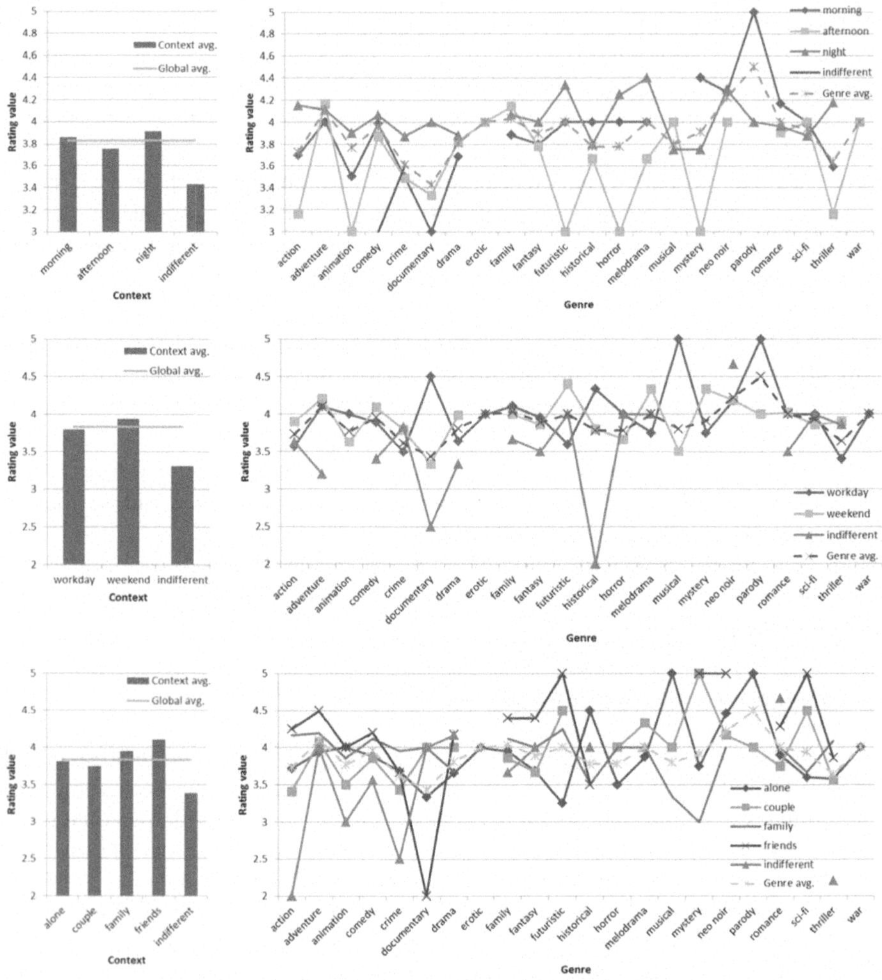

Fig. 1. Average movie rating values computed over different contexts and movie genres on the context-enriched dataset collected in our study

globally and per movie genre. As shown in the figure, there are important variations in average rating values between different contexts. These results show that time and social context information has an impact on user preferences in the movies domain, and thus, can be useful in the rating prediction task.

3.3 Evaluated Context-Aware Recommender Systems

We evaluated several pre-filtering, post-filtering and contextual modeling approaches. In the pre-filtering case, we used the exact pre-filtering strategy suggested by

Adomavicius and colleagues [1], and the Item Splitting technique proposed by Baltrunas and Ricci [4, 7, 8]. In the post-filtering case, we used the filtering strategy presented by Panniello and colleagues in [9]. Finally, in the contextual modeling case, we evaluated several classifiers developed by the Machine Learning community, including Naïve Bayes, Random Forest, MultiLayer Perceptron (MLP), and Support Vector Machine (SVM) algorithms [20, 21]. All the classifiers were built with vectors of content-based attributes corresponding to user and item genre information, and different contextual signals.

In exact pre-filtering (PeF), only ratings relevant to the target context are used to compute rating predictions with a context-unaware recommendation algorithm. Specifically, the k-nearest neighbor (kNN) algorithm [22] was used as underlying recommendation algorithm.

Item Splitting (IS) is a variant of context pre-filtering. This method divides (i.e., splits) preference data for items according to the context in which such data were generated, in cases where there exist significant differences in the user preferences received by items among contexts. In order to determine whether such differences are significant, an impurity criterion is used. When an item is split, two new (artificial) items are created, each one with a subset of the preference data from the original item, according to the associated context value. One of these new items corresponds with the preferences generated on one contextual condition, and the other (artificial) item corresponds with the remainder preferences. The original item is removed from the dataset, and afterwards, any non-contextualized recommendation algorithm is performed on the modified dataset.

In order to decide whether to split the set of ratings given to an item i, we utilized several impurity criteria, based on Baltrunas and Ricci's findings [4]. An impurity criterion $ic(i, s)$ returns a score of the differences between the ratings given to an item i in a split $s \in S$, where S represents the set of possible contextual splits.

The selected impurity criteria were: $ic_{IG}(i, s)$, which measures the information gain given by s to the knowledge of item i rating; $ic_M(i, s)$, which estimates the statistical significance of the difference in the means of ratings associated to each context in s using the t-test; and $ic_P(i, s)$, which estimates the statistical significance of the difference between the proportion of high and low ratings in each context of s using the two-proportion z-test. A set of item ratings is split if the corresponding criterion returns a score above certain threshold. If several splits obtain a score above the threshold, the split with highest score is used. Note that by using this heuristic, when more than one context variable is used for splitting (e.g. *time of the day* and *period of the week*), the impurity score lets select dynamically the best context variable for performing the split of a given item –the one that maximizes the differences in item rating patterns among contextual conditions. We used kNN and matrix factorization (MF) [17] collaborative filtering algorithms separately as recommendation strategies after IS.

In contextual post-filtering (PoF), rating predictions are generated by a context-unaware algorithm in a first stage, and then the predictions are contextualized according to the target context. We used the same kNN rating prediction algorithm used with pre-filtering approaches. The contextualization of rating predictions was performed by a filtering strategy presented in [9], which penalizes the recommendation of items that are not relevant in the target context as follows. The relevance of an item i for the target user u in a particular context c is approximated by the probability $P_c(u,i,c) = \frac{|U_{u,i,c}|}{k}$, where k is the number of neighbors used by kNN and $U_{u,i,c} = \{v \in N(u) | r_{v,i,c} \neq \emptyset\}$, that is, the user's neighbors v in the neighborhood of u, $N(u)$, who have rated/consumed item i in context c. The item relevance is determined by a threshold value τ_{P_c} (set to 0.1 in our experiments) that is used to contextualize the ratings as follows:

$$F(u,i,c) = \begin{cases} F(u,i) & \text{if} \quad P_c(u,i,c) \geq \tau_{P_c} \\ F(u,i) - 0.5 & \text{if} \quad P_c(u,i,c) < \tau_{P_c} \end{cases}$$

where $F(u,i)$ denotes the context-unaware rating prediction given by a RS, and $F(u,i,c)$ denotes the context-aware rating prediction.

The Machine Learning algorithms used for contextual modeling provide a score distribution for a rating (class label) in the space of rating values 1, 2, 3, 4 and 5. These algorithms were trained with a set of patterns composed of attributes describing user and item characteristics, and attributes containing contextual information. The algorithms exploit these patterns to compute score distributions. In this way, preferences of individual users were exploited in a collaborative way. The analyzed user and item characteristics correspond to movie genres. For each user u, the value of attribute a_m was the number of u's liked/preferred items with genre m. For each item i, the value of attribute a_n was 1 if i had the genre n, and 0 otherwise.

4 Experiments and Results

To determine which contextualization approach performs the best, we evaluated the CARS described in Section 3.3 on the context-enriched dataset collected in our study, and using the contextual information described in Section 3.2. In this section we detail the followed experimental setting, and discuss the obtained results.

4.1 Experimental Setting

We performed 10-fold cross-validation in all the experiments. In the pre-filtering and post-filtering cases, we used the kNN and MF implementations provided by the Apache Mahout project[3], with $k = 30$ and the Pearson Correlation for kNN, and 60 factors for the MF algorithm. To obtain full coverage, in cases where an algorithm was unable to compute a prediction, the average dataset rating was provided as prediction. In the contextual modeling cases, we used the classifier implementations provided in Weka[4].

We computed the accuracy of the evaluated recommendation approaches in terms of the correct classification rate for each rating value (*acc1*, *acc2*, *acc3*, *acc4*, and *acc5*), and the weighted overall correct classification rate (*acc*) [23]. We also computed the Area under the Curve (*AUC*) metric [24]. These metrics allow us to observe the performance of the tested approaches taking the pattern's class distribution into account.

[3] http://mahout.apache.org/

[4] http://www.cs.waikato.ac.nz/ml/weka/

4.2 Results

Table 1 shows the best results obtained for each of the tested approaches on our context-enriched dataset. The results are grouped according to the contextualization approach (pre- and post-filtering or contextual modeling), and the type of profile data provided to

Table 1. Performance values obtained by the pre-filtering, post-filtering and contextual modeling-based recommender systems built with different profile types. Global top values are in bold, and best values for each profile type are underlined.

	Profile type	Classifier	acc1	acc2	acc3	acc4	acc5	acc	AUC
Contextual Pre- and Post-Filtering	*user and item genres*	*kNN*	23.077	5.405	6.522	87.442	8.871	43.659	0.494
		MF	0.000	21.622	23.913	67.442	30.645	44.283	0.626
	user and item genres + time contexts	*PeF*	7.692	0.000	1.087	99.070	0.000	44.699	0.466
		IS_ic_{IG} + *kNN*	23.077	2.703	4.348	87.442	8.871	43.035	0.493
		IS_ic_{M} + *kNN*	23.077	5.405	4.348	86.047	10.484	43.035	0.514
		IS_ic_{P} + *kNN*	23.077	5.405	3.261	88.372	8.871	43.451	0.504
		IS_ic_{IG} + *MF*	0.000	21.622	23.913	66.512	31.452	44.075	0.625
		IS_ic_{M} + *MF*	0.000	21.622	25.000	66.977	32.258	44.699	0.636
		IS_ic_{P} + *MF*	0.000	18.919	25.000	66.977	33.065	44.699	0.635
		PoF	23.077	5.405	6.522	88.372	8.871	44.075	0.510
	user and item genres + social context	*PeF*	0.000	0.000	1.087	95.814	1.613	43.451	0.468
		IS_ic_{IG} + *kNN*	0.000	2.703	5.435	88.837	9.677	43.451	0.508
		IS_ic_{M} + *kNN*	23.077	5.405	6.522	87.442	8.871	43.659	0.494
		IS_ic_{P} + *kNN*	7.692	2.703	5.435	85.581	6.452	41.372	0.486
		IS_ic_{IG} + *MF*	0.000	21.622	25.000	66.512	29.839	43.867	0.625
		IS_ic_{M} + *MF*	0.000	21.622	23.913	67.442	29.839	44.075	0.626
		IS_ic_{P} + *MF*	0.000	**24.324**	22.826	67.907	32.258	44.906	0.639
		PoF	23.077	5.405	6.522	86.512	8.871	43.243	0.493
	user and item genres + all contexts	*PeF*	0.000	0.000	0.000	**100.000**	0.000	44.699	0.462
		IS_ic_{IG} + *kNN*	0.000	2.703	4.348	88.372	8.871	42.827	0.510
		IS_ic_{M} + *kNN*	23.077	5.405	4.348	86.047	10.484	43.035	0.514
		IS_ic_{P} + *kNN*	7.692	2.703	3.261	88.372	4.839	41.788	0.489
		IS_ic_{IG} + *MF*	0.000	21.622	25.000	66.047	29.839	43.659	0.625
		IS_ic_{M} + *MF*	0.000	21.622	25.000	66.977	32.258	44.699	0.636
		IS_ic_{P} + *MF*	0.000	21.622	22.826	68.372	33.871	45.322	0.642
		PoF	23.077	5.405	6.522	86.977	8.871	43.451	0.499
Contextual Modeling	*user and item genres*	*Naïve Bayes*	**38.462**	0.000	6.522	73.488	31.452	43.243	0.615
		Random Forest	0.000	21.622	25.000	62.791	51.613	**47.817**	0.669
		MLP	0.000	13.514	**29.348**	59.070	46.774	45.114	0.646
		SVM	0.000	16.216	20.652	54.884	37.903	39.501	0.554
	user and item genres + time contexts	*Naïve Bayes*	**38.462**	0.000	8.696	72.093	32.258	43.243	0.613
		Random Forest	15.385	13.514	23.913	61.395	48.387	45.946	0.649
		MLP	0.000	8.108	**29.348**	54.419	43.548	41.788	0.648
		SVM	23.077	16.216	21.739	59.535	40.323	43.035	0.573
	user and item genres + social context	*Naïve Bayes*	**38.462**	0.000	6.522	71.628	33.871	43.035	0.619
		Random Forest	0.000	16.216	20.652	60.930	**54.032**	46.362	**0.672**
		MLP	7.692	13.514	23.913	57.674	41.935	42.412	0.631
		SVM	7.692	10.811	18.478	59.070	41.129	41.580	0.563
	user and item genres + all contexts	*Naïve Bayes*	**38.462**	0.000	8.696	71.163	33.871	43.243	0.617
		Random Forest	7.692	13.514	22.826	63.721	44.355	45.530	0.666
		MLP	7.692	18.919	21.739	57.209	44.355	42.827	0.631
		SVM	15.385	13.514	17.391	63.721	37.903	43.035	0.568

each recommendation algorithm. In the IS approaches, we tested different threshold values for the considered impurity criteria. We finally used 0.8, 2.1 and 1.2 as threshold values for ic_{IG}, ic_M and ic_P respectively. We also tested different settings for specific parameters of each classifier used in contextual modeling, obtaining similar results.

We observe that the results of the ***AUC* metric** are close and above 0.5 for most of the approaches, with the exception of kNN and PeF, which got the worst performance. Moreover, the results obtained by PeF are worse than those obtained by kNN without contextualization in all cases. We also observe that **IS pre-filtering** improves the results provided by the underlying recommendation algorithm, particularly when it is used with the ic_P impurity criterion and the MF recommender. When using kNN, the ic_M impurity criterion improves the base recommendation algorithm. PoF shows a slightly better AUC than kNN. The Random Forest contextual modeling method obtains the best values of AUC, followed by MLP. The latter results are similar to those obtained by the IS + MF method.

For the ***acc* metric**, we observe that the **contextual modeling** approaches in general obtain the best values, although this may be due to the accuracy of the classifiers, as can be observed from the results using only genre profile data. On the other hand, the IS approach is not useful for improving kNN results. We observe that for PeF the good results are related with an almost perfect result on *acc4* metric. This is due to the low coverage induced by PeF, which forces to present the dataset average rating (3.83) as prediction in many cases, which is associated to the class label 4, but with near zero accuracy for the other rating values. On the other hand, PoF and contextual modeling approaches show a better balance of accuracy among the different rating values, as contextual modeling approaches also do.

Regarding the contribution of the contextual signals, we observe that **the evaluated CARS take advantage differently from each type of context information**. IS pre-filtering shows better performance by using all contextual signals. PoF, differently, shows better performance when it uses only time context information. In the case of the contextual modeling approaches, Naïve Bayes and Random Forest algorithms show better *AUC* when exploiting social context, although *acc* is not improved when using such contextual signal. SVM, on the other hand, shows better performance when it uses time context information, and MLP obtains only a slight improvement on *AUC* from using time context information. Interestingly, using all contextual signals does not lead to consistent improvements of the contextual modeling approaches.

One possible reason for the low performance obtained when using all the contextual signals is the increased dimensionality introduced by the additional information that must be handled by the CARS. This higher dimensionality is traduced in increased data sparsity in the case of PeF-based CARS (because PeF uses rating data only from the same context), and overfitting in the case of the Machine Learning-based contextual modeling CARS analyzed here, due to the increased number of pattern attributes.

Summing up, based on the reported results, we could conclude that **there is no unique superior CARS for improving rating predictions on the movie domain**, and that performance improvements have a strong dependency with the underlying recommendation algorithm used with the contextualization approach. Moreover, **no contextual signal seems to be more informative than other** for all the evaluated

CARS. Similarly to findings in previous research comparing some CARS approaches on e-commerce applications [9], the identification of the best performing approach requires a time-consuming evaluation and comparison of several CARS on the target data. Finally, we could also conclude that **using larger number of contextual signals does not necessarily lead to better CARS performance**, and the contribution given to a contextual signal depends on the particular combination of contextualization approach and recommendation algorithm used.

5 Conclusions and Future Work

In this paper we have compared diverse CARS, including various pre-filtering, post-filtering and contextual modeling approaches. To address the lack of available context-enriched data, we conducted a user study, and collected a dataset of movie ratings and information about the time and the social company preferred by the users for watching the rated movies.

The results obtained in our experiments show that there is not a CARS clearly superior to others, since performance values depend to a large extent on the particular combination of the contextualization approach and the underlying recommendation algorithm used to instantiate the approach. We observed that an **Item Splitting pre-filtering using Matrix Factorization**, as well as a **Random Forest-based contextual modeling** had a general good performance on the collected dataset, independently of the contextual information used, and thus, may represent good choices for the movie domain when different contextual signals are available (**RQ1**).

The analysis of contextual information also showed that the highest contribution is not given consistently by any of the signals alone, nor their combination. Thus, we conclude that **using all available context information does not have to be the best solution**, due to the higher dimensionality introduced by the context information (the "curse of dimensionality" [20]). Despite this fact, the **Item Splitting-based approach was able to properly deal with the combination of context signals**, possibly due to its ability of not discarding rating data, but splitting them according to the context only in cases where a significant difference is observed (**RQ2**).

The study reported in this paper has some limitations. In particular, the used dataset have a limited number of ratings, and experiments with a much larger dataset (and additional datasets) should be conducted, in order to test whether results obtained in this work are general or not. Nonetheless, we remind that in our dataset (and differently to publicly available datasets with rating timestamps), the contextual information associated to each rating corresponds to the actual context in which users watched movies (at least as informed by them), and thus, represent confident contextual signals.

Apart from using more experimental data, next steps in our research will consider analyzing additional contextual signals, and evaluating more complex contextual modeling strategies, particularly those that are able to take advantage of combinations of contextual signals.

Acknowledgements. This work was supported by the Spanish Government (TIN2011-28538-C02) and the Regional Government of Madrid (S2009TIC-1542).

References

1. Adomavicius, G., Sankaranarayanan, R., Sen, S., Tuzhilin, A.: Incorporating contextual information in recommender systems using a multidimensional approach. ACM Transactions on Information Systems 23, 103–145 (2005)
2. Adomavicius, G., Tuzhilin, A.: Context-aware recommender systems. In: Ricci, F., Rokach, L., Shapira, B., Kantor, P.B. (eds.) Recommender Systems Handbook, pp. 217–253 (2011)
3. Dey, A.K.: Understanding and using context. Personal and Ubiquitous Computing 5, 4–7 (2001)
4. Baltrunas, L., Ricci, F.: Experimental evaluation of context-dependent collaborative filtering using item splitting. User Modeling and User-Adapted Interaction (2013)
5. Adomavicius, G., Tuzhilin, A.: Toward the next generation of recommender systems: a survey of the state-of-the-art and possible extensions. IEEE Transactions on Knowledge and Data Engineering 17, 734–749 (2005)
6. Baltrunas, L., Amatriain, X.: Towards time-dependant recommendation based on implicit feedback. In: Proceedings of the 2009 Workshop on Context-Aware Recommender Systems (2009)
7. Baltrunas, L., Ricci, F.: Context-based splitting of item ratings in collaborative filtering. In: Proceedings of the 3rd ACM Conference on Recommender Systems, pp. 245–248 (2009)
8. Baltrunas, L., Ricci, F.: Context-dependent items generation in collaborative filtering. In: Proceedings of the 2009 Workshop on Context-Aware Recommender Systems (2009)
9. Panniello, U., Tuzhilin, A.: Experimental comparison of pre- vs. post-filtering approaches in context-aware recommender systems. In: Proceedings of the 3rd ACM Conference on Recommender Systems, pp. 265–268 (2009)
10. Oku, K., Nakajima, S., Miyazaki, J., Uemura, S.: Context-aware SVM for context-dependent information recommendation. In: Proceedings of the 7th International Conference on Mobile Data Management, pp. 109–109 (2006)
11. Karatzoglou, A., Amatriain, X., Baltrunas, L., Oliver, N.: Multiverse recommendation: n-dimensional tensor factorization for context-aware collaborative filtering. In: Proceedings of the 4th ACM Conference on Recommender Systems, pp. 79–86 (2010)
12. Rendle, S., Gantner, Z., Freudenthaler, C., Schmidt-Thieme, L.: Fast context-aware recommendations with factorization machines. In: Proceedings of the 34th International ACM SIGIR Conference on Research and Development in Information, pp. 635–644 (2011)
13. Panniello, U., Gorgoglione, M., Palmisano, C.: Comparing pre-filtering and post-filtering approach in a collaborative contextual recommender system: an application to e-commerce. In: Proceedings of the 10th International Conference on E-Commerce and Web Technologies, pp. 348–359 (2009)
14. Panniello, U., Gorgoglione, M.: Incorporating context into recommender systems: an empirical comparison of context-based approaches. Electronic Commerce Research 12, 1–30 (2012)
15. Panniello, U., Tuzhilin, A., Gorgoglione, M.: Comparing Context-Aware Recommender Systems in Terms of Accuracy and Diversity. User Modeling and User-Adapted Interaction (in press, 2013)
16. Campos, P.G., Díez, F., Cantador, I.: Time-Aware Recommender Systems: A Comprehensive Survey and Analysis of Existing Evaluation Protocols. User Modeling and User-Adapted Interaction (in press, 2013)

17. Koren, Y.: Collaborative filtering with temporal dynamics. In: Proceedings of the 15th ACM SIGKDD International Conference on Knowledge Discovery and Data Mining, pp. 447–456 (2009)
18. Woerndl, W., Groh, G.: Utilizing Physical and Social Context to Improve Recommender Systems. In: Proceedings of the 2007 IEEE/WIC/ACM International Conferences on Web Intelligence and Intelligent Agent Technology - Workshops, pp. 123–128 (2007)
19. He, J., Chu, W.W.: A social network-based recommender system (SNRS). In: Data Mining for Social Network Data 2010, Annals of Information Systems, vol. 12, pp. 47–74 (2010)
20. Bishop, C.M.: Pattern Recognition and Machine Learning. Springer (2006)
21. Breiman, L.: Random Forests. Machine Learning 45, 5–32 (2001)
22. Herlocker, J.L., Konstan, J.A., Borchers, A., Riedl, J.: An algorithmic framework for performing collaborative filtering. In: Proceedings of the 22nd Annual International ACM SIGIR Conference on Research and Development in Information Retrieval, pp. 230–237 (1999)
23. Witten, I.H., Frank, E.: Data Mining: Practical Machine Learning Tools and Techniques, 2nd edn. Morgan Kaufmann Publishers Inc., San Francisco (2005)
24. Ling, C.X., Huang, J., Zhang, H.: AUC: A Better Measure than Accuracy in Comparing Learning Algorithms. In: Xiang, Y., Chaib-draa, B. (eds.) AI 2003. LNCS (LNAI), vol. 2671, pp. 329–341. Springer, Heidelberg (2003)

Matching Ads in a Collaborative Advertising System

Giuliano Armano and Alessandro Giuliani

University of Cagliari
Department of Electrical and Electronic Engineering
{armano,alessandro.giuliani}@diee.unica.it

Abstract. Classical contextual advertising systems suggest suitable ads to a given webpage, without relying on further information – i.e. just analyzing its content. Although we agree that the target webpage is important for selecting ads, in this paper we concentrate on the importance of taking into account also information extracted from the webpages that link the target webpage (inlinks). According to this insight, contextual advertising can be viewed as a collaborative filtering process, in which selecting a suitable ad corresponds to estimate to which extent the ad matches the characteristics of the "current user" (the webpage), together with the characteristics of similar users (the inlinks). We claim that, in so doing, the envisioned collaborative approach is able to improve classical contextual advertising. Experiments have been performed comparing a collaborative system implemented in accordance with the proposed approach against (i) a classical content-based system and (ii) a system that relies only on the content of similar pages (disregarding the target webpage). Experimental results confirm the validity of the approach.

1 Introduction

Web 2.0 users need suggestions about online contents (e.g., news and photos), people (e.g., friends in social networks), goods for sale (e.g., books and CDs), and/or services and products (e.g., suitable ads), depending on their preferences and tastes. In this scenario, Information Filtering (IF) techniques, aimed at presenting only *relevant* information to users, need to be improved to make them more robust, intelligent, effective, and applicable to a broad range of real life applications. To this end, the corresponding research activities are focused on defining and implementing intelligent techniques rooted in several research fields, – including machine learning, text categorization, evolutionary computation, and semantic web [1].

IF is typically performed by using Recommender Systems (RS). Here, recommendations are typically provided by relying on Collaborative Filtering (CF), which consists of automatically making predictions (*filtering*) about the interests of a user by collecting preferences or tastes from similar users (*collaboration*). The underlying idea is that similar users have similar tastes.

C. Huemer and P. Lops (Eds.): EC-Web 2013, LNBIP 152, pp. 150–161, 2013.

Several CF systems have been developed to suggest items and goods [2]. Some proposals suggest to use CF also for Contextual Advertising (CA), i.e., for suggesting suitable ads to a webpage [3,4,5]. In fact, suggesting an ad to a webpage can be viewed as the task of recommending an item (the ad) to a user (the webpage) [6]. In classical CA systems an ad is typically suggested after matching the target webpage with the contents of candidate ads. Although we agree that the target webpage is important for selecting ads, in this paper we concentrate on the importance of taking into account also information extracted from the webpages that link the target webpage (inlinks). According to this insight, CA can be viewed as a collaborative filtering process, in which selecting a suitable ad corresponds to estimate to which extent the ad matches the characteristics of the "current user" (the webpage), together with the characteristics of similar users (the inlinks). We claim that, in so doing, the envisioned collaborative approach is able to improve classical contextual advertising.

Experiments have been performed comparing a collaborative system implemented in accordance with the proposed approach against (i) a classical content-based system and (ii) a system that relies only on the content of similar pages (disregarding the target webpage).

The remainder of the paper is organized as follows: Section 2 illustrates the proposed approach and the implemented system. Section 3 presents the adopted dataset, the evaluation metrics, and the baseline system. In Section 4, results are showed and discussed. Section 5 gives an overview of the related work. Section 6 concludes the paper sketching future work.

2 The Proposed Approach and the Corresponding System

It has been shown that the best performances in RS are obtained by adopting hybrid solutions, which make use of both collaborative and content-based techniques [7]. On the other hand, a preliminary study about the adoption of hybrid techniques (in particular those typically applied for RS) has been proposed in the work of Vargiu et al.[8]. This insight has also been investigated in the work

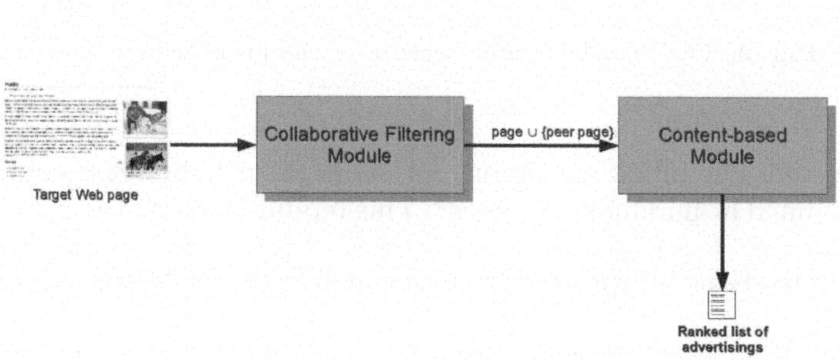

Fig. 1. The interaction between the CF module and the content-based module

of Armano et al. [9], focusing on the feasibility of devising a RS a la mode of CA, and vice versa.

In agreement with this view, we implement a CA system that uses hybrid techniques, taken from RS. We know that RS uses CF by relying on *peer users* (i.e., users with similar tastes). Hence, the proposed approach uses CF by relying on *peer pages* (i.e., at least in principle, pages related to the target webpage). The approach is sketched in Figure 1.

Given a target webpage p in which to display an ad, the proposed approach uses CF to extract information from webpages related to p and then classifies them according to a given taxonomy. In particular, the CF module uses the *collaboration* of p by retrieving a subset of its peer pages. The content of p and of its retrieved peer pages is then analyzed by a content-based module that is in charge of suggesting suitable ads to p. Suitable peer pages appear to be all the *inlinks* of p (also called *backlinks*). The underlying motivation is that most likely an inlink contains information strictly related to the topic of p [10]. However, we used the inlink's snippet[1], instead of taking into account the whole page. It is worth pointing out that the decision of using snippets is a trade-off between two conflicting issues: the need for retaining relevant information and the need for limiting the latency time (for more information on these issues see, for example, [8,11]).

Figure 2 depicts high-level architecture of the proposed system, composed of four modules: (i) *Inlink extractor*, (ii) *BoW builder*, (iii) *Classifier*, and (iv) *Matcher*.

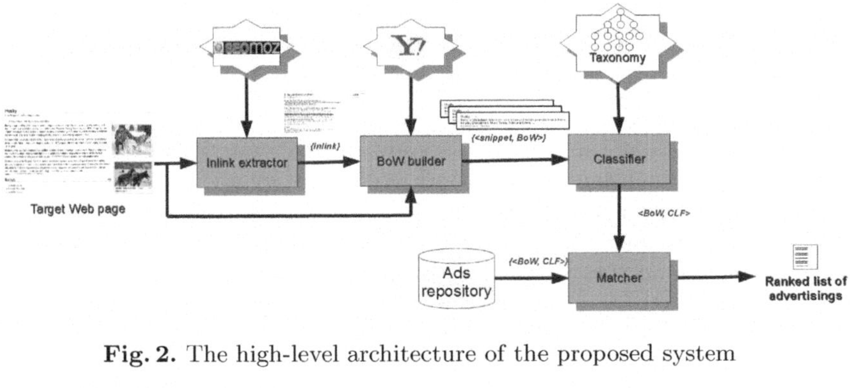

Fig. 2. The high-level architecture of the proposed system

Inlink Extractor. The inlink extractor represents the collaborative component of the system, aimed at finding peer pages[2]. This module collects the first 10 inlinks

[1] A snippet is the page excerpt provided by a search engines following the query of the user.

[2] In principle, also *outlinks* could be taken into account, as in fact, an outlink in p to q is an inlink to q from p. However, in the current version of the system we consider only inlinks, as they appear to be more informative than outlinks. This conjecture has been experimentally investigated in a preliminary study by Armano et al. [11].

of a given page by performing a query to SeoMoz[3], a special online service for Search Engine Optimization tasks.

BoW Builder. This module represents the content-based component of the system, aimed at extracting and analyzing snippets. The Bow builder first extracts the snippet of the target webpage and the snippets of its inlinks by querying Yahoo! (the content of each query is the URL of the link under analysis). This module outputs a vector representation of the original text as bag of words (*BoW*), each word being weighted by its TFIDF [12]. Let us recall that the effectiveness of snippets for text summarization has been experimentally proven in [13].

Classifier. This module is aimed at categorizing the target webpage and its inlinks according to a relevant taxonomy. The *Classifier* computes the so-called Classification Features (CLF), in accordance with the work of Broder et al. [14]. CLF are weighted and represented as a vector, whose generic feature w_j reports the averaged score given by the classifier to the target webpage (represented by the current BoW) for the category j. The module outputs a $\langle Bow, CLF\rangle$ pair – i.e., the bag of words and the classification features of the target webpage.

The classifier is trained according to the Rocchio algorithm [15]. In particular, for each category of the taxonomy, all relevant snippets are used to evaluate its centroid, with only positive examples and no relevance feedback. In formula:

$$\vec{c_j} = \frac{1}{|C_j|} \sum_{\vec{d} \in C_j} \frac{\vec{d}}{\left\|\vec{d}\right\|} \tag{1}$$

where $\vec{c_j}$ is the centroid for class C_j and d (i.e., the BoW representation of snippet in terms of its TFIDF encoding) ranges over the documents of a particular class. The classification of a snippet is based on the cosine of the angle between the snippet s and the centroid of the class C_j. In formula:

$$C^* = \underset{c_j \in C}{argmax} \left(\frac{\vec{c_j}}{\left\|\vec{c_j}\right\|} \cdot \frac{\vec{s}}{\left\|\vec{s}\right\|} \right) = \underset{c_j \in C}{argmax} \frac{\sum_{i \in F} c_j^i \cdot s^i}{\sqrt{\sum_{i \in F} \left(c_j^i\right)^2} \sqrt{\sum_{i \in F} \left(s^i\right)^2}} \tag{2}$$

where F is the set of features. To produce comparable scores, each score is normalized with the snippet and the class length. The terms c_j^i and s^i represent the weight of the ith feature, based on the standard TFIDF formula, in the jth class centroid and in the s snippet, respectively.

Matcher. This module assigns a score s to each ad according to its similarity with the given target webpage, according to the following formula:

$$s(p, a) = \alpha \cdot sim_{BoW}(p, a) + (1 - \alpha) \cdot sim_{CLF}(p, a) \tag{3}$$

[3] `http://www.seomoz.org`

in which α is a global parameter that permits to control the impact of BoW with respect to CLF, whereas $sim_{BoW}(p, a)$ and $sim_{CLF}(p, a)$ are cosine similarity scores between the target page (p) and the ad (a) using BoW and CLF, respectively. For $\alpha = 0$ only semantic analysis is considered, whereas for $\alpha = 1$ only syntactic analysis is considered.

After ranking categories, the matcher selects the first k categories (k is a fixed parameter that depends on the agreement between publisher and advertiser).

Each ad, which in our work is represented by the description (the so-called *creative*) of a product or service company's webpage (*landing page*), is processed in a similar way and it is represented by suitable BoW and CLF, where the CLF are computed only for the landing page's snippet. To choose the ads relevant to the target page, the :

3 Experiments Set Up

To assess the effectiveness of the proposed approach, we performed comparative experiments with a content-based system that does not implement any collaborative approach and with a system that analyzes only the content of similar pages.

The Adopted Dataset

We first trained the classifier with a subset of DMOZ[4]. Let us recall that DMOZ is the collection of HTML documents referenced in a Web directory developed in the Open Directory Project (ODP). Experiments have been performed on 21 selected categories, arranged in a hierarchy with depth 3.

As for the ads, we built a suitable repository in which they are manually classified according to the given taxonomy. We created the repository focusing on the DMOZ subtree rooted by the "Shopping" category. In this repository each ad is represented by the creative and the title of the landing webpage.

Evaluation Measures

Given a page p and an ad a, the corresponding $\langle p,\ a\rangle$ pair has been scored on a 1 to 3 scale, defined as follows (see Figure 3):

1 **Relevant (Figure 3-a)**. Occurs when a is directly related to the main subject of p. This case holds when both p and a belong to the same class (F).
2 **Somewhat relevant**. Three cases may occur: (i) a is related to a similar subject of p (*sibling*, Figure 3-b.1); (ii) a is related to the main topic of p in a more general way (*generalization*,Figure 3-b.2); or (iii) a is related to the main topic of p in a very specific way (*specialization*, Figure 3-b.3).
3 **Irrelevant (Figure 3-c)**. When the ad is unrelated to the page, i.e., they are in different branches of the taxonomy.

[4] http://www.dmoz.org

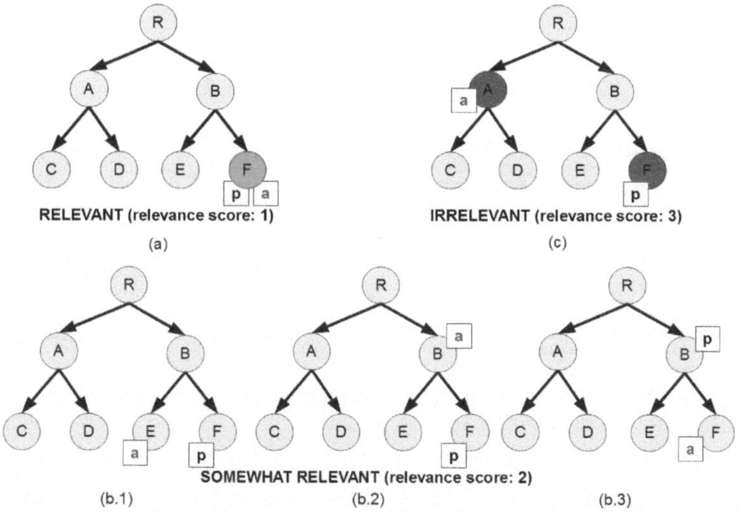

Fig. 3. The adopted policy for calculating relevance scores

According to state-of-the-art (e.g., [14]), we considered as True Positives (TP) pairs scored 1 or 2, and as False Positives (FP) pairs scored 3. In so doing, we are able to calculate the precision p of a system in the classical way.

As we rely on a graded relevance scale of evaluation, to measure the effectiveness of the approach we also made comparisons by relying on two further evaluation metrics: Normalized Discounted Cumulative Gain (nDCG)[16] and Expected Reciprocal Rank (ERR)[17].

Let us note that we do not have any information regarding the Click-through Rate (CTR) and no further comparison measures can be provided (in fact, this information is not given by companies that develop advertising systems, e.g., Yahoo!, Google, or Microsoft).

The Systems Adopted for Comparisons

As we are interested in studying the impact of CF on CA tasks, to perform experiments we devised a content-based system in which the target webpage is classified with the same *Classifier* adopted in the proposed system, but without resorting to any collaborative approach. The corresponding system, depicted in Figure 4, is compliant with the system proposed by Anagnostopoulos et al.[18], in which only classification features are considered in the matching phase (let us remark that creating a snippet is an extraction-based text summarization technique). The system takes the target webpage as input. The *BoW builder*

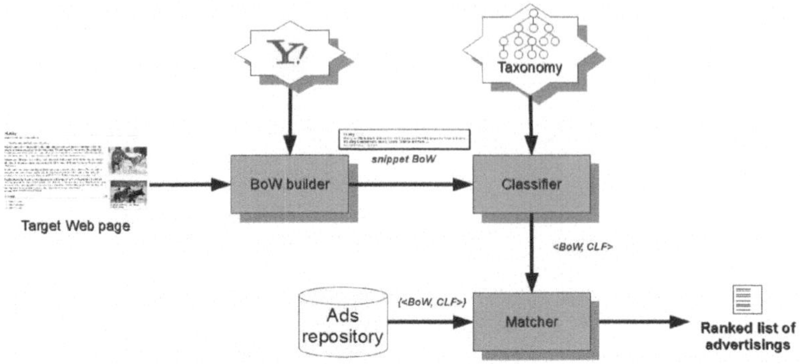

Fig. 4. The baseline system

first retrieves the snippet of the page and then removes stop-words and performs stemming. Starting from the *BoW* provided by the *BoW builder*, the *Classifier* classifies the page's snippet according to the given taxonomy by adopting a centroid-based approach. Finally, the *Matcher* ranks the ads contained in the *Ads repository* according to equation 3.

To study the impact of the peer pages alone (i.e., without taking into account the target webpage), we modified the proposed hybrid system removing the content of the target webpage from the input of the *BoW builder* module. In other words, in the system depicted in Figure 2 the target webpage is not given as input to the *BoW builder*, meaning that only inlinks have been processed.

4 Results

As pointed out, all systems embed the same *Classifier*, which has been trained by using the same training set. A total of about 2100 webpages, each belonging to one category, has been adopted to train and test the systems and to make experimental comparisons. Experiments have been performed by running 10-fold cross-validation.

We evaluated the performance of each system by running five different experiments, in which from 1 to 5 ads are selected for the target page, respectively. In Figure 5, each chart reports the precision of systems while varying α. According to equation 3, a value of 0.0 means that only semantic analysis is considered, whereas a value of 1.0 considers only syntactic analysis. The three systems are, respectively, our CF proposal (***Page + Inlinks***), the proposal in which only peer pages are taken into account (***Inlinks***), and the content-based baseline system (***Page***). As expected, the best performance in each chart is provided by the adoption of page and inlinks snippets. Furthermore, in each chart, the peak of precision is obtained with low values of α (ranging from 0 to 0.5). Observing the charts, we can state that, in this kind of problem, the CLF have the discriminant

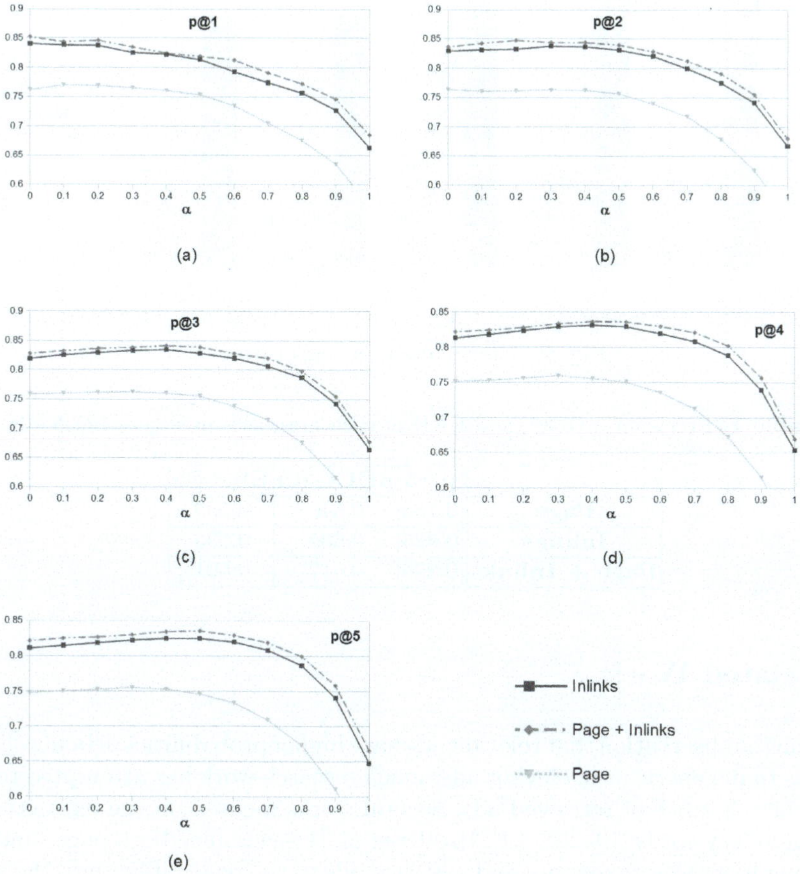

Fig. 5. The results in terms of p@k while varying α

impact at low values of k, whereas the *BoW* could help to improve the performance for higher value of k. This behavior is in accordance with previous works, meaning that the semantic information has more impact than the syntactic one.

For the sake of clarity we report in Figure 6 the precision of the systems, for each value k, according to the best value of α. Figure 6 highlights that the adoption of inlinks improves the performance of the baseline system.

Finally, Table 1 shows the performance of each system in suggesting 5 ads, in terms of precision, nDCG and ERR, confirming the assumption that linking documents can be helpful.

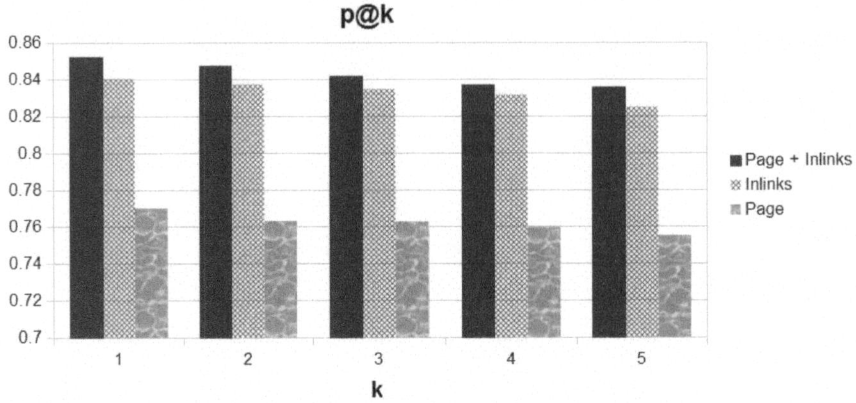

Fig. 6. The results in terms of p@k

Table 1. Precision, nDCG, and ERR of each approach in suggesting 5 ads

	p@5	**nDCG@5**	**ERR@5**
Page	0.755	0.540	0.539
Inlinks	0.825	0.605	0.593
Page + Inlinks	0.836	0.617	0.601

5 Related Work

Based on the observation that relevant ads have higher probabilities of being clicked by users than generic or irrelevant ads, much research work has attempted to improve the relevance of retrieved ads. Several works focused on the extraction of meaningful keywords [19] [20] [21]. Broder et al. [14] classified both pages and ads according to a given taxonomy and matched ads to the page falling into the same node of the taxonomy, giving rise to a semantic analysis. Another approach that combines syntax and semantics has been proposed in [22]. The corresponding system, called ConCA (Concepts on Contextual Advertising), relies on ConceptNet, a semantic network able to provide commonsense knowledge [23]. The choice of the classifier is in accordance with these works. Nowadays, ad networks need to deal in real time with a large amount of data, at least in principle, involving billions of pages and ads. Hence, efficiency and computational costs are crucial factors in the choice of methods and algorithms. Anagnostopoulos et al. [18] presented a methodology for Web advertising in real time, focusing on the contributions of the different fragments of a webpage. This methodology allows to identify short but informative excerpts of the webpage by means of several text summarization techniques, used in conjunction with the model developed in [14]. According to this view, Armano et al. [24] [25] studied the impact of text summarization in CA, showing that effective text summarization techniques may help to improve the behavior of a CA system. The adoption of snippets is compliant with these works; in fact, a snippet is usually a summary of the webpage's content. In RS, different ways of combining collaborative and content-based methods have been adopted [2]: (i) implementing collaborative and content-based methods separately and combining their predictions; (ii) embedding some content-based characteristics into a collaborative approach; (iii) embedding some collaborative characteristics into a content-based approach; and (iv) devising a unifying model able to incorporate both content-based and collaborative characteristics. As the best performances in RS are achieved by adopting CF in conjunction with content-based approaches [7], we propose the hybrid CA system that uses CF in a content-based setting according to the third approach. Many researchers investigated the role of links in information retrieval. In particular, links have been used to (i) enhance document representation [26], (ii) improve document ranking by propagating document score [27], (iii) provide an indicator of popularity [28], and (iv) find hubs and authorities for a given topic [29]. Our choice to rely on inlinks is consistent with link-based ranking algorithms, which are based on the assumption that linking documents have related content [10].

6 Conclusions and Future Work

It is well known that the best performances in recommender systems are obtained by adopting collaborative filtering, in conjunction with content-based approaches. In this paper, we proposed a collaborative advertising system which makes use oh hybrid techniques, in particular, collaborative filtering. To suggest an ad to a target webpage, we perform a direct matching between the webpage and each ad. We adopt the collaboration of suitable pages related thereto, i.e., pages similar to the target webpage, at least in the topics. We performed comparative experiments with a content-based and with a system that takes into account only the peer pages (while disregarding the target one). Experiments have been performed on about 2100 webpages from the Open Directory Project. Results indicate the effectiveness of the proposed approach and show that the proposed hybrid contextual advertising system performs better than the baseline system.

As for future work, we are currently studying how to improve the collaborative and/or the content-based module. As for the former, further techniques for selecting similar pages are under study, for instance link prediction methods [30] and the adoption of clustering techniques. As for the latter, we are planning to modify the classifier by adopting a hierarchical approach, such as the one proposed in [31]. In fact, in our view, taking into account the taxonomic relationship among categories should improve overall classifier performance.

References

1. Armano, G., de Gemmis, M., Semeraro, G., Vargiu, E.: Intelligent Information Access. SCI, vol. 301. Springer, Heidelberg (2010)
2. Adomavicius, G., Tuzhilin, A.: Toward the next generation of recommender systems: A survey of the state-of-the-art and possible extensions. IEEE Transactions on Knowledge and Data Engineering 17(6), 734–749 (2005)

3. Broder, A.Z., Ciccolo, P., Fontoura, M., Gabrilovich, E., Josifovski, V., Riedel, L.: Search advertising using web relevance feedback. In: Proc. of 17th. Int. Conference on Information and Knowledge Management, pp. 1013–1022 (2008)
4. Anastasakos, T., Hillard, D., Kshetramade, S., Raghavan, H.: A collaborative lter-ing approach to ad recommendation using the query-ad click graph. In: Proc. of the 18th ACM Conference on Information and Knowledge Management, CIKM 2009, pp. 1927–1930. ACM, New York (2009)
5. Vargiu, E., Urru, M.: Exploiting web scraping in a collaborative ltering-based approach to web advertising. Artificial Intelligence Research 2(1), 44–54 (2013)
6. Armano, G., Vargiu, E.: A unifying view of contextual advertising and recommender systems. In: Proc. of Int. Conference on Knowledge Discovery and Information Retrieval (KDIR 2010), pp. 463–466 (2010)
7. Burke, R.: Hybrid recommender systems: Survey and experiments. User Modeling and User-Adapted Interaction 12(4), 331–370 (2002)
8. Vargiu, E., Giuliani, A., Armano, G.: Improving contextual advertising by adopting collaborative filtering. ACM Transaction on the Web (in press, 2013)
9. Armano, G., Giuliani, A., Vargiu, E.: Intelligent Techniques in Recommender Systems and Contextual Advertising: Novel Approaches and Case Studies. In: Intelligent Techniques in Recommendation Systems: Contextual Advancements and New Methods, pp. 105–128. IGI Global (2012)
10. Koolen, M., Kamps, J.: Are semantically related links more effective for retrieval? In: Clough, P., Foley, C., Gurrin, C., Jones, G.J.F., Kraaij, W., Lee, H., Mudoch, V. (eds.) ECIR 2011. LNCS, vol. 6611, pp. 92–103. Springer, Heidelberg (2011)
11. Armano, G., Giuliani, A., Vargiu, E.: Are related links effective for contextual advertising? a preliminary study. In: Int. Conference on Knowledge Discovery and Information Retrieval (2012)
12. Salton, G., McGill, M.: Introduction to Modern Information Retrieval. McGraw-Hill Book Company (1984)
13. Armano, G., Giuliani, A., Vargiu, E.: Using snippets in text summarization: A comparative study and an application. In: IIR 2012: 3rd Italian Information Retrieval (IIR) Workshop (2012)
14. Broder, A., Fontoura, M., Josifovski, V., Riedel, L.: A semantic approach to contextual advertising. In: SIGIR 2007: Proc. of the 30th annual Int. ACM SIGIR Conference on Research and Development in Information Retrieval, pp. 559–566. ACM, New York (2007)
15. Rocchio, J.: Relevance feedback in information retrieval. In: The SMART Retrieval System: Experiments in Automatic Document Processing, pp. 313–323. Prentice-Hall (1971)
16. Järvelin, K., Kekäläinen, J.: IR evaluation methods for retrieving highly relevant documents. In: Proc. of the 23rd Int. ACM SIGIR Conference on Research and Development in Information Retrieval, SIGIR 2000, pp. 41–48. ACM, New York (2000)
17. Chapelle, O., Metlzer, D., Zhang, Y., Grinspan, P.: Expected reciprocal rank for graded relevance. In: Proc. of the 18th ACM Conference on Information and Knowledge Management, CIKM 2009, pp. 621–630. ACM, New York (2009)
18. Anagnostopoulos, A., Broder, A.Z., Gabrilovich, E., Josifovski, V., Riedel, L.: Just-in-time contextual advertising. In: CIKM 2007: Proc. of the Sixteenth ACM Conference on Information and Knowledge Management, pp. 331–340. ACM, New York (2007)

19. Ribeiro-Neto, B., Cristo, M., Golgher, P.B., Silva de Moura, E.: Impedance coupling in content-targeted advertising. In: SIGIR 2005: Proc. of the 28th Int. ACM SIGIR Conference on Research and Development in Information Retrieval, pp. 496–503. ACM, New York (2005)
20. Lacerda, A., Cristo, M., Gonçalves, M.A., Fan, W., Ziviani, N., Ribeiro-Neto, B.: Learning to advertise. In: SIGIR 2006: Proc. of the 29th Int. ACM SIGIR Conference on Research and Development in Information Retrieval, pp. 549–556. ACM, New York (2006)
21. Yih, W.T., Goodman, J., Carvalho, V.R.: Finding advertising keywords on web pages. In: WWW 2006: Proc. of the 15th Int. Conference on World Wide Web, pp. 213–222. ACM, New York (2006)
22. Armano, G., Giuliani, A., Vargiu, E.: Semantic enrichment of contextual advertising by using concepts. In: Int. Conference on Knowledge Discovery and Information Retrieval (2011)
23. Liu, H., Singh, P.: Conceptnet: A practical commonsense reasoning tool-kit. BT Technology Journal 22, 211–226 (2004)
24. Armano, G., Giuliani, A., Vargiu, E.: Experimenting text summarization techniques for contextual advertising. In: IIR 2011: Proc. of the 2nd Italian Information Retrieval (IIR) Workshop (2011)
25. Armano, G., Giuliani, A., Vargiu, E.: Studying the impact of text summarization on contextual advertising. In: 8th Int. Workshop on Text-based Information Retrieval (2011)
26. Picard, J., Savoy, J.: Enhancing retrieval with hyperlinks: a general model based on propositional argumentation systems. Journal of the American Society for Information Science and Technology 54, 347–355 (2003)
27. Frei, H.P., Stieger, D.: The use of semantic links in hypertext information retrieval. Information Processing and Management 31, 1–13 (1995)
28. Brin, S., Page, L.: The anatomy of a large-scale hypertextual web search engine. Comput. Netw. ISDN Syst. 30, 107–117 (1998)
29. Chakrabarti, S., van den Berg, M., Dom, B.: Focused crawling: a new approach to topic-specific Web resource discovery. Computer Networks 31(11-16), 1623–1640 (1999)
30. Liben-Nowell, D., Kleinberg, J.: The link-prediction problem for social networks. Journal of the American Society for Information Science and Technology 58, 1019–1031 (2007)
31. Addis, A., Armano, G., Vargiu, E.: Assessing progressive filtering to perform hierarchical text categorization in presence of input imbalance. In: Proc. of Int. Conference on Knowledge Discovery and Information Retrieval, KDIR 2010 (2010)

Confidence on Collaborative Filtering and Trust-Based Recommendations

Simon Meyffret[1,2], Lionel Médini[1,3], and Frédérique Laforest[1,4]

[1] Université de Lyon, CNRS
[2] INSA-Lyon, LIRIS, UMR5205, F-69621, France
simon.meyffret@liris.cnrs.fr
[3] Université Lyon 1, LIRIS, UMR5205, F-69622, France
lionel.medini@liris.cnrs.fr
[4] Telecom Saint-Etienne, LT2C, F-42000, France
frederique.laforest@telecom-st-etienne.fr

Abstract. Memory-based collaborative filtering systems predict items ratings for a particular user based on an aggregation of the ratings previously given by other users. Most systems focus on prediction accuracy, through MAE or RMSE metrics. However end users have seldom feedback on this accuracy. In this paper, we propose confidence on predictions in order to depict the belief from the system on the pertinence of those predictions. This confidence can be returned to the end user in order to ease his/her final choice or used by the system in order to make new predictions. It takes into account some characteristics on the aggregated ratings, such as number, homogeneity and freshness of ratings as well as users weight. We present an evaluation of such a confidence by applying it on different collaborative filtering systems of the literature using two datasets with different characteristics.

Keywords: recommendation, confidence, evaluation, dataset.

1 Introduction

Recommender systems are one solution classically proposed to help users select items among a lot of possibilities [13]. In this paper, we focus on memory-based collaborative filtering recommender systems that rely on relations between users to predict items that best fit their interests.

More and more e-commerce and collaborative websites include a recommendation system that proposes items or actions adapted to the user. Collaborative filtering is notably used on the Amazon website. The evaluation of such systems in the literature is mainly based on accuracy and coverage. These criteria are valuable for the comparison of systems and for the selection of the most efficient one. But when the system is deployed, end-users require other indications on the value of recommendations. Recommendations explanations can be provided using traces of the computation, but they are qualitative and difficult to interpret by naive end-users.

C. Huemer and P. Lops (Eds.): EC-Web 2013, LNBIP 152, pp. 162–173, 2013.

A quantitative confidence value, provided by the system as an indicator of the reliability of the recommendations, is easier to interpret. A study of the literature has shown that few systems propose a notion of confidence associated to their predictions. The few systems we have found just compute very simple confidence, for example with a standard deviation of the gathered ratings. In order to enrich the confidence notion, and to make it more valuable to the end-user, we propose a confidence formula dedicated to collaborative filtering recommender systems that takes into account five different confidence axes. Confidence should be provided with each prediction proposed to the end-user.

We also provide an evaluation of the proposed confidence so as to verify whether it is correlated with predictions accuracy. This evaluation is done using two different datasets extracted from two real websites with different characteristics. These datasets include data required for this evaluation as well as additional information gathered for wider purpose.

This paper is structured as follows. After a rapid tour of the literature, we define the five axes of confidence, as well as a synthetic confidence formula. We then describe our datasets and our evaluation protocol that measures the correlation between the confidence and accuracy of recommender systems predictions. Finally, we show the results of this evaluation on five different systems of the literature before concluding.

2 Related Work

Collaborative filtering systems predict item ratings for a particular user based on the items previously rated by other users [1]. To do so, they usually aggregate other users' ratings with the following function:

$$r_{a,i} = \frac{\sum_{a' \in \mathcal{A}_i} \omega_{a,a'} \times r_{a',i}}{\sum_{a' \in \mathcal{A}_i} \omega_{a,a'}} \tag{1}$$

where $r_{a,i}$ is the rating given by user a to item i, $\mathcal{A}_i$ is the set of users having rated item i (*aka.* "advisors") and $\omega_{a,a'}$ is a weight between a and a', typically a similarity coefficient. In this paper, we call **UserBasedCF** (respectively **ItemBasedCF**) the collaborative filtering algorithm defined in eq.1 where the ω coefficient is calculated using the Pearson's correlation coefficient between two users' ratings (resp. two items' ratings) [2].

Trust-based recommender systems build a subclass of collaborative filtering based on different links between users: users state that they trust the ratings expressed by other users [11,8,6]. For such systems, equation 1 is modified so that ω represents trust instead of similarity. Trust is implemented as a value in $[0, 1]$ that weights the links between users. Trust is the belief of one user in the usefulness of information provided by another user [5].

In the literature, very few collaborative filtering and trust-based systems use the notion of confidence. We present here the two best known trust-based systems as well as our previous work. We briefly explain the prediction principle and the associated confidence if any.

MoleTrust [8] predicts the trust value of a source user to a target user by gradually propagating trust in the user graph, up to a given depth k. In order to stop the propagation at some point, it defines a trust horizon, *i. e.* a maximum depth propagation k, being the maximum distance between u and v [9]. Beyond that distance, trust is not computed. MoleTrust does not provide confidence.

TrustWalker [3] is a random walk model combining trust-based and item-based recommendation. Each random walk returns a trusted user's rating on the item or on similar items, to depth k. Random walks are aggregated to produce the final prediction. TrustWalker associates a confidence value with each prediction, using the standard deviation of all T walks r_i (section 3.1 "variance confidence"):

$$confidence = 1 - \frac{\sigma^2}{\sigma^2_{max}} \quad \text{with} \quad \sigma^2 = \frac{\sum_{i=1}^{T} (r_i - \bar{r})^2}{T} \tag{2}$$

In **CoTCoDepth** [10], we use a trust or social network to propagate and aggregate ratings in a P2P manner up to a certain depth k. In [10], we have introduced a first version of our confidence coefficient, which takes into account previous confidence (recursively) and variance of rating predictions. This confidence is aggregated and transmitted at each hop.

As stated in the following, confidence is a composed notion that requires more attention. The next section presents a complete confidence formula.

3 Confidence

As shown in equation 1, collaborative filtering recommender systems usually aggregate ratings from trusted of similar users, *aka.* "advisors". This aggregation, or prediction, is returned as is to the final user, without justifying its accuracy. We think that all predictions should not be treated equally by the end user. For example, users cannot rely on a prediction computed from only one recommender as much as on a prediction computed from many advisors giving similar ratings.

In this section, we define a quantitative confidence coefficient associated with each prediction, in order to indicate to the final users which predictions are likely to be accurate. The higher the confidence, the higher the probability of the recommendation to be accurate, according to the system. Confidence is transmitted to the end user in order to justify the recommendation.

Definition 1 (Confidence). *The confidence* $c_{a,i} \in [0, 1]$ *of the system on the prediction provided to user* a *on item* i *depicts the belief from the system on the accuracy of this prediction.* 0 *means that the prediction is not likely to be accurate,* 1 *means that the system is confident on the accuracy. This coefficient is associated with each prediction.*

We extend this definition in order to attach confidence to any rating, not only prediction. That means that the system also deals with ratings differently during the final confidence computation. To better define confidence, we consider the following conditions to provide accurate predictions, therefore high confidence:

Size: many ratings are aggregated to provide the prediction,
Variance: aggregated ratings are homogeneous,
Advisors' confidence: ratings are associated with high confidence values,
Advisors' weight: ratings come from a well trusted advisors,
Freshness: ratings are recent.

In the following subsections, we provide a mathematical definition of confidence coefficients that take into account these conditions and aggregate those coefficients into a complete confidence formula.

3.1 Confidence Coefficients

Size Confidence (c^{size}) takes into account the number of advisors. The more advisors, the higher the confidence on the prediction.

We have chosen a logistic function (*c.f.* eq.3) to model that confidence: it is a monotonic increasing function. The initial growth (for positive values) is approximately exponential, followed by a slowing down until reaching value 1.

$$sigmoid(x) = \frac{1}{1+e^{-x}} \tag{3}$$

We define the following properties to adapt the logistic function to our case:

- 0.5 is the lowest size confidence, *i. e.* the confidence with only one advisor (flip-coin prediction),
- x is set so that a sufficient number of advisors leads to a high confidence[1].

The size confidence of user a on i's rating is defined in eq.4. It goes from 0.5 with only one advisor to about 1 with 7 advisors or more.

$$c_{a,i}^{size} = sigmoid(|\mathcal{A}_i| - 1) \tag{4}$$

Variance Confidence (c^{σ}) takes into account the variance of advisors' ratings. The higher the variance, *i. e.* the more different the recommendations, the lower the confidence on the prediction. This coefficient is similar to the one defined in equation 2. However our approach refines it by using a weighted variance, taking into account users' weights:

$$c_{a,i}^{\sigma} = 1 - \frac{\sigma_{a,i}^2}{\sigma_{max}^2} \tag{5}$$

$$\sigma_{a,i}^2 = \frac{\sum_{a' \in \mathcal{A}_i} \omega_{a,a'} \times (r_{a',i} - \mu^*)^2}{\sum_{a' \in \mathcal{A}_i} \omega_{a,a'}} \tag{6}$$

μ^* is the advisors' ratings weighted mean. σ_{max}^2 is the maximum possible variance and is used to normalize the confidence. As stated by [3], $\sigma_{max}^2 = \frac{Range^2}{4}$ for a dataset with a finite rating range denoted $Range^2$.

---

[1] Our experimentations show that five advisors are enough to provide good accuracy, therefore high confidence.

[2] In our datasets, ratings are in $[1, 5]$, so $Range = 4$ and $\sigma_{max}^2 = 4$.

Advisors' Confidence ($c^{\mathcal{A}}$) is implemented as the mean of advisors' confidence on their ratings, weighted by their ω coefficients:

$$c^{\mathcal{A}}_{a,i} = \frac{\sum_{a' \in \mathcal{A}_i} \omega_{a,a'} \times c_{a',i}}{\sum_{a' \in \mathcal{A}_i} \omega_{a,a'}}$$

The lower advisors are confident on their ratings, the lower $c^{\mathcal{A}}$. In the meantime, advisors with high coefficients are more likely to influence this confidence. However, if all advisors have a high confidence on their ratings but all ω between them and the user are low, advisors' confidence will still be high.

Weight Confidence (c^{ω}) copes with the advisors' confidence drawback described previously. We consider that if all advisors that provide a rating have a low ω coefficient, the confidence should remain low. Therefore we define the weight confidence as the maximum of advisors' weights ω:

$$c^{\omega}_{a,i} = \max_{a' \in \mathcal{A}_i} \omega_{a,a'} \tag{7}$$

If at least one weight is high, the associated confidence will impact more the advisors' confidence coefficient, which handles cases with mixed high and low weights. Otherwise it will remain low. This coefficient takes into account cases where a prediction comes from many advisors highly confident on their recommendations, but where the links between them and the user have low weights.

Freshness Confidence (c^t). This confidence aims at taking into account rating obsolescence. It is specific to timestamped explicit ratings and does not consider predicted ones, as explained in section 3.2.

Freshness is function of the age of the rating: the older the less confident on a rating. We bound freshness to $]0.5, 1]$ with the following assumptions:

1. 1 is the highest confidence: when the rating has just been made,
2. it remains greater than 0.5: an old explicit rating is still an explicit rating made by the user.

These assumptions are generic but the freshness should be specific to items since some items ratings become obsolete faster than others. Therefore we define two parameters allowing us to tune the freshness according to the kind of recommended items:

- the half-life λ is the period of time after which the confidence lost about half its amplitude, *i. e.* equals 0.75 or so,
- the time unit $\mathcal{T}$, or scale, give the lifetime of a recommendation: minutes, days, months, etc.

In order to model the freshness function, we have also chosen a logistic function based on the *sigmoid* function defined in eq.3 page 165 (t is in $\mathcal{T}$ unit). The freshness is function of the age of the rating and monotonically decreasing. To satisfy the conditions 1 and 2, we define c^t as:

$$c^t_{a,i} = \frac{sigmoid(\lambda - t_{a,i})}{2 \times sigmoid(\lambda)} + 0.5 \tag{8}$$

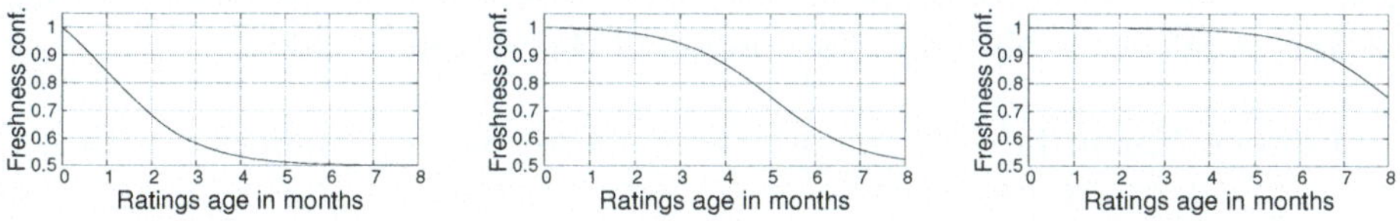

(a) $\lambda = 1$ (b) $\lambda = 5$ (c) $\lambda = 8$

Fig. 1. Freshness confidence depending on ratings age with different values for λ

Figure 1 shows some examples with different λ and a unit time $\mathcal{T}$ in months.

Since λ and $\mathcal{T}$ are dependant on the kind of recommended items, they should be defined either by the users or the items category. We can assume that a tweet will have a low λ coefficient and a time unit $\mathcal{T}$ in hours or days, whereas a movie will have higher λ and $\mathcal{T}$.

3.2 Confidence Aggregation

Before returning confidence to the end user, the system aggregates the confidence coefficients. We consider two different cases: either it is an explicit rating made by the user, or it is a computed prediction. Depending on the situation, the confidence is not computed the same way.

Explicit Rating Confidence. If a user has rated an item, only the freshness confidence has a meaning, if the rating is timestamped. In that case, users' confidence on their own rating is the freshness confidence: $c_{a,i} = c^{t}_{a,i}$. Otherwise the confidence is 1, as we assume users to be confident on their own ratings.

Computed Prediction Confidence. When a user has not rated an item, the confidence on the computed prediction aggregates the other coefficients: size, advisors, weight and variance confidences.

If all coefficients are maximum (respectively minimum), then the aggregated confidence should be maximum (respectively minimum). But those coefficients are not independent from one another. The more advisors return ratings, the more advisors, weight and variance confidences are reliable.

The size confidence should influence the aggregation specifically: a high size confidence implies that the other coefficients are reliable, so we should use them; a low size confidence implies that the overall confidence should be low, since the other coefficients are not reliable enough.

Therefore we define the aggregated confidence c as follows:

$$c_{a,i} = c^{size}_{a,i} * \frac{c^{\mathcal{A}}_{a,i} + c^{\omega}_{a,i} + c^{\sigma}_{a,i}}{3} \quad (9)$$

With a high size confidence (near 1), the overall confidence is mainly computed using the advisors, weight and variance confidence. With a low size confidence (near 0.5), the overall confidence is low, no matter the other coefficients. Then the size confidence is always the maximum of the overall confidence.

Confidence Formula. The complete formula to compute confidence is then:

$$c_{a,i} = \begin{cases} c^{t}_{a,i} & \text{if } \exists r_{a,i} \\ c^{size}_{a,i} * \dfrac{c^{\mathcal{A}}_{a,i} + c^{\omega}_{a,i} + c^{\sigma}_{a,i}}{3} & \text{if } \nexists r_{a,i} \wedge \mathcal{A}_i \neq \emptyset \\ \perp & \text{otherwise} \end{cases} \tag{10}$$

4 Evaluation

In the previous section, we have defined confidence coefficients compatible with collaborative filtering recommender systems. This section evaluates the relevance of those coefficients in existing systems: UserBasedCF, ItemBasedCF, MoleTrust and CoTCoDepth, *c. f.* section 2. We also compare them with the confidence defined in TrustWalker [4].

Section 4.1 describes two datasets that we have built for the evaluation and comparison of collaborative filtering and trust-based systems. Section 4.2 depicts our evaluation metrics using those datasets. Section 4.3 provides a comparison between our coefficients on existing systems and the TrustWalker's one. It shows that confidence is correlated with accurate predictions.

4.1 Datasets

In this section, we introduce two datasets we have extracted from two different websites: Epinions and Appolicious.

Rich Epinions Dataset (RED). The Epinions[3] website contains reviews made by users on items, where users build their web of trust within the community. A web of trust is a list of trusted or distrusted users.

The dataset contains 131 228 users, 317 755 items and 1 127 673 reviews, that is a 0.003 % density. 113 629 users have at least one rating. 47 522 users have at least one trust relation. 31 000 users have at least one similarity computed toward another user. 21 910 users have at least one review, one trust relation and one computed similarity. 4 287 users have neither reviews nor trust relation.

In average, a user has less than one trusted user with a computable similarity: intersection between trusted users and similar users is very small. The output and input trust are equally distributed and follow a power law. This is common to social network datasets.

[3] `http://www.epinions.com`

The ratings count distribution follows a power law, a few users made a lot of ratings whereas most users made few ratings. Similarly, few items have been reviewed many times whereas most items were reviewed a few times. The ratings distribution is as follows: 7.2 % of 1, 7.4 % of 2, 12 % of 3, 30 % of 4 and 43.4 % of 5. We can see the particular distribution of the dataset. It is similar to the Trustlet [7] and Alchemy [12] datasets, also extracted from Epinions, and corresponds to the real distribution of the Epinions website.

Appolicious Dataset (AD). The Appolicious[4] website contains reviews made by users on mobile applications. Users follow other users of the community. Here, "Follow" means the same thing as "trust" in the Epinions website.

The dataset contains 4 058 users, 8 935 items (applications), 28 963 ratings and 12 546 reviews, with 10 605 common ratings/reviews, that is a 0.08 % density. 1 007 users have at least one rating. All users follow at least one other user.

There are 20 815 following links, that is 5 following/follower per user in average. The output and input following links are equally distributed and follow a power law. This is common to social network datasets.

The ratings distribution is as follows: 2.5 % of 1, 5.1 % of 2, 20 % of 3, 37 % of 4 and 35.4 % of 5. The ratings count distribution follows a power law, a few users made a lot of ratings whereas most users made few ratings. Similarly, few items have been reviewed many times whereas most items were reviewed a few times.

4.2 Metrics

Confidence as defined in this paper has no impact on predictions, therefore evaluating using RMSE or coverage makes no sense. Traditional recommender systems evaluations usually try to detect which recommender systems provide with the best accuracy or coverage. In order to highlight the impact of our confidence on predictions, we measure ρ as the correlation between confidence and accuracy. The greater ρ, the more confidence is correlated with accuracy, the more relevant the confidence, *i. e.* high confidences are associated with accurate predictions.

We compute ρ as the opposite of the Pearson correlation coefficient between confidence and error:

$$\rho = -\frac{\sum_{n=1}^{N}(c_n - \bar{c})(e_n - \bar{e})}{\sqrt{\sum_{n=1}^{N}(c_n - \bar{c})^2} \times \sqrt{\sum_{n=1}^{N}(e_n - \bar{e})^2}} \quad (11)$$

Let N be the total number of predictions. e_n is the error of prediction p_n on rating r_n: $e_n = |r_n - p_n|$. c_n is the confidence of the nth rating prediction.

4.3 Results and Discussion

In order to evaluate our confidence coefficient on existing systems, we have implemented UserBasedCF, ItemBasedCF, MoleTrust2, and CoTCoD2 using a

[4] `http://www.appolicious.com`

propagation at depth 2 for the latter and run them on our datasets[5]. We have implemented TrustWalker2 to compare its confidence, noted "only variance", with ours. We have also implemented our confidence without the size coefficient, in order to evaluate the impact of the number of advisors on the confidence.

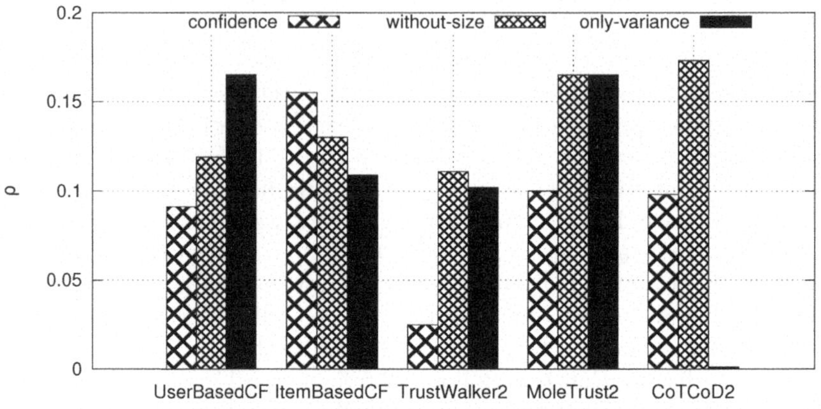

Fig. 2. Confidence correlation with prediction accuracy on RED

Figure 2 indicates ρ, the Pearson correlation coefficient between confidence and accuracy on RED. First of all, the *only variance* version is not correlated at all with the accuracy on CoTCoD2. CoTCoDepth is a trust-based recommender system propagating and aggregating ratings in a social network. Since ratings are aggregated, the number of advisors is usually low and produces a quite small variance, this latter being therefore not relevant. However this confidence is quite good with UserBasedCF. This approach aggregates ratings from similar users, *i. e.* users with homogeneous ratings. Moreover RED contains a lot of users, enhancing the chances to compute similarity.

We have evaluated our confidence with and without size confidence. We expected some improvements when taking into account the size but it seems that this is not always the case. Using RED, the size coefficient improves confidence correlation only with ItemBasedCF. Since RED is sparse, similarity between items is seldom computable, less than with users. Predictions using only few items are, as expected, less likely to be accurate.

Moreover, trust-based approaches provide the highest correlation between confidence and accuracy, especially with CoTCoD2. Sparse networks make similarity difficult to compute, prevailed by trust.

Figure 3 indicates the Pearson correlation coefficient between confidence and accuracy on AD. Clearly, size confidence is not compatible with TrustWalker. The latter aggregates ratings until the variance is low enough. With a dense

[5] Using a 99 % "training set" campaign on RED with a 4-cross validation and a "leave one out" campaign on Appolicious dataset.

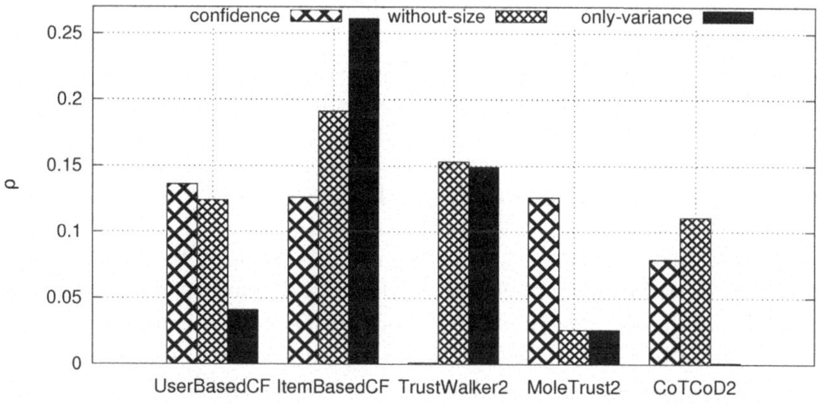

Fig. 3. Confidence correlation with prediction accuracy on AD

dataset such as AD, it does not need a lot of walks, therefore making predictions with few ratings. This implies a size confidence always low and adding noise in the confidence computation.

Using this dataset, our confidence is more relevant with UserBasedCF, but not with ItemBasedCF. AD contains much more items than users, letting ItemBasedCF use more items to compute predictions. Our coefficient produces higher correlation with UserBasedCF and MoleTrust with size confidence and TrustWalker / CoTCoDepth without.

This evaluation shows that confidence coefficients should be selected regarding the system and the dataset. Systems aggregating few ratings, such as CoTCoDepth, are not compatible with a simple variance, they require more sophisticated coefficients such as the ones we propose in this paper. On the other hand, TrustWalker performs better without size confidence, since their random walks aggregation is very heterogeneous, varying from few ratings up to 10 000 ones.

Regarding dataset density, size confidence is more relevant with dense datasets (AD) than with sparse ones (RED). It is more effective to distinguish predictions using lots of ratings.

5 Conclusion

In this paper, we introduce a confidence coefficient that aims to foresee predictions accuracy regarding some characteristics of the predictions, such as number, homogeneity and freshness of ratings as well as weights between users. Unlike traditional works on recommendation, we are not focusing on enhancing accuracy but on anticipating it. Our confidence is compatible with main classical collaborative filtering systems (UserBasedCF and ItemBasedCF) as well as trust-based systems. By definition, it is compatible with any approach aggregating ratings using weights or not.

End users may take into account this confidence as a second indicator, besides ratings. Existing systems already provide the number of ratings for each item, letting the user decide if an item with one excellent rating is more relevant than an item with many fairly good ratings. Confidence allows users to consider ratings number as well as other dimensions when selecting items.

The evaluation shows that our confidence is correlated with accuracy. Even if this correlation could be improved by further researches, it is most of the time higher than the state of the art's one. We show that some coefficients are more adapted than others to some system and/or dataset characteristics.

Confidence is composed of several coefficients defined in section 3, some of which are specific to ratings (freshness) and can be used during the aggregation in order to promote ratings that are likely to be accurate. In [10], we use this confidence during ratings propagation. We can extend existing recommender systems to propose a new function aggregating ratings, similarly to eq.1, considering weights between users and confidence on ratings:

$$r_{a,i} = \frac{\sum_{a' \in \mathcal{A}_i} f(\omega_{a,a'}, c_{a',i}) \times r_{a',i}}{\sum_{a' \in \mathcal{A}_i} f(\omega_{a,a'}, c_{a',i})} \tag{12}$$

With f a function of ω and c. In [10], we have used $\omega \times c$. This function should promote ratings that are likely to be accurate for the final prediction.

Finally we can imagine a meta-recommender system selecting the right prediction from several recommender systems using their confidence on predictions. The prediction with the higher confidence being returned to the end-user.

References

1. Adomavicius, G., Tuzhilin, A.: Toward the next generation of recommender systems: A survey of the state-of-the-art and possible extensions. IEEE Transactions on Knowledge and Data Engineering 17(6), 734–749 (2005)
2. Breese, J.S., Heckerman, D., Kadie, C.: Empirical analysis of predictive algorithms for collaborative filtering. In: Proceedings of the 14th Conference on Uncertainty in Artificial Intelligence, Madison, Wisconsin, pp. 43–52. Morgan Kaufmann Publishers Inc. (1998)
3. Jamali, M., Ester, M.: TrustWalker: a random walk model for combining trust-based and item-based recommendation. In: Proceedings of the 15th ACM SIGKDD International Conference on Knowledge Discovery and Data Mining, pp. 397–406. ACM (2009)
4. Jamali, M., Ester, M.: A matrix factorization technique with trust propagation for recommendation in social networks. In: Proceedings of the Fourth ACM Conference on Recommender Systems, pp. 135–142. ACM (2010)
5. Lee, D.H., Brusilovsky, P.: Does Trust Influence Information Similarity? In: Proceedings of Workshop on Recommender Systems & the Social Web, the 3rd ACM International Conference on Recommender Systems, pp. 3–6. Citeseer (2009)
6. Ma, H., King, I., Lyu, M.R.: Learning to recommend with social trust ensemble. In: Proceedings of the 32nd International ACM SIGIR Conference on Research and Development in Information Retrieval, pp. 203–210. ACM, New York (2009)

7. Massa, P., Avesani, P.: Trust-aware bootstrapping of recommender systems. In: Proceedings of the ECAI 2006 Workshop on Recommender Systems, pp. 29–33 (2006)
8. Massa, P., Avesani, P.: Trust-aware recommender systems. In: Proceedings of the 2007 ACM Conference on Recommender Systems, pp. 17–24. ACM, New York (2007)
9. Massa, P., Avesani, P.: Trust metrics on controversial users: balancing between tyranny of the majority and echo chambers. International Journal on Semantic Web and Information Systems 3(1), 39–64 (2007)
10. Meyffret, S., Médini, L., Laforest, F.: Trust-based local and social recommendation. In: Proceedings of the 4th ACM RecSys Workshop on Recommender Systems and the Social Web - RSWeb 2012, Dublin, Ireland, pp. 53. ACM Press (2012)
11. O'Donovan, J., Smyth, B.: Trust in recommender systems. In: Proceedings of the 10th International Conference on Intelligent User Interfaces, pp. 167–174. ACM, New York (2005)
12. Richardson, M., Domingos, P.: Mining knowledge-sharing sites for viral marketing. In: Proceedings of the Eighth ACM SIGKDD International Conference on Knowledge Discovery and Data Mining, pp. 61–70. ACM, New York (2002)
13. Schafer, J.B., Konstan, J., Riedi, J.: Recommender systems in e-commerce. In: Proceedings of the 1st ACM Conference on Electronic Commerce - EC 1999, pp. 158–166. ACM Press, New York (1999)

Smoothly Extending e-Tourism Services with Personalized Recommendations: A Case Study

Paolo Cremonesi and Franca Garzotto

Department of Electronics, Information, and Bioengineering - Politecnico di Milano
Via Ponzio 34/5 – Milan (Italy)
{paolo.cremonesi,franca.garzotto}@polimi.it

Abstract. Our research explores the influence of recommendations on the quality of the user experience (UX) in the e-tourism domain.. We are interested in the effects of smoothly introducing recommenders in *existing* commercial e-tourism system and to explore the benefits of recommendations in different conditions of *availability* of tourism services (which has a dynamic nature and typically depends on tourism flows in different seasons). The paper presents a wide empirical study (240 participants) that addresses the above issues and has been carried on in cooperation with a large hotel reservation provider (*Venere.com* – a company of *Expedia* Inc.).

Keywords: Recommender systems, E-tourism, Evaluation.

1 Introduction

Theoretical arguments and empirical evidence (mostly in the domain of e-commerce [15]) suggest that Recommender Systems (RSs) improve the user experience (UX) with web services that offer large amounts of digital content. This paper explores this issue in the context of online tourism services. Our work takes into account one peculiar features of the tourism domain, the *dynamic nature* of the availability of services (e.g., accommodations). In online hotel booking, for example, it is likely that most accommodations are fully booked during high-season, and the user has difficulty in finding the solution (s)he is looking for. Users may interpret the scarcity of resources in a given period as a weakness of the catalogue of services and ascribe the phenomenon to the service provider rather than objective contingent situations. This experience can reduce trust on the provider, and even induce users to leave the current online service and try a different one. Hence it is interesting to study the effects of RSs in different conditions of resources availability and to investigate how personalized recommendations play in relation the potentially negative effects of scarcity of resources. In addition, differently from previous works in e-tourism evaluating RSs systems that are *totally* built "*ex novo*", in terms of interface and functionality, we are interested to explore the effects of RSs on the UX from a "conservative" perspective, i.e., when recommendations represent the *only* modification to the interface and functional characteristics of an *existing* service. To address this issue, we carried on an

C. Huemer and P. Lops (Eds.): EC-Web 2013, LNBIP 152, pp. 174–181, 2013.

empirical study on the hotel e-booking service of *Venere.com* (www.venere.com), a company of the Expedia group). Venere.com is one of the worldwide leaders in the hotel booking market, featuring more than 120,000 hotels, bed and breakfasts and vacation rentals in 30,000 destinations worldwide. The goal of our study was to empirically explore the effects, on the UX with Venere.com, of the smooth, "conservative" introduction of recommendations generated with *four different recommendation algorithms* and in *two different conditions of room availability*.

2 Related work

The potential benefits of RSs in e-tourism have motivated some domain-specific researches. Some works used travel recommender systems to emulate offline travel agents [4,12] or to recommend product bundles (e.g., journey, hotel, car rental, packages with multiple destinations) instead of single items [10,12,13,16]. Other works describe conversational recommender systems used in the travel domains [7,14]. Few works investigate which factors can potentially influence the decision-making process in tourism recommender systems [12]. Ricci et al. in [12] developed and tested NutKing, an online system that helps the user to construct a travel plan by recommending attractive travel products or by proposing complete itineraries. The NutKing system was empirically evaluated in a preliminary between subject study showing that users receiving recommendations spent more time in examining information rather than moving through pages. Levi et al. in [9] describes a recommender system for online hotel booking, which was evaluated on 150 subjects. Zanker et al. [16] present an interactive travel assistant designed for an Austrian spa resort. Preference and requirement elicitation is explicitly performed via a sequence of question/answer forms. Field analysis confirmed an increase from 3.5% to 9% in the conversion rate (percentage of users requesting availability information at the spa resort). Delgado et al. in [4] describe the application of a collaborative attribute-based recommender system to the Sky-Europe.com web site, specialized in winter sky vacations. Elicitation is performed using a question-and-answer conversation. Recommendations are produced by taking into account both implicit and explicit user feedbacks. According to a field study, the recommender system was able to quadruplicate the conversion rate (percentage of visitors requesting a quotation for a vacation).

3 The Empirical Study

3.1 Research Hypotheses and Variables

Prior studies (see [2] for a survey) in e-commerce pinpoint that recommendations generated by different algorithms have different effects on the UX. We are interested to explore if the same is true in the hotel online booking domain when recommendations are smoothly introduced in an existing system. In addition, we want to investigate if the dynamic characteristics of resources availability interfere with these effects. Our study focuses on two research hypotheses:

H1: The effects on UX of the "conservative introduction" of personalized recommendations in online booking depend on the algorithm

H2: The effects on UX of the "conservative introduction" of personalized recommendations in online booking are influenced by room availability

We operationalize the *effects* on the UX associated to the introduction of recommendations using the a subjective variable - *choice satisfaction* (measured using a questionnaire) and 3 objective variables - execution time, extent of hotel search, and list view interaction (be measured using interaction logs) that are related to the *effort* requested to meet the user's goal (making a reservation) and the efficacy of the decision making process [15]. *Choice satisfaction* is the subjective judgment of quality/value for the user in relationship to the final choice, i.e., the reserved hotel. *Execution time* is the time taken for the user to explore the product offer, search for hotel information, and make a final decision. *Extent of hotel search* is the number of hotels that have been searched and for which detailed information has been acquired. *List view interactions* is the number of times the user *changed the ordering* of hotels in the list view of hotels matching some specified characteristics (e.g., stars, price, accommodation type). Ordering change is a measure of the *efficacy* of recommendations in situations where conversion rate, i.e., the percentage of recommended items that are actually purchased by users, cannot be assessed [16]. This typically happens when a system does not present a *separate* list of recommended items, but recommendations are rendered by sorting items in descending order of relevance as estimated by the recommender algorithm and the "top-N" items represent the "de facto" recommendation list.

The effects of recommendations are explored under *eight* different experimental conditions, defined by the combination of two manipulated variables: *hotel availability* and *recommendation algorithm*. Hotel availability can assumes two values: *high availability* - all hotels have rooms available in the dates specified by the user; *low availability* - some of the hotels that the user tries to reserve have no room available in the selected period. Concerning algorithms, we consider *one* non-personalized algorithm, *HighestRated*, and *three* personalized RSs representative of three different classes of algorithms: *PureSVD* (collaborative) *DirectContent* (content-based), and *Interleave* (hybrid).

HighestRated is the most common approach of online booking systems, which provides the user with non personalized lists of hotels matching some the chosen product attributes, and presents items in decreasing order of average user rating. *PureSVD* is a recently proposed latent factor algorithm based on conventional SVD [3]. Latent factor models, also informally known as Singular Value Decomposition (SVD) models, try to explain ratings by characterizing items and users with factors that are automatically inferred from a user's feedback. *DirectContent* is a simplified version of the content-based LSA algorithm described in [2]. Content-based algorithms recommend items whose content is similar to the content of items the user has positively rated or visited in the past. *Interleave* is a hybrid algorithm and generates a list of recommended hotels alternating the results from *PureSVD* and *DirectContent*. Interleave has been proposed in [1] with the name "mixed hybridization" and, although trivial in its formulation, has been shown to improve diversity of recommendations.

Table 1. Dataset statistics

Hotels	Total	3,164
	With reviews	2,884
Users (reviewers)	Total	209,704
	Venere	72,347
	TripAdvisor	137,357
Reviews ratings	Total	245,939
	Venere	80,562
	TripAdvisor	165,377
Hotel content	Unique features	481

3.2 Instrument

For the purpose of our study, we have developed PoliVenus, a web-based testing framework for the hotel booking field, which can be easily configured to facilitate the execution of controlled empirical studies in e-tourism services. PoliVenus implements the same layout as Venere.com online portal and simulates all of its functionality (with the exception of payment functions). The Polivenus framework is based on a modular architecture and can be easily customized to different datasets and types of recommendation algorithms. Venere.com provided us with a catalog of more than 3,000 hotels and 80,000 related users' reviews. We have enriched the dataset with additional reviews extracted from the TripAdvisor.com web site using a web crawling tool. Each accommodation is provided with a set of 481 features concerning, among the others: accommodation type (e.g., residence, hotel, hostel, B&B) and service level (number of stars), location (country, region, city, and city area), booking methods, average single-room price, amenities (e.g., cinema), and added values (e.g., in-room dining). User's reviews associated to each accommodation consist of a numeric rating and a free-text. Table 1 reports detailed statistics of the subset of data used in our experiments.

PoliVenus can operate in two different configurations. The *Baseline Configuration* corresponds to the existing Venere.com portal. Users can filter the hotel catalogue according to hotel characteristics (e.g., budget range, stars, accommodation type, city area) and retrieve non-personalized results. The *default* sorting criterion for the list of filtered hotels is "user average rating" but users can also sort the list by popularity, service level, or price. In the *Personalized Configuration*, the only difference is the default sorting criterion: filtered hotels are ordered on the basis of the personalized recommendations.

The user profile required by the algorithms to provide recommendations contains implicit hotel that are dynamically calculated on the basis of the user's current interaction with the system (*implicit elicitation*) [5, 6, 8, 11, 12]. This choice is motivated by two reasons: (i) we want to support users who have no rating history or who are not interested in logging into the system; (ii) we want to explore a smooth, *conservative* integration of personalized recommendations in Venere.com: to enable explicit elicitation would require the introduction of an intrusive add-on. Lack of space prevents us to provide details of Polivenus implicit elicitation mechanism.

Finally, to control for *resources availability*, PoliVenus can be configured to simulate *two different situations*, achieved by shrinking or widening the set of hotels which have rooms available for the dates selected by the user. In the "high availability" configuration, all hotels always have rooms available. In the "low availability" configuration, the first 4 hotels for which the user checks for room availability are "forced" to result fully booked.

3.3 Participants

The total number of recruited subjects who completed the task and filled the questionnaire was *240*. They were aged between 20 and 40, had some familiarity with the use of the web and had never used Venere.com before the study. To encourage participation and to induce participants to play for real, we used a lottery incentive [17]. Participants had the chance of winning a prize, consisting of a discount coupon of the value of 150€, to be used at the hotel reserved using PoliVenus. All participants were not aware of the goal of the experiment and were given the following instructions when accessing Polivenus: "*Imagine that you are planning a vacation in Rome and are looking for an accommodation for three days during Christmas season; choose an hotel where you would like to stay and make a reservation; dates and accommodation characteristics (stars, room type, services, location) are at your discretion. After confirming the reservation (simulated), please complete the final questionnaire*".

4 Results

N-way ANOVA indicates that algorithm and availability have a significant impact on almost all of the dependent variables ($p < 0.05$) with the exception of the number of explored hotels. Regardless the presence of recommendations and the availability of hotels, the *number of explored hotels* is between 5 and 8 for almost all of the users. In other words, customers wish to compare in details at least 5 and no more than 8 alternative choices before committing to a final decision.

We ran multiple pair-wise comparison post-hoc tests using Tukey's method on all of the remaining variables. The results are shown in Figures 2 and 3, where the mean is represented by a bar and the 95% confidence interval as a line.

Figure 2 highlights the combined effects of *algorithm* and *resources availability* on choice *satisfaction*. It shows that the usage of *content and hybrid algorithms* in the online booking system *increases user's satisfaction*. Not surprisingly, in the *low-availability* scenario the user's satisfaction is on average lower (because of the difficulties in booking a hotel and the potential disappointment due to resources scarcity). Still, both *content and hybrid algorithms are able to increase user's satisfaction to the same level* of users not using recommendations in conditions of low-season/high availability. The improvement does not happen with the collaborative algorithm: users receiving collaborative recommendations have, on average, the same level of satisfaction of users who did not received personalized recommendations.

The increased user satisfaction when using RSs is not always correlated with the user effort. Figure 3 plots the execution time by algorithm in the 2 different conditions

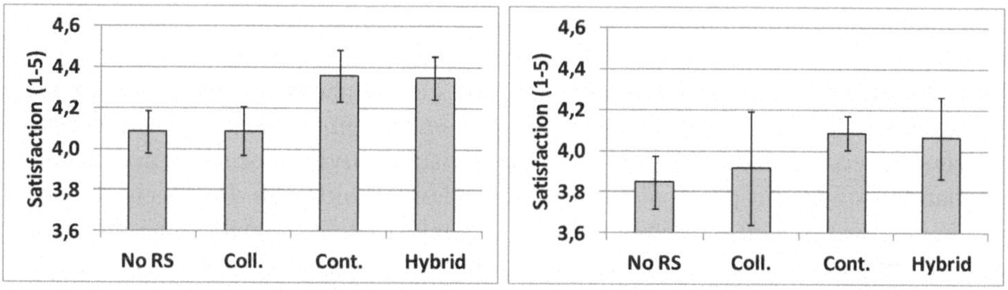

(a) High Availability (b) Low Availability

Fig. 1. User satisfaction

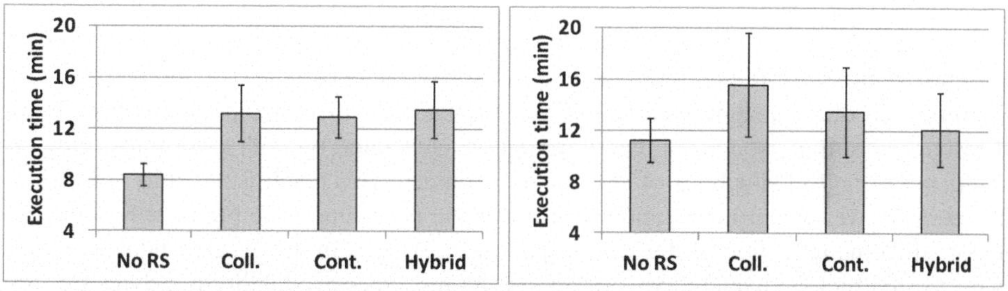

(a) High Availability (b) Low Availability

Fig. 2. Task execution time

of resources availability. Users with low availability intuitively require a longer execution time with respect to users with high availability. Less intuitively, users receiving recommendations require more time than users not receiving recommendations..

Behavioral data emerging from users' interaction log files provides some interesting results. As mentioned in sect. 3.1., we have estimated the *efficacy* of the RS by measuring how many users changed the default sorting options (recommended items first) by setting other parameters (e.g., price, popularity, stars). The results show that only *37%* of the users with personalized recommendations changed the sorting of hotels, as compared to *54%* of the users in the baseline configuration, but no significant difference in the efficacy variable exists between different conditions of resources availability.

5 Discussion and Conclusions

Our findings show that *hypothesis 1 is confirmed*, with different algorithms inducing different effects on UX quality (in line with prior results, e.g., [1]). With respect to the baseline algorithm (no personalized recommendations) the hybrid and content algorithms *improve* choice satisfaction, while the collaborative one has no significant perceived effect. Our interpretation is that collaborative algorithms, although able to provide relevant recommendations, are not always able to provide novel recommendations – e.g., collaborative algorithms are biased toward "obvious" recommendations

[2]. In contrast, there is *no significant variation among personalized algorithms with respect to objective effort*: none of them statistically differ from the baseline in terms of execution time and extent of product search, i.e., number of explored hotel pages. Our results show a *mismatch between satisfaction* and *effort*: users exposed to hybrid and content recommendations perceived the decision activity process as more satisfying than those without personalized recommendations, although they spent the more time in the process. Our interpretation is that, thanks to the personalized recommendations, the presented hotels are more interesting for the users who spend more time in evaluating the different alternatives. This result is partially in line with previous work hypothesizing that, thanks to RSs, users spend less time in searching for items and more time in the more satisfactory activity of exploring information related to the choice process [12].

Hypothesis 2 is also confirmed. Hotel availability influences the effects of personalized recommendations. More precisely, the introduction of the content and hybrid personalized algorithms produces a significant *increment* of satisfaction in situations of *full* availability of resources. Still, personalized recommendations generated by both algorithms bring *no significant benefit* in situations of scarcity of resources. This result is not fully surprising: RSs perform well when information overload is the prevailing trait, but their benefits decrease when the reduction of the search space size, such as in the experimental condition characterized by low availability of resources. As resources availability is a dynamic characteristic of several domains outside the control of service providers, online operators are looking for ways to mitigate the negative effects induced by scarcity of resources in specific periods. The role of recommender systems in these situations deserves further investigation in order to design recommenders that can work well also in conditions of both abundance and scarcity of resources.

Overall, our findings extend our understanding of the potential of introducing recommendations to improve the UX quality with commercial e-tourism services, and differs from previous work in this domain for a number of aspects. We adopt a *conservative* approach that can promote the acceptance and adoption of recommenders in the e-tourism business. Differently from most previous works in this field where the evaluated RSs create new "ad hoc" user experiences, we assess the effect of recommendations on UX quality by *smoothly extending* a *commercial* online booking system (Venere.com) with personalized recommendations, without creating any major modifications to the "standard" interaction flow and overall user experience. In particular, we consider recommenders involving *implicit* elicitation, while most of existing studies in the e-tourism domain address recommenders with (more intrusive) explicit elicitation. In addition, we compare *three different algorithms* against the baseline scenario without recommendations and against each other. Previous works limit their analysis to a single recommendation algorithm evaluated against a non personalized baseline. Furthermore, it is worth noticing that an implicit assumption of most existing studies on Recommender System (RS) evaluation is that all items are always available, regardless the number of users who have "consumed" (bought, used) them. Still, in many domains, e.g., online services related to travel, clothing, or events, items are or involve physical resources that have constrained availability, i.e., the same product can be consumed by a limited number of users. To our knowledge our work is the first one that investigates this concept for recommender evaluation.

Finally, the *research design* of our empirical study is per se a strength of our work: for the number of variables measured in a single experiment – larger than most existing studies in e-tourism and other domains; for the sophisticated technological instrument used (the PoliVenus framework); for the vast size of the involved subjects (240); and for the lottery based incentive mechanisms adopted to motivate users and commit them to realistic and sound task execution.

References

1. Burke, R.: Hybrid web recommender systems. In: Brusilovsky, P., Kobsa, A., Nejdl, W. (eds.) Adaptive Web 2007. LNCS, vol. 4321, pp. 377–408. Springer, Heidelberg (2007)
2. Cremonesi, P., Garzotto, F., Turrin, R.: Investigating the Persuasion Potential of Recommender Systems from a Quality Perspective: an Empirical Study. ACM Transactions on Interactive Intelligent Systems 2(2), 1–41 (2012)
3. Cremonesi, P., Koren, Y., Turrin, R.: Performance of recommendation algorithms on top-n recommendation tasks. In: Proc. RecSys 2010, pp. 39–46. ACM, New York (2010)
4. Delgado, J., Davidson, R.: Knowledge bases and user profiling in travel and hospitality recommender systems, 2002. In: Proc. ENTER 2002, pp. 1–16. Springer, Wien (2002)
5. Drenner, S., Sen, S., Terveen, L.: Crafting the initial user experience to achieve community goals. In: Proc. of RecSys 2008, pp. 187–194. ACM, New York (2008)
6. Golbandi, N., Koren, Y., Lempel, R.: On bootstrapping recommender systems. In: Proc. CIKM 2010, pp. 1805–1808. ACM, New York (2010)
7. Jannach, D., Zanker, M., Jessenitschnig, M., Seidler, O.: Developing a conversational travel advisor with advisor suite. In: Proc. ENTER 2007, pp. 43–52. Springer, Wien (2007)
8. Jones, N., Pu, P.: User technology adoption issues in recommender systems. In: Proc. NAEC 2007, pp. 379–394 (2007)
9. Levi, A., Mokryn, O., Diot, C., Taft, N.: Finding a needle in a haystack of reviews: cold start context-based hotel recommender system. In: Proc. RecSys 2012, pp. 115–122. ACM, New York (2012)
10. Xie, M., Lakshmanan, L.V.S., Wood, P.T.: Comprec-trip: A composite recommendation system for travel planning. In: Proc. ICDE, pp. 1352–1355. IEEE (2011)
11. Rashid, A.M., Karypis, G., Riedl, J.: Learning preferences of new users in recommender systems: an information theoretic approach. In: SIGKDD Explorer Newsletter, vol. 10, pp. 90–100 (2008)
12. Ricci, F., Missier, F.: Supporting travel decision making through personalized recommendation. In: Karat, C., Blom, J., Karat, J. (eds.) Designing Personalized User Experiences in eCommerce. HCI Interaction Series, vol. 5, pp. 231–251. Springer, Netherlands (2004)
13. Schumacher, M., Rey, J.-P.: Recommender systems for dynamic packaging of tourism services. In: Proc. ENTER 2011, pp. 13–23. Springer, Wien (2011)
14. Mahmood, T., Ricci, F., Venturini, A., Höpken, W.: Adaptive recommender systems for travel planning. In: Proc. ENTER 2008, pp. 1–11. Springer, Wien (2008)
15. Xiao, B., Benbasat, I.: E-commerce product recommendation agents: use, characteristics, and impact. Management Information Systems Quarterly 31(1), 137–209 (2007)
16. Zanker, M., Fuchs, M.W., Tuta, M.H., Müller, N.: Evaluating recommender systems in tourism - a case study from Austria. In: Proc. ENTER 2008, pp. 24–34. Springer, Wien (2008)
17. Porter, S.R., Whitcomb, M.E.: The Impact of Lottery Incentives on Survey Response Rates. Research in Higher Education 44(4), 389–407 (2003)

Exploiting Big Data for Enhanced Representations in Content-Based Recommender Systems

Fedelucio Narducci[2], Cataldo Musto[1], Giovanni Semeraro[1], Pasquale Lops[1], and Marco de Gemmis[1]

[1] Department of Computer Science
University of Bari Aldo Moro, Italy
name.surname@uniba.it

[2] Department of Information Science, Systems Theory, and Communication
University of Milano-Bicocca, Italy
narducci@disco.unimib.it

Abstract. The recent explosion of Big Data is offering new chances and challenges to all those platforms that provide personalized access to information sources, such as recommender systems and personalized search engines. In this context, social networks are gaining more and more interests since they represent a perfect source to trigger personalization tasks. Indeed, users naturally leave on these platforms a lot of data about their preferences, feelings, and friendships. Hence, those data are really valuable for addressing the cold start problem of recommender systems. On the other hand, since content shared on social networks is noisy and heterogeneous, information extracted must be hardly processed to build user profiles that can effectively mirror user interests and needs.

In this paper we investigated the effectiveness of external knowledge derived from Wikipedia in representing both documents and user profiles in a recommendation scenario. Specifically, we compared a classical keyword-based representation with two techniques that are able to map unstructured text with Wikipedia pages. The advantage of using this representation is that documents and user profiles become richer, more human-readable, less noisy, and potentially connected to the Linked Open Data (LOD) cloud. The goal of our preliminary experimental evaluation was twofolds: 1) to define the representation that best reflects user preferences; 2) to define the representation that provides the best predictive accuracy.

We implemented a news recommender for a preliminary evaluation of our model. We involved more than 50 Facebook and Twitter users and we demonstrated that the encyclopedic-based representation is an effective way for modeling both user profiles and documents.

Keywords: User Profiling, Social Network Analysis, Explicit Semantic Analysis, Personalization, Facebook, Twitter, Recommender System.

C. Huemer and P. Lops (Eds.): EC-Web 2013, LNBIP 152, pp. 182–193, 2013.

1 Introduction

Social networks have rapidly changed the interaction among people, thus becoming a real hub of information shared on the Web. A recent statistic reports that 91% of online adults use regularly social networks: every minute 100k tweets are sent and 684,478 pieces of content are shared on Facebook[1]. Even though the original aim of social networks was merely to allow friends to keep in touch, nowadays these platforms are becoming really valuable mines of information about user preferences, which can be exploited by personalization systems. On the other hand, content shared on social networks is noisy and heterogeneous, and must be deeply processed to extract information which mirrors effectively the preferences and interests of users. However, even though the gathering and representation of user interests play a crucial role, equally important is the representation of items to be recommended.

In this paper we investigated the effectiveness of a representation based on Wikipedia concepts (articles) both for user profiles and items in a recommendation scenario. Accordingly, we associated to each user profile a set of Wikipedia concepts most related with the user interests. The same process was performed on the items (i.e., news). We guess that this kind of representation brings in different advantages such as: producing more transparent and human-readable user profiles, removing noise, making profiles and items ready to be easily connected to the Linked Open Data (LOD) cloud.

We thus analyze two different aspects: first, we try to define the best model for representing user interests; second, we compare different groups of recommended news by representing content in different ways.

The rest of this paper is organized as follows. Section 2 analyzes the state of the art. Section 3 introduces the techniques adopted for obtaining a Wikipedia-based representation of content. Section 4 defines the representation of profiles and documents, and in Section 5 the recommendation model is introduced. Finally, experimental results are presented in Section 6, and in Section 7 the conclusion and the future work are summarized.

2 Related Work

In literature, several works try to model user profile by mining data extracted from social networks. In [7] the authors present a methodology for building multifaceted user models from raw Twitter data. Tweets are also exploited in [11] to model users in a news recommendation scenario. In the same domain, Abel et al. [1] model user interests in terms of entities, hashtags and topics a tweet refers to. Next, in [10] the authors propose a methodology for modeling profiles of user interests by extracting information by Facebook, Twitter, and LinkedIn as well. The most distinguishing aspect of our approach lies in the fact that we adopt a Wikipedia-based text representation which allows the construction of

[1] `http://thesocialskinny.com/216-social-media-and-internet-statistics september-2012/`

more transparent and human-readable user profiles, rather than using a simple keyword-based representation of the content extracted from the social networks. A strategy for linking user interests to Wikipedia is presented in [14], where the authors elicit user preferences by analyzing their personal folksonomy on delicio.us, then tags are connected to Wikipedia categories. Another strength that comes from the adoption of a Wikipedia-based representation of user interests is that each facet of the user profile can be easily linked to the LOD cloud by exploiting DBPedia[2], thus enabling a sort of reasoning on the information stored in a user model. Furthermore, a system that adopts a more understandable representation can lead towards a more transparent personalization process. For example, a recommender system that uses a human-understandable profile could easily explain the reason for a suggestion, and, as stated in [12], transparency is an essential feature of personalization tasks. Differently from the approach presented in [10], where a reasoning process leverages domain ontologies for inducing new implicit interests, our strategy for the generation of new topics exploits Explicit Semantic Analysis (ESA)[6].

Wikipedia-based document representations are adopted in different areas such as document similarity, information retrieval, and clustering. In [5] ESA is adopted for computing semantic relatedness between documents. Authors demonstrated that the proposed Wikipedia-based representation is more effective than a keyword-based one for that specific task. Similar results are also confirmed in [9,15] . A Wikipedia-based representation leverages ESA and outperforms a keyword-based document representation [2] also in an information retrieval scenario. Wikipedia is effectively exploited for cross-lingual and multilingual information retrieval, as well [13]. Finally, in [8] authors show that clustering performance significantly improves by enriching document representation with Wikipedia concepts and categories. To the best of our knowledge there are no work in literature that exploit a Wikipedia-based representation for addressing personalization tasks.

3 Wikipedia-Based Text Representation

Two different techniques were exploited for obtaining Wikipedia-based content representation: the anchor disambiguation algorithm implemented in Tag.me[3] and the Explicit Semantic Analysis (ESA) [6].

Tag.me - TAG.ME is an online tool developed by the University of Pisa (Italy) that implements an *anchor disambiguation* algorithm. It produces a Wikipedia-based representation of short text fragments, where the most relevant concepts occurring in the text are mapped to the Wikipedia articles they refer to, according to inter-relations between Wikipedia pages, as well as other heuristics. More details about the approach are provided in [4].

ESA - ESA is a vectorial representation of text, proposed by Gabrilovich and Markovitch [6], that uses Wikipedia as a space of concepts explicitly defined

[2] DBpedia is a RDF-based mapping of Wikipedia - `http://dbpedia.org`

[3] `http://tagme.di.unipi.it/`

and described by humans. The idea is that the meaning of a generic term (e.g. *London*) can be described by a list of concepts it refers to (e.g. the Wikipedia articles for: *London Eye, Big Ben, River Thames*). Formally, given the space of Wikipedia concepts (articles) $C = \{c_1, c_2, ..., c_n\}$, a term t_i can be represented by its *semantic interpretation vector* $v_i =< w_{i1}, w_{i2}, ..., w_{in} >$, where weight w_{ij} represents the strength of the association between t_i and c_j. Weights are obtained from a matrix T, called ESA-*matrix*, in which each of the n columns corresponds to a concept (Wikipedia article), and each row corresponds to a term of the Wikipedia vocabulary, i.e. the set of distinct terms in the corpus of all Wikipedia articles. Cell $T[i, j]$ contains w_{ij}, the TF-IDF value of term t_i in the article (concept) c_j. The semantic interpretation vector for a text fragment f (i.e. a sentence, a document, a tweet, a Facebook post) is obtained by computing the centroid of the semantic interpretation vectors associated with terms occurring in f.

The main difference between the two approaches is that ESA can generate *new* features related to the text to be indexed, while TAG.ME simply detects Wikipedia concepts that actually occur in the text. Hence, the former performs a *feature generation* process, while the latter performs a sort of *feature selection*.

4 Profile and Document Representation

We exploited TAG.ME and ESA in order to semantically annotate user profile and news. In the former case the input are the data about the user interests extracted from Facebook and Twitter, in the latter the input is a set of news titles coming from RSS feeds.

4.1 Wikipedia-Based Profile Representation

In the following, we describe a component called *Social Data Extractor* designed for this purpose. It is able to extract the following textual information about user activities on Facebook and Twitter:

- FACEBOOK: title and description of liked groups, title and description of attended events, title and description of liked pages, personal statuses, liked statuses, title and summary of shared links;
- TWITTER: personal tweets, tweets of followings, favorite tweets, direct messages.

For the sake of simplicity, all the aforementioned pieces of information will be identified hereafter by the expression *social items*. Three different kinds of profile representations are obtained by processing social items with the techniques described in the previous section. Examples of profiles, shown as tag clouds, are given in Figure 1.

Fig. 1. Examples of user profiles

Social Profile - This is the simplest representation since it is based merely on the keywords occurring in the social items collected for the user: only tokenization and stopword elimination were applied, while the weight associated with each keyword is just its TF-IDF score. The social profile is the baseline for the other models.

Tag.me Profile - This representation leverages the algorithm implemented in TAG.ME to identify the Wikipedia concepts that occur in the social profile. Given a set of social items for user u, TAG.ME identifies those that can be mapped to Wikipedia concepts. All the titles of the identified Wikipedia concepts are included into the TAG.ME profile of u. The weight of each Wikipedia concept is the TF-IDF score of the keyword it refers to.

ESA Profile - This representation exploits the semantic interpretation vectors associated with keywords in the social items in order to identify *new* keywords which can be included in the profile. For each social item, the feature generation process is performed and the corresponding semantic interpretation vector is built (as described in Section 3 for text fragments). The 10 most relevant concepts, i.e. those with the highest weights in the semantic interpretation vector, are selected and the *titles* of the corresponding Wikipedia pages are included in the profile, together with their TF-IDF scores.

As an example, let's consider some statuses posted by a Facebook's user: *I'm in trepidation for my first riding lesson!*, *I'm really anxious for the soccer match :(* , *This summer I will flight by Ryanair to London!*, *Ryanair really cheapest company!*, *Ryanair lost my luggage :(*, *These summer holidays are really amazing!*, *Total relax during these holidays!*. The *Social Data Extractor* extracts and processes that information, by producing the profiles reported in Figure 1 (please consider that also other *social items* contribute to build those tag clouds). It emerges at-a-glance that the *social* profile is the richest one, since it also contains many non-relevant concepts, such as those referring to user moods (anxious, trepidation, etc.). On the other hand, the TAG.ME profile contains the terms that already occur into the *social* profile (horse, London, soccer, etc.), but their weights are higher since all the noise coming from non-relevant keyword has already been filtered out. Finally, in the ESA profile there are some topics in some way related to the other profiles (riding horse, trip, Vienna[4]), but not *explicitly* mentioned in the Social profile. This is due to the fact that ESA enriches the basic representation with novel concepts associated with social items.

4.2 Wikipedia-Based Document Representation

Also for the documents, we compared a keyword-based representation with two Wikipedia-based models.

Keyword - This representation is only based on keywords. A *bag of words* is built for each news title. Tokenization, stemming and stopword elimination are performed on the text.

Tag.me - This representation is based on Wikipedia-concepts. The news title is the input to TAG.ME. Hence, TAG.ME identifies the Wikipedia concepts occurring in that text fragment.

Tag.me + ESA - This representation is obtained by combining TAG.ME and ESA results. The previously shown TAG.ME-based representation is enriched of Wikipedia concepts generated by ESA. Therefore, every news is represented by merging the Wikipedia concepts identified by TAG.ME and the Wikipedia concepts generated by ESA. The input to ESA is the news title and the 10-most related Wikipedia concepts are extracted from its semantic interpretation vector.

The motivation behind the combination of ESA with TAG.ME in a single profile is that sometimes ESA is not able to generate concepts for very short text fragment (several heuristics are applied in order to reduce the ESA-matrix dimension). Hence, we decided to have TAG.ME as basic representation and enrich it with the ESA concepts.

Since we need an unified representation both for documents and user profile, for each document representation we exploited the corresponding user profile built in the same way. Therefore, the *Social* profile is used to recommend news represented by the *Keyword* representation; the *Tag.me* profile is used to recommend news represented by the *Tag.me* model, and finally a profile obtained by merging the *Tag.me* and the *ESA* profile is used for recommending news adopting the *Tag.me + ESA* representation.

As an example, given the news title[5] "*At Facebook, Still the Undisputed Boss*". TAG.ME only identifies the Wikipedia page FACEBOOK; conversely the semantic interpretation vector generated by ESA contains the following Wikipedia concepts: FACEBOOK PLATFORM (the platform which enables third-party developers to integrate with the social network), SOCIAL GRAPH (term coined to describe "the global mapping of everybody and how they're related", on wich Facebook is based on), MARK ZUCKERBERG (the *undisputed boss* the news title refers to), DUSTIN MOSKOVITZ (co-founder of Facebook). This example confirms that ESA

[4] In Vienna is located the most world famous riding school.

[5] Extracted from the online version of The New York Times.

performs a feature generation process, while TAG.ME produces a sort of feature selection.

5 Learning Method

We implemented our recommender system as a text classifier. Hence, for each user we learned a classifier by exploiting the data extracted from social networks. The recommendation is thus a binary text classification task where the two classes are *like* and *dislike*. Subsequently, the learned classifier is used for deciding which items (i.e., news) are interesting (belonging to the class *like*) for a specific user. User feedback are exploited for updating the user profile and learning a new classifier. Probability as output is a really valuable feature in this context, since the recommender is able to perform a ranking of the suggested items (according to the probability to belong to the class *like*).

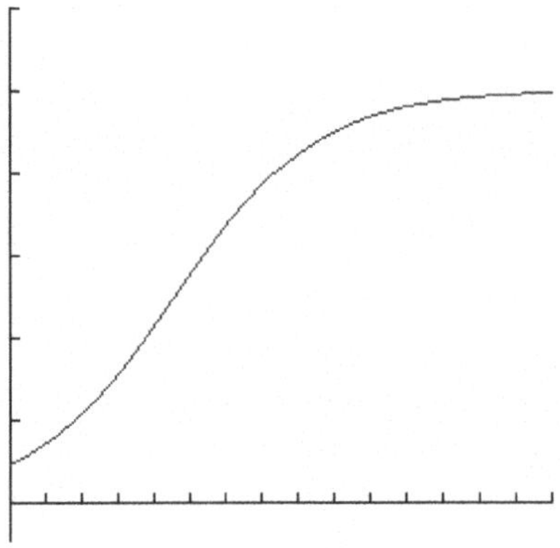

Fig. 2. Example of logistic function

We decided to use LOGISTIC REGRESSION as text classifier. LR belongs to the category of supervised learning methods. It is able to analyze data and recognize patterns and are used for classification and regression analysis. LR and its variants have been applied in several areas to solve classification problems. In [16] LR showed an accuracy comparable to SUPPORT VECTOR MACHINEs for several datasets with the advantage of yielding a probability model. The classification is performed by learning a logistic function on the training examples, that is represented by a sigmoid curve.

By analyzing Figure 2, on the x-axis we have the observed variable (e.g., the TF-IDF value), and on the y-axis we have the probability value (e.g., to belong to the class *like*). This is the simplest case in which we have only one feature, but it is easily extensible to more features.

After the model has been learned, new examples are mapped in the same previously built space and the correct class is chosen based on the value of the learned function.

In our experiments we use the LIBLINEAR library [3], an open-source library for large-scale linear classification (for datasets with a huge number of features and instances) that supports LR and SVMs with linear kernel.

6 Experimental Evaluation

We designed two different experimental sessions. The first one investigates the best model for representing user interests. In this session we are not interested in defining the user profile that achieve the best predictive accuracy, but we only focus our attention on the representation of user interests. The second session compares different groups of recommended news by representing content in different ways. We also evaluated the impact of the relevance feedback on the recommendation accuracy.

In order to avoid a cognitive overload of users, we invited a different group for each session. Each group was composed of 100 Italian Internet users. From the first group 51 users agree to participate to the first session: 36 gave us the consent to extract social items only from Facebook (71%), 4 only from Twitter (8%), 11 (21%) from both social networks. In the second session users were more unbalanced. 63 users of the second group accepted to participate: 62 Facebook users and only 1 Twitter user.

During the experiment users were driven by a wizard. Each session has been carried out for two weeks. Users were asked to login and to extract their data from their own Facebook and/or Twitter accounts (Figure 3). Next, in the first session, three user profiles were built according to the extracted data. Users were asked to rate the three profiles. In the second session, four groups of Italian news were proposed and users were asked to rate each group (Figure 4). After this step the user profiles were updated by exploiting the user feedback and four other news groups are proposed to rate. More details in the next sections. The two experiments took no more than five minutes per user. User votes were expressed by using a 5-star rating scale. The Wilcoxon Matched Pairs Test ($p < 0.05$) is used to test the significance of results (no assumption on the data distribution).

6.1 Session 1: Representation of Interests

The goal of the experiment was to identify which kind of user profile, among those discussed in Section 4.1, is the best representation for user interests. For each kind of profile, we defined the *transparency* as the overlap between actual user interests and keywords shown in the profile. For each user, the SOCIAL, ESA, and TAG.ME profiles were built and shown to her as tag clouds. Then, users were asked to answer to the following question, by using a 5-star rating scale:

1. How much the keywords in this profile reflect your personal interests and describe them in an accurate way?

For each representation, average rating, minimum and maximun ratings, and standard deviation are shown in Table 1. The representation obtained by TAG.ME

Fig. 3. Data Acquisition

describes the user interests in a better way than the other representations, as shown by the statistically significant differences among average ratings related to the transparency question. SOCIAL and ESA profiles obtained quite similar results (no statistically significant difference between them), while the ESA-based representation shows the highest standard deviation. Hence, it seems that this profile receives heterogeneous evaluations from users (also confirmed by the gap between MIN and MAX ratings). Indeed, ESA introduces new topics in the user profile, and this sort of *unexpectedness* is likely differently evaluated by the users.

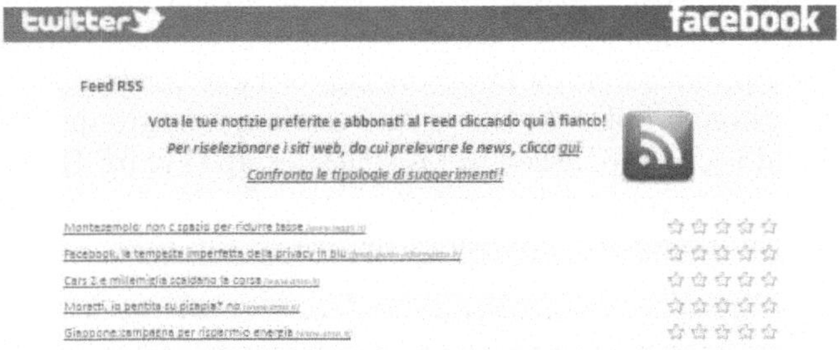

Fig. 4. List of recommended news

6.2 Session 2: Representation of Documents

In this session we investigate how the document representation can affect the predictive accuracy of our recommender. Afterwards, we evaluated the impact of relevance feedback on the predictive accuracy. Also in this case we compare a keyword-based model with Wikipedia-based representations. Users were asked to evaluate four groups of recommendations, and for each group, five news were suggested. Each group of recommendations is generated by using one of the representation models defined in Section 4.2; the fourth group is the baseline of our experiment and is represented by random recommendations.

Results of this experimental session are reported in Table 2. The first outcome is that all the configurations have a statistically significant improvement with

Table 1. Results of Transparency and Serendipity Evaluation

Transparency				
Representation	Avg Rating	Min Rating	Max Rating	Stand. deviation
SOCIAL	1.33	0	3	0.65
TAG.ME	**3.88**	2	5	0.82
ESA	1.16	0	4	1.00

Table 2. Predictive Accuracy

1st cycle (without relevance feedback)				
Representation	Avg Rating	Min Rating	Max Rating	Stand. deviation
RANDOM	1.49	0	5	1.22
KEYWORD	1.89	0	5	1.47
TAG.ME	**2.86**	1	5	1.3
TAG.ME+ESA	2.59	0	5	1.37
2nd cycle (with relevance feedback)				
Representation	Avg Rating	Min Rating	Max Rating	Stand. deviation
RANDOM	1.49	0	5	1.12
KEYWORD	2.61	0	5	1.49
TAG.ME	**3.23**	1	5	1.35
TAG.ME+ESA	3.00	1	5	1.41

respect to RANDOM recommendations. For the first cycle, the highest average rating is achieved by using the TAG.ME representation. Differences between TAG.ME and both KEYWORD and TAG.ME+ESA representations are statistically significant. Hence, we can state that TAG.ME is an effective strategy for filtering out noise from the gathered content. The same results are confirmed in the second cycle (that exploits the user feedback), but in this case TAG.ME has a statistically significant difference only with the KEYWORD representation. TAG.ME+ESA shows a statistically significant difference with respect to KEYWORD, as well. Furthermore, also the difference between results of the first cycle and results of the second cycle is statistically significance. Finally, we can observe that there are not strong differences in terms of standard deviation and MIN/MAX rating among the different representations.

By summing up, even tough user feedback actually improve the predictive accuracy of the recommender, in a first stage where we have no explicit evidence from the user, the proposed Wikipedia-based representations are quite effective in modeling interests (gathered from social networks) and items of a recommender system.

7 Conclusions and Future Work

In this experimental evaluation we investigate different methods for representing user interests, and different methods for representing very short text (social items and news titles).

From a preliminary evaluation it emerged that users prefer a representation of their own interests expressed in terms of encyclopedic concepts with respect to simple keywords. The main outcome of the evaluation is that an encyclopedic-based representation of user interests that merges TAG.ME and ESA might lead to *unexpected* and transparent user profiles.

As regards the document representations, TAG.ME is an effective strategy for modeling items and user profiles. Also ESA significantly outperform the KEYWORD representation. Furthermore, the Wikipedia-based representations give the advantage of easy linking items and profiles to the LOD cloud.

In the future, we will investigate several weighing strategies in order to understand how the concepts coming from different sources can be merged. Furthermore, we want evaluate whether new topics introduced by ESA in the user profile can lead to serendipitous and unexpected recommendations. Finally, a comparison with other approaches based on the relationships encoded in the LOD cloud will be investigated.

Acknowledgments. This work fulfills the research objectives of the projects PON 02_00563_3470993 VINCENTE (A Virtual collective INtelligenCe ENvironment to develop sustainable Technology Entrepreneurship ecosystems) and PON 01_00850 ASK-Health (Advanced system for the interpretations and sharing of knowledge in health care) funded by the Italian Ministry of University and Research (MIUR).

References

1. Abel, F., Gao, Q., Houben, G.-J., Tao, K.: Analyzing user modeling on twitter for personalized news recommendations. In: Konstan, J.A., Conejo, R., Marzo, J.L., Oliver, N. (eds.) UMAP 2011. LNCS, vol. 6787, pp. 1–12. Springer, Heidelberg (2011)
2. Egozi, O., Markovitch, S., Gabrilovich, E.: Concept-based information retrieval using explicit semantic analysis. ACM Trans. Inf. Syst. 29(2), 8:1–8:34 (2011)
3. Fan, R.-E., Chang, K.-W., Hsieh, C.-J., Wang, X.-R., Lin, C.-J.: LIBLINEAR: A library for large linear classification. Journal of Machine Learning Research 9, 1871–1874 (2008)
4. Ferragina, P., Scaiella, U.: Tagme: on-the-fly annotation of short text fragments (by wikipedia entities). In: Proceedings of the 19th ACM International Conference on Information and Knowledge Management, CIKM 2010, pp. 1625–1628. ACM, New York (2010)
5. Gabrilovich, E., Markovitch, S.: Computing semantic relatedness using wikipedia-based explicit semantic analysis. In: Proceedings of the 20th International Joint Conference on Artifical Intelligence, IJCAI 2007, pp. 1606–1611. Morgan Kaufmann Publishers Inc., San Francisco (2007)
6. Gabrilovich, E., Markovitch, S.: Wikipedia-based semantic interpretation for natural language processing. Journal of Artificial Intelligence Research (JAIR) 34, 443–498 (2009)
7. Hannon, J., McCarthy, K., O'Mahony, M.P., Smyth, B.: A multi-faceted user model for twitter. In: Masthoff, J., Mobasher, B., Desmarais, M.C., Nkambou, R. (eds.) UMAP 2012. LNCS, vol. 7379, pp. 303–309. Springer, Heidelberg (2012)

8. Hu, X., Zhang, X., Lu, C., Park, E.K., Zhou, X.: Exploiting wikipedia as external knowledge for document clustering. In: Proceedings of the 15th ACM SIGKDD International Conference on Knowledge Discovery and Data Mining, KDD 2009, pp. 389–396. ACM, New York (2009)
9. Huang, L., Milne, D., Frank, E., Witten, I.H.: Learning a concept-based document similarity measure. J. Am. Soc. Inf. Sci. Technol. 63(8), 1593–1608 (2012)
10. Ma, Y., Zeng, Y., Ren, X., Zhong, N.: User interests modeling based on multi-source personal information fusion and semantic reasoning. In: Zhong, N., Callaghan, V., Ghorbani, A.A., Hu, B. (eds.) AMT 2011. LNCS, vol. 6890, pp. 195–205. Springer, Heidelberg (2011)
11. Phelan, O., McCarthy, K., Bennett, M., Smyth, B.: Terms of a feather: Content-based news recommendation and discovery using twitter. In: Clough, P., Foley, C., Gurrin, C., Jones, G.J.F., Kraaij, W., Lee, H., Mudoch, V. (eds.) ECIR 2011. LNCS, vol. 6611, pp. 448–459. Springer, Heidelberg (2011)
12. Sinha, R., Swearingen, K.: The role of transparency in recommender systems. In: CHI 2002: CHI 2002 Extended Abstracts on Human Factors in Computing Systems, pp. 830–831. ACM, New York (2002)
13. Sorg, P., Cimiano, P.: Exploiting wikipedia for cross-lingual and multilingual information retrieval. Data Knowl. Eng. 74, 26–45 (2012)
14. Szomszor, M., Alani, H., Cantador, I., O'Hara, K., Shadbolt, N.R.: Semantic modelling of user interests based on cross-folksonomy analysis. In: Sheth, A.P., Staab, S., Dean, M., Paolucci, M., Maynard, D., Finin, T., Thirunarayan, K. (eds.) ISWC 2008. LNCS, vol. 5318, pp. 632–648. Springer, Heidelberg (2008)
15. Yeh, E., Ramage, D., Manning, C.D., Agirre, E., Soroa, A.: Wikiwalk: random walks on wikipedia for semantic relatedness. In: Proceedings of the 2009 Workshop on Graph-based Methods for Natural Language Processing, TextGraphs-4, Stroudsburg, PA, USA, pp. 41–49. Association for Computational Linguistics (2009)
16. Zhang, T., Oles, F.J.: Text categorization based on regularized linear classification methods. Information Retrieval 4, 5–31 (2000)

Recommendations Based on Different Aspects of Influences in Social Media

Chin-Hui Lai[1], Duen-Ren Liu[2], and Mei-Lan Liu[3]

[1] Department of Information Management, Chung Yuan Christian University, Taiwan
chlai@cycu.edu.tw

[2,3] Institute of Information Management, National Chiao Tung University, Taiwan
dliu@iim.nctu.edu.tw, meilan0913@gmail.com

Abstract. Among the applications of Web 2.0, social networking sites continue to proliferate and the volume of content keeps growing; as a result, information overload causes difficulty for users attempting to choose useful and relevant information. In this work, we propose a novel recommendation method based on different types of influences: social, interest and popularity, using personal tendencies in regard to these three decision factors to recommend photos in a photo-sharing website, *Flickr*. Because these influences have different degrees of impact on each user, the personal tendencies related to these three influences are regarded as personalized weights; combining influence scores enables predicting the scores of items. The experimental results show that our proposed methods can improve the quality of recommendations.

Keywords: Web 2.0, Social media, Social network, Recommender System, Social Influence, Collaborative filtering.

1 Introduction

As social networking sites continue to proliferate and the volumes of their content keep growing, information overload causes users to experience difficulty in choosing useful and relevant information. In order to overcome the information overload problem, a recommender system [1] plays an important role in providing users with personalized recommendations on items.

People's preferences for items may be affected by three decision factors: social friends, personal interest and item popularity. For example, some users may like an item because their friends also like it, or they are interested in such items, or it is generally popular. However, most researches only utilize users' preference, the content of items or social influence to make recommendations. Although these methods can recommend the proper items to users, they do not take advantage of different types of influences, including social, interest and popularity influences in making recommendations in social media such as *Flickr*. Moreover, these decision factors have different impacts on each user. Each user has his/her personal tendency in regard to the influences of the three decision-related factors.

C. Huemer and P. Lops (Eds.): EC-Web 2013, LNBIP 152, pp. 194–201, 2013.

In this work, we propose a novel recommendation method based on different types of influences, including: social, interest and popularity, as well as the personal tendency related to these three decision-related factors to recommend photos in a photo-sharing website. Social influence means that users are affected by their friends and friends' friends; interest influence means that people are influenced by users with similar interests; and popularity influence signifies that users are affected by popular items. Additionally, we consider the perspectives of both an influenced user and an influential user with different weights in computing social influence and interest influence. Because those influences have different degrees of impact on each user, we exploit personal tendency in regard to the influence of social, interest and popularity as personalized weights, to combine these 3 decision-related factors in recommendation methods. Those photos with high predicted scores will be recommended to the target users. The experimental results show that applying the personalized tendency towards different types of influences in a recommendation method can improve prediction accuracy and quality of recommendation in social media. Because of better recommendation performance, users can save time in looking for relevant photos, and social media can attract more people to share photos, resulting in greater business opportunities.

The remainder of the paper is organized as follows. Section 2 introduces the works related to social networks, and recommender systems. In Section 3, we introduce the proposed recommendation methods based on social, interest and popularity influences, respectively. Section 4 shows the experimental results and evaluations of our methods. Finally, in Section 5, we discuss our results and conclude the paper.

2 Related Work

Social networking sites, such as *Facebook*, *Twitter* and *Flickr*, are popular business models that allow users to share information, publish articles and post photos. With the emergence of social networks, social recommender systems became helpful for users to acquire relevant and useful information. The goal of social recommender systems (SRSs) is to mitigate the problem of information overload for users of social media. Unlike traditional CF recommender systems, social recommender systems take advantage of explicit and implicit relationships among users, items or social contexts in order to make recommendations.

Social influence means that a user's behavior is affected by his/her friends [2]. However, most of the research estimates the social influence in recommender systems by taking a single perspective instead of the perspectives of both the influenced and influential user. Additionally, information can be disseminated quickly through those influential users, and the items recommended by those influential users are easily accepted by others. Several researchers combine social influence with traditional recommendation methods to make recommendations [3]. Nevertheless, they still do not take other influence factors, such as interest influence and popularity influence, into account. In this work, we adopt personalized tendency towards three decision factors: social influence, interest influence and popularity influence in our proposed approach for improving recommendation performance in social media.

3 Recommendation Based on Different Types of Influences

3.1 Overview

Because of the emergence of Web 2.0 technologies, users can post articles or share feelings in social networking sites such as *Facebook*, *Twitter* or *Flickr*. In *Flickr*, users can upload photos, mark photos as favorites, comment on photos and join specific groups to converse and share content. However, it is difficult for users to find relevant photos because of the volume of user-generated content and photos. Hence, more and more recommender systems are applied to social networks to filter out irrelevant information. Generally, recommendation methods in social networks use users' preferences, general acceptance of items and influence from social friends to provide recommendations [4]. However, because of differing personalities and behavior, users may be affected by different types of influences in making decisions, such as social influence, interest influence and popularity influence. Social influence refers to the ability of a user who follows his/her friends' footsteps to add their favorite photos into his/her favorite list. Interest influence means that a user is affected by users with similar interests; for example, a user may mark a photo as a favorite because similar users have added it to their lists. Popularity influence refers to the effect of popularity on a user's behavior.

In this work, we propose recommendation methods based on personalized tendencies towards different types of influence in the social media. Our proposed framework includes data collection, decision factor analyses, and recommendation phases. In the data collection phase, we collected a dataset from the *Flickr* website by using Flickr API to obtain information on photos and users. Then, the social, interest and popularity analyses are used to measure users' influences. Finally, according to a user's tendency to the influence of social, interest and popularity, we propose user-based collaborative filtering methods to recommend photos for users. Our methods not only provide personalized recommendations to users but also improve the performance of recommendations in social media.

3.2 Social Analysis

Social Influence from Direct Friends

We built social influence networks based on social influence links (SIL). If user u_c marks a photo as a favorite, which user u_f has marked, and u_c and u_f are friends, then we create a SIL from user u_c to u_f, which means user u_c is influenced by u_f or u_f influences u_c. The weight of SIL, the degree of social influence, indicates the degree of influence of user u_f over user u_c. Additionally, we take both perspectives, that of the influential and influenced users, into account, and then linearly combine the two values derived from these two perspectives.

User u_f's social influence on user u_c derived from the perspective of user u_c, i.e., the first part of Eq. (1), where $|FAV_{u_c}|$ is the number of favorite photos of user u_c; $FAV_{u_c F u_f} = \{i \mid i \in FAV_{u_c} \cap FAV_{u_f} \text{ and } t(u_c,i) > t(u_f,i)\}$ is the set of photos marked as favorites by user u_c after user u_f has marked the photos; and $t(u_c,i)$ is the time when u_c marks photo i. Additionally, user u_f's social influence on user u_c derived from the perspective of user u_f, i.e., the second part of Eq. (1), where $|FAV_{u_f}|$ is the number of favorite photos marked by user u_f. The parameter α ($0 \le \alpha \le 1$) is used to adjust the relative importance of the social influence derived from two different perspectives.

$$SI(u_c,u_f) = \alpha \times \frac{|FAV_{u_c Fu_f}|}{|FAV_{u_c}|} + (1-\alpha) \times \frac{|FAV_{u_c Fu_f}|}{|FAV_{u_f}|}, \tag{1}$$

Social Influence from Propagation

Because a target user and his/her direct friends may have no co-favorite photos, there is no direct social influence from friends on a target user. Social influence propagation can be used to infer the social influence on a target user through indirect social influence. Let user u_c denote the target (source) user; $SIP(u_c, u_f)$ denotes the social influence of user u_f on target user u_c derived from the influence propagation on a social network. If there is no direct social influence from user u_f on u_c, the propagation score of user u_f on user u_c based on the social influence is the average of the direct social influence of user u_f on user u_k, i.e., $SI(u_k, u_f)$ (Eq. (1)), weighted by the social influence propagation $SIP(u_c, u_k)$, as shown in Eq. (2) where $u_k : u_k \rightarrow u_f$ means that u_f has direct social influence on u_k, and $SIP(u_c, u_k)$ is the influence of user u_k on user u_c derived from the influence propagation of the social influence network:

$$SIP(u_c,u_f) = \frac{\sum_{u_k:u_k \rightarrow u_f} SIP(u_c,u_k) \times SI(u_k,u_f)}{\sum_{u_k:u_k \rightarrow u_f} SIP(u_c,u_k)}, \tag{2}$$

The Weight of Social Influence

Because each user may be affected by his/her friends to differing degrees, we use a weight to represent the personalized tendency towards social influence of each user. The weight of social influence is based on the proportion of the number of favorite photos which have been marked by both user u_c and user u_c's friends. Let $W_{u_c,SI}$ denote the weight of social influence for target user u_c; FRI_{u_c} be a set of friends of target user u_c; $\left|\bigcup_{u_f \in FRI_{u_c}} FAV_{u_c Fu_f}\right|$ be the number of photos that user u_c marks as favorite photos after u_c's friends have marked these photos as favorites.

$$W_{u_c,SI} = \frac{\left|\bigcup_{u_f \in FRI_{u_c}} FAV_{u_c Fu_f}\right|}{|FAV_{u_c}|}, \tag{3}$$

3.3 Interest Analysis

Interest Influence

Interest influence means that users who have similar or common interests may affect the behavior of one another; it is derived from the influential user, who is similar to the influenced user, on the influenced user. Again, as in the social influence discussed in Section 3.2, interest influence is also derived from both the perspectives of the influential and influenced users.

The interest influence of user u_x on user u_c from user u_c perspective, i.e., the first part of Eq. (4), where $|FAV_{u_c}|$ is the number of favorite photos of user u_c, and $FAV_{u_cFu_x} = \{i \mid i \in FAV_{u_c} \cap FAV_{u_x} \text{ and } t(u_c,i) > t(u_x,i)\}$ is the set of photos marked as favorite by user u_c after user u_x has marked them as favorite. Similarly, the Second part of Eq. (4) is used to obtain the interest influence derived from user u_x's perspective, where $|FAV_{u_x}|$ is the number of favorite photos of user u_x. Then, these two parts of interest influence are linearly combined by using a parameter β ($0 \le \beta \le 1$) to evaluate user u_x's total interest influence on user u_c,

$$II(u_c,u_x) = \beta \times \frac{|FAV_{u_cFu_x}|}{|FAV_{u_c}|} + (1-\beta) \times \frac{|FAV_{u_cFu_x}|}{|FAV_{u_x}|}, \tag{4}$$

The Weight of Interest Influence

Not all users express interest in the photos in the 'favorite' lists of similar users; i.e., every user has a personalized tendency towards interest influence. Given this, we used a weight to represent the personalized tendency towards interest influence for each user. The weight of interest influence is based on a proportion of the number of favorite photos marked by both user u_c and his/her similar users, that is, when user u_c and his/her similar users have common photos in their favorites lists. For those common photos, user u_c's similar users marked them before user u_c marked them. Eq. (5) is used to measure the weight of interest influence for user u_c, where $W_{u_c,II}$ is the weight of interest influence for user u_c; NBR_{u_c} is a set of Top-K similar users of target user u_c; and $\left|\bigcup_{u_x \in NBR_{u_c}} FAV_{u_cFu_x}\right|$ is the number of favorite photos that user u_c marked after user u_c's similar users marked them.

$$W_{u_c,II} = \frac{\left|\bigcup_{u_x \in NBR_{u_c}} FAV_{u_cFu_x}\right|}{|FAV_{u_c}|}, \tag{5}$$

3.4 Popularity Analysis

Popularity Influence

Popularity is also a factor that affects users' behavior; especially on social networking sites. The score of popularity influence is used to measure the degree of popularity of a photo in a period of time. If the popularity score of a photo is high in this period, the photo is popular. The score of popularity influence, as defined in Eq. (6), is a ratio of the total favorite count of each photo to the maximal favorite count of all photos, where PI_i is the score of popularity influence of photo i; FC_i is the total favorite count of photo i; and $\max_j(FC_j)$ is the maximal favorite count of all photos collected in the dataset.

$$PI_i = \frac{FC_i}{\max_j \left(FC_j \right)}, \tag{6}$$

The Weight of Popularity Influence

The popularity of items has a different impact on each user. Therefore, we define a weight to represent personalized tendency towards popularity influence for each user. The weight of popularity influence is based on the number of popular photos in a user's favorite list, as defined in Eq. (7). Let $W_{u_c,PI}$ denote the weight of popularity influence, which is a ratio of the number of photos that are included in the favorite count before u_c has marked them, with those that exceed the threshold of the number of photos marked as favorite by user u_c, and N_{u_c} denotes the number of photos that their favorite counts exceed a threshold before user u_c has marked the photos.

$$W_{u_c,PI} = \frac{N_{u_c}}{\left| FAV_{u_c} \right|}, \tag{7}$$

3.5 Recommendation

In this section, we propose a recommendation method based on our decision factor analyses, including social, interest and popularity influences. We combined these three types of influences with the personalized weights to predict the score of photo *i* for the target user u_c, i.e., $PS(u_c, i)$, as defined in Eq. (8). The influence scores of social, interest and popularity on a particular photo *i* are derived from Eqs. (1), (2), (3), (4), (5), (6) and (7). The predicted score of photo *i* is defined as follows where $W_{u_c,SI}$, $W_{u_c,II}$ and $W_{u_c,PI}$ are the weights of social, interest and popularity influences, respectively, for target user u_c; and *timefactor*(*i*) is a time factor of photo *i*, ranging from 0 to 1. A higher time weight is assigned to a photo marked in the recent past and, conversely, lower time weights are assigned to older photos. Finally, Top-*N* photos with the highest predicted scores, i.e. $PS(u_c, i)$, will be recommended to the target user.

$$PS(u_c,i) = \left(W_{u_c,SI} \times \sum_{u_f \in FRI_{u_c}, i \in FAV_{u_f}} SIP(u_c,u_f) + W_{u_c,II} \times \sum_{u_x \in NBR_{u_c}, i \in FAV_{u_x}} II(u_c,u_x) + W_{u_c,PI} \times PI_i \right) \times timefactor(i), \tag{8}$$

4 Experiment and Evaluations

In our experiment, we collected a data set from the famous social networking website *Flickr*. *Flickr* is a popular photo-sharing social media site where users can upload photos, add photos into their favorites list and make friends through the web platform. The data set consists of photos analyzed from Aug 15, 2011 to Nov 15, 2011. Our dataset was composed of 50,000 similar users, about 90,000 users and over 2 million photos. We then divided the data set: 75% for training, 10% for tuning and 15% for testing. The training set was used to implement our proposed method and generate recommendation lists, while the testing set was used to verify the quality of these recommendations. The tuning set was used to determine parameters for our methods. To compare the prediction accuracy of the proposed methods, we employed *F1*-metric [5, 6], which are widely used in recommender systems to evaluate the quality of recommendations.

4.1 Comparison of Different Variations of the Proposed Methods

Different variations of the proposed methods are compared in this experiment. The S-IF method predicts photos by only considering social influence with the time factor; the I-IF method makes recommendations by using interest influence with the time factor; and the P-IF method takes the popularity influence into account. In addition, the combination of any two decision factors is utilized in the recommendation methods, i.e., SI-IF, SP-IF and IP-IF, for improving the accuracy of prediction. The SI-IF method recommends photos by integrating the influence of social and interest; the SP-IF method recommends photos based on the combination of both social and popularity influences; and the IP-IF method makes recommendations based on the composite of both interest and popularity. Besides these 6 methods, the SIP-IF method, which makes predictions based on the combination of all three decision factors, is also compared and evaluated. All parameters in these recommendation methods are derived from the experimental results based on the pretesting data. That is, α is set as 0.6, β is set as 0.5, the number of neighbors is 40, τ equals to 1/10. The average F1 value, calculated over various top-N (top-5, top-10, top-20, top-40, top-60) recommendations, is used to measure the recommendation quality.

Fig. 1 shows the experimental results by averaging the F1 values of the S-IF, I-IF, P-IF, SI-IF, SP-IF, IF-IF and SIP-IF methods, respectively. For the methods which make recommendations based on one decision factor, the S-IF method outperforms the I-IF and P-IF methods. The performance of the SI-IF model is better than both the IP-IF and SP-IF methods. Combining two decision factors is better than using only

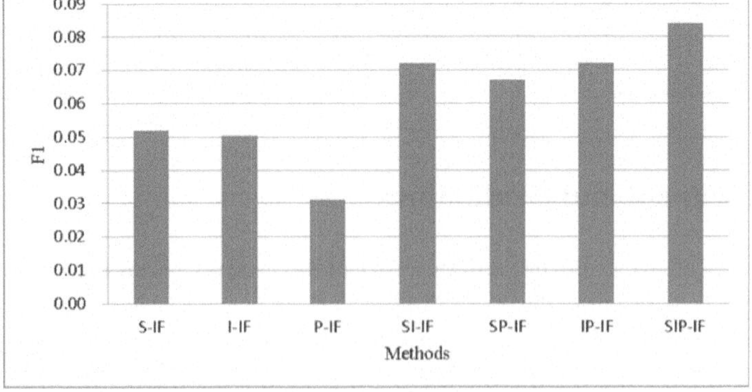

Fig. 1. The evaluation of different variations of the proposed methods

one decision factor in recommendation methods. Additionally, the SIP-IF method, which predicts photos based on the integration of social, interest and popularity influences and considers the personalized tendency towards such influences, has the best performance among these compared methods. In summary, the proposed decision influence types: social, interest and popularity, are useful and effective in making recommendations.

5 Conclusions

In this work, we proposed novel recommendation methods based on different types of influences: social, interest and popularity, and personalized tendency towards these three decision factors to recommend photos in a photo-sharing website *Flickr*. The perspectives of both the influenced user and the influential user were taken into account when computing the influence of social friends and interest. In addition, because these three decision factors have differing degrees of impact on each user, the personalized tendencies of these users towards these three decision factors were regarded as personalized weights to combine the influence scores for predicting the scores of items. The experimental results show that considering both of these perspectives when computing social and interest influences effectively enhances recommendation quality. Moreover, our proposed methods, which apply the personal tendency towards different types of influences as weights to combine the influence scores to make recommendations, indeed outperform other methods.

Acknowledgements. This research was supported by the National Science Council of the Taiwan under the grant NSC 101-2410-H-033-022-MY2.

References

1. Jannach, D., Zanker, M., Felfernig, A., Friedrich, G.: Recommender Systems: An Introduction. Cambridge University Press (2010)
2. Friedkin, N.E.: A structural theory of social influence. Cambridge University Press (1998)
3. Crandall, D., Cosley, D., Huttenlocher, D., Kleinberg, J., Suri, S.: Feedback effects between similarity and social influence in online communities. In: Proceedings of the 14th ACM SIGKDD International Conference on Knowledge Discovery and Data Mining, pp. 160–168. ACM, Las Vegas (2008)
4. He, J., Chu, W.W.: A social network-based recommender system (SNRS). In: Memon, N., Xu, J.J., Hicks, D.L.L., Chen, H. (eds.) Data Mining for Social Network Data, pp. 47–74. Springer US (2010)
5. Salton, G., Harman, D.: Information retrieval. John Wiley and Sons Ltd. (2003)
6. Sarwar, B., Karypis, G., Konstan, J., Riedl, J.: Analysis of recommendation algorithms for e-commerce. In: Proceedings of the 2nd ACM Conference on Electronic Commerce, pp. 158–167. ACM, Minneapolis (2000)

Robustness Analysis of Naïve Bayesian Classifier-Based Collaborative Filtering

Cihan Kaleli and Huseyin Polat

Computer Engineering Department, Anadolu University,
Eskisehir, 26470, Turkey
ckaleli,polath@anadolu.edu.tr

Abstract. In this study, binary forms of previously defined basic shilling attack models are proposed and the robustness of naïve Bayesian classifier-based collaborative filtering algorithm is examined. Real data-based experiments are conducted and each attack type's performance is explicated. Since existing measures, which are used to assess the success of shilling attacks, do not work on binary data, a new evaluation metric is proposed. Empirical outcomes show that it is possible to manipulate binary rating-based recommender systems' predictions by inserting malicious user profiles. Hence, it is shown that naïve Bayesian classifier-based collaborative filtering scheme is not robust against shilling attacks.

Keywords: Shilling, Naïve Bayesian classifier, Robustness, Prediction.

1 Introduction

In e-commerce applications, one of the most popular method for producing predictions is collaborative filtering (CF). By employing CF services, online vendors provide personalized referrals to their customers to boost their sales. Online vendors need to collect users' preferences about several products that they previously purchased or showed interest. Such preferences can be expressed in binary form in which ratings must strictly belong to one of two classes, like or dislike. Naïve Bayesian classifier (NBC)-based CF is widely used algorithm to produce binary recommendations, which is proposed by [1]. NBC-based CF considers all users' data for estimating a prediction for a target item (q) for an active user (a).

Malicious users can insert bogus profiles, referred to as shilling attacks, in a very straightforward way into recommender systems' databases to manipulate the estimated predictions on behalf of their advantages. The advantage helping people be part of recommender systems easily then becomes a vulnerability for the systems. Consequently, CF algorithms can be faced with various profile injection attacks [2,3]. In a traditional example of attacking scenario, any product producer may want to increase its product's popularity. To do so, it tries to insert fake user profiles into the system in which the target product is extremely liked. In another scenario, the same producer might intend to decrease the popularity of one of its competitor's product by creating and inserting bogus profiles.

C. Huemer and P. Lops (Eds.): EC-Web 2013, LNBIP 152, pp. 202–209, 2013.

CF algorithms suffer from shilling attacks. Thus, researchers introduce several studies examining the robustness of CF algorithms against them [4,5]. However, previous works examine numerical ratings-based CF algorithms and there is no work covering the case when the ratings are in binary form. Hence, we primarily focus on how the common basic attack models can be applied to NBC-based CF. All users having rating for the target item participate in recommendation process in NBC-based scheme. Thus, vulnerability of NBC-based CF algorithm might increase against profile injection attacks. We particularly introduce binary forms of six mostly implemented attack types, i.e., segmented attack intends to push a product, reverse bandwagon and love/hate attacks are employed as nuke attacks, while random, average, and bandwagon attacks can be considered for achieving both goals. We investigate how robust NBC-based CF algorithm under such attacks. For the purpose of measuring success of binary attacks, we propose a new metric. We perform real data-based experiments and their results clearly show that the proposed binary forms of shilling attacks are capable of biasing prediction results of NBC-based CF algorithm in the direction of their aims.

2 Related Work

Dellacoras [6] discusses negative effects of fraudulent behaviors of users on online reputation systems inspiring shilling attacks concept. O'Mahony et al. [2,3] introduce the first works about shilling attacks, where the authors analyze vulnerabilities of CF systems against biasing prediction results. Initially, shilling attack strategies are discussed by O'Mahony [7]. The proposed attacks are performed by inserting fake user data to the CF systems. Later, Lam and Riedl [8,9] introduce four open questions related to effectiveness of shilling attacks. Mobasher et al. [10,11] determine attack strategies and present the basic attack types such as random, average, bandwagon, and love/hate attacks. Burke et al. [4] examine bandwagon and popular item attacks. Burke et al. [5] propose a different attack type called segmented attack targeting a set of particular users. Cheng and Hurley [12] propose diverse and obfuscated attack models to be effective on model-based CF schemes. To bias users' reputation, copied-item injection attack is presented by Oostendorp and Sami [13]. Gunes et al. [14] present a comprehensive survey about shilling attack studies explaining attack descriptions, detection methods, designing robust recommender algorithms, and evaluation metrics and data sets.

The studies presented above study various attack models and investigate the robustness of numerical ratings-based CF schemes against such attacks. However, CF systems might employ binary ratings rather than numerical ratings; and there is no work analyzing robustness of CF systems with binary preferences. Therefore, in this study, we distinctively focus on robustness analysis of NBC-based CF algorithm, which is proposed to estimate binary ratings-based recommendations. We also propose a new metric to measure the effects of shilling attacks on binary systems.

Miyahara and Pazzani [1] utilize NBC to provide binary predictions. The "naïve" assumption states that features are independent given the class label.

Table 1. Generic Attack Profiles

Attack Type	I_F		I_S		$I_\emptyset$	i_t
	Items	Ratings	Items	Ratings		
Random	Random	System mean	N/A		$I - I_F$	r_{max}
Average	Random	Item mean	N/A		$I - I_F$	r_{max}
Bandwagon	Random	System mean	Popular	r_{max}	$I - \{I_F U I_S\}$	r_{max}
Segmented	Random	r_{min}	Segmented	r_{max}	$I - \{I_F U I_S\}$	r_{max}
Reverse Bandwagon	Random	System mean	Unpopular	r_{min}	$I - \{I_F U I_S\}$	r_{min}
Love/Hate	Random	r_{max}	N/A		$I - \{I_F U I_S\}$	r_{min}

Hence, the probability of an item belonging to $class_j$, where $j \in \{like, dislike\}$, given its n feature values, can be written, as follows:

$$p(class_j|f_1, f_2, \dots f_n) \propto p(class_j) \prod_{u}^{n} p(f_u|class_j), \quad (1)$$

where f_u corresponds the feature value of q for user u. The probability of each class is computed and q is assigned to the class with the highest probability.

Generic attack profile is depicted in Fig. 1 [11]. It consists of filler items (I_F), selected items (I_S), and the rest of the items, which are left unrated but attacked item (i_t). Items in I_F are selected randomly with a function θ. I_S is determined according to items' popularity by using the rating function δ and i_t is chosen with a function Υ. We analyze random, average, bandwagon, segmented, reverse bandwagon, and love/hate [14]. Their profile details are given in Table 1.

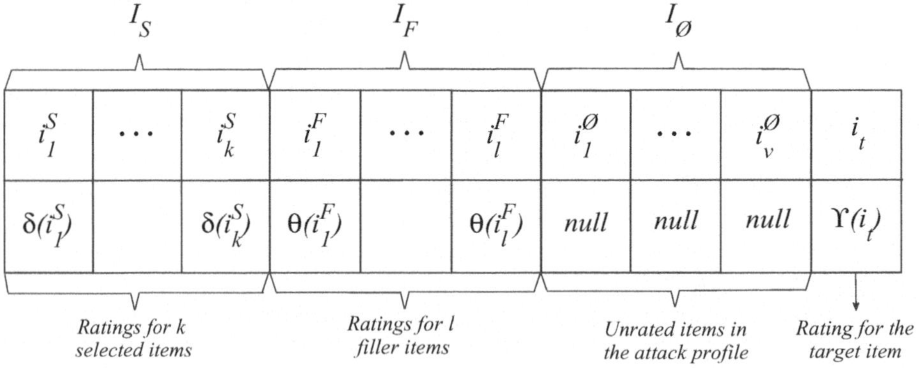

Fig. 1. General form of an attack profile

3 Designing Binary Attacks Against NBC-Based CF

We propose new attack design strategies for attacking databases including binary ratings. We first discuss binary forms of attacks without I_S. Random attack can be considered as the base model for other attack models [4]. If an attacker knows the system rating mean, she can perform random attack. However, an attacker cannot choose a rating value around the system mean for binary votes. Moreover, if the attacker chooses one as the rating values, it must fill all I_F values with the same value, which ends up with a detectable attack profile. The same scenario is valid for item means. Thus, in binary ratings-based systems, ratings of I_F cannot be selected around item means in average attack, as well. However, since all items do not have the same mode value, it is possible to employ item modes directly in binary attack profiles. Unlike random and average attack strategies, since I_F is filled with the maximum rating in numerical ratings-based love/hate attack, its methodology can be directly applied in the case of binary ratings. Thus, binary forms of random, average, and love/hate attacks have common steps but filling I_F items. Methodology of generating such attacks using binary ratings can be characterized, as follows:

1. Number of filler items (I_F) is determined with respect to a predefined range.
2. Filler items in I_F are uniformly randomly chosen among all items except i_t.
3. All other items (I_S and $I_\emptyset$) are left unrated.
4. For each attack type, do the followings:
   - If the attack type is random, in order to fill each item i in I_F, the attacker generates a random number α_i between 0 and 1. If α_i is greater than 0.5, then item i is filled with 1, otherwise it is filled with 0.
   - If the attack type is average, items in I_F is filled with their mode values.
   - If the attack type is love/hate, items in I_F is filled with maximum rating value, which is 1.
5. The attacker can employ random and average attacks for both pushing and nuking i_t. If the goal is pushing, i_t is filled with 1, otherwise it is filled with 0. Since love/hate is a nuke attack, i_t is assigned to 0 only.
6. Finally, the attacker determines number of all bogus user profiles and generates them by following the above steps.

We then discuss binary forms of attacks with I_S. To perform effective attacks, bandwagon, segmented, and reverse bandwagon attack models utilize I_S item set to increase correlations between fake and genuine users. Bandwagon and reverse bandwagon attacks utilize popular and unpopular items in CF systems, respectively. In segmented attack, the attacker selects a subset of users having an interest to a certain kind of products as target. Such segment of users is constituted by users who have maximum rating value for selected items. In the binary form of these attacks, items in I_S can be filled with either maximum or minimum rating value. On the other hand, strategy of filling items in I_F is changed and the methodology in binary attacks without I_S is employed. The overall methodology of creating binary forms of bandwagon, segmented, and reverse bandwagon attacks can be described, as follows:

1. For each attack type, do the followings:
   - In case of binary bandwagon attack, k of the most popular items are selected as I_S and they are filled with rating value 1.

- For binary segmented attack, m of the most popular items in the selected segment of users are chosen as I_S and they are filled with rating value 1.
- If the attack is binary reverse bandwagon attack, k of the most unpopular items are selected as I_S and they are filled with rating value 0.

2. Number of filler items (I_F) is determined with respect to a predefined range.
3. Filler items are uniformly randomly selected among all items except $\{I_S \cup i_t\}$.
4. All other items ($I_\emptyset$) are left unrated.
5. For all attack types, in order to fill each item i in I_F, the attacker generates a random number α_i between 0 and 1. If α_i is greater than 0.5, then item i is filled with 1, otherwise it is filled with 0.
6. Since binary bandwagon attack can be performed for pushing and nuking purposes, i_t gets either 1 or 0 value according to aim of the attack. Unlike binary bandwagon attack, binary segmented and reverse bandwagon attacks are applied only for one purpose. Thus, i_t is filled with 1 in binary segmented attack, while it is assigned to 0 in binary reverse bandwagon attack.
7. Lastly, the attacker determines number of all bogus user profiles and generates them by following the above steps.

Prediction shift is defined as the average changes in the predicted rating before and after the attack for an attacked item. It is utilized to measure success of an attack [14]. However, it works on only numerical ratings. Thus, we propose a new metric, called *ratio shift*, which measures the ratio of 1's in prediction results before and after attack. The metric can be formulated, as follows:

$$Ratio\ Shift = Ratio\ of\ 1s\ after\ attack - Ratio\ of\ 1s\ before\ attack, \quad (2)$$

where $ratio\ of\ 1s\ after\ attack$ represents the percentage of 1's in the produced predictions for an attacked item after an attack while $ratio\ of\ 1s\ before\ attack$ indicates the same percentage in predictions of the corresponding item before it is attacked. We computed only 1's ratio. If the target item is aimed to be pushed, *ratio shift* for that item is a positive value for a successful attack. Conversely, if the attacker's goal is to nuke an item, then *ratio shift* becomes a negative value.

4 Experimental Evaluation

In our trials, we used MovieLens Public (MLP) data set collected by GroupLens research team at the University of Minnesota (http://www.grouplens.org). It includes 100,000 discrete ratings of 943 users about 1,682 movies. We performed experiments for varying *attack size* and *filler size* values. *Attack size* is the percentage of shilling attack profiles in the system while *filler size* represents the percentage of items to be filled with fake ratings in bogus profiles to form I_F.

We labeled items as 1 if the numerical rating for the item was bigger than 3, or 0 otherwise in MLP. We followed all-but-one experimentation methodology in which one of the users acts as an active user and the rest of them forms training set during all iterations. To select two distinct target items, we analyzed 1's and 0's ratio. We finally randomly selected 50 movies for push and nuke attacks.

We chose target items for push attack from the items having zero ratings more than ones, conversely, target items for nuke attack were chosen from items having mostly one ratings. To constitute I_S sets in binary forms of bandwagon and reverse bandwagon attacks, we determined 10 most popular and unpopular items to set k. We targeted a segment of users and selected five of the popular items for that segment for binary segmented attack to set m.

For all items in both target item sets, we produced predictions for all users who do not have a rating for those items. We computed 1's ratio values for each of the target items. All target items were attacked individually for all users in the system. We estimated *ratio shift* values for each item and and overall averages for all target items were presented for each binary attack type. We first varied *attack size* from 1% to 15% and kept *filler size* fixed at 15%. Secondly, *attack size* was kept fixed at 15% and *filler size* values were varied from 1% to 15%. We displayed the outcomes in Fig. 2 and Fig. 3. As shown in Fig. 2 and Fig. 3, average and bandwagon binary push attacks are significantly effective. Binary forms of such push attacks achieve 56.75% and 39% *ratio shift* values when attack and filler sizes are set to 15%. When an attacker aims to push a target item whose 1's ratio is 30%, she can successfully push the item and 1's ratio can be increased to 86.75% if binary average push attack is employed. The result will be 69% if binary bandwagon push attack is chosen. Binary segmented and random push attacks can push a target item; however, their impacts are comparably smaller. At some attack sizes, random attack is not successful. With increasing attack and filler sizes, the success of binary attacks also increases. Improvements in *ratio shift* are noticeable for smaller attack and filler sizes. They then become stable as attack and filler sizes become larger.

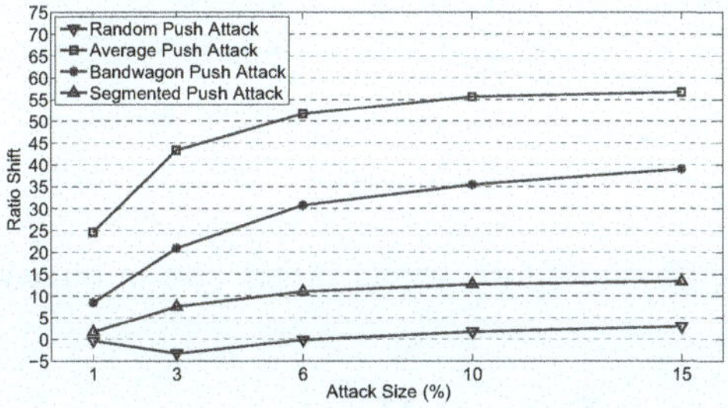

Fig. 2. *Ratio shift* values for varying *attack size* in binary push attack

We performed another set of experiments for binary nuke attacks. All attack types but segmented attack were employed. We followed the same methodology used in previous trials. Since *ratio shift* values are negative numbers for successful nuke attacks, we displayed absolute values of the outcomes. Since obtained similar outcomes, we showed outcomes for varying attack sizes only in Fig. 4. As seen from Fig. 4, we observed similar outcomes as in push attacks. For smaller attack and filler sizes, improvements in *ratio shift* are significant. However, as they

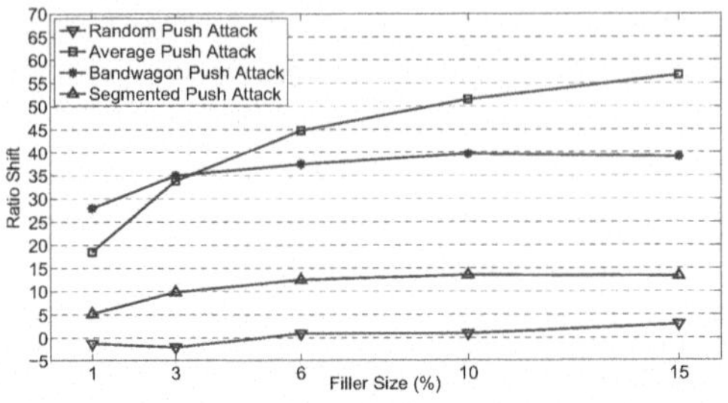

Fig. 3. *Ratio shift* values for varying *filler size* in binary push attack

become larger, such improvements become stable. Binary average nuke attack is the most successful attack type for nuking an item. Bandwagon, love/hate, and reverse bandwagon nuke attacks can be employed for nuking. However, their success ratio is smaller. Although the results for varying attack sizes are similar with binary push attacks' results, the outcomes for varying filler sizes for binary nuke attacks differentiate from the values in push attacks. With increasing filler sizes, *ratio shift* decreases for random and bandwagon binary nuke attacks. However, they can still manipulate an item's popularity for nuking purposes if controlling parameters are set to smaller values.

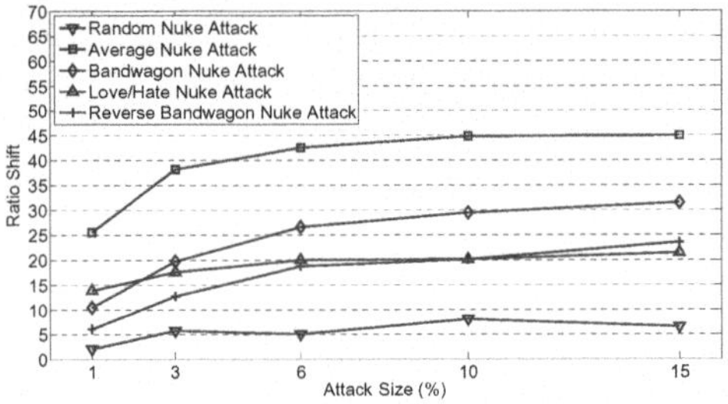

Fig. 4. *Ratio shift* values for varying *attack size* in binary nuke attack

5 Conclusions and Future Work

We proposed binary form of six shilling attack types and assessed their effects on NBC-based CF. We proposed a new metric, *ratio shift*, to measure the success of the proposed attacks. We performed real data-based trials and the outcomes indicated that it is possible to manipulate predictions. Thus, NBC-based CF is not a robust algorithm. We also pointed out that average and bandwagon attacks are the most successful attack for pushing. Average attacks achieves the best outcomes for nuking. As future studies, we plan to introduce new binary attack types and examine their effects on predictions. Also, we plan to analyze robustness of privacy-preserving NBC-based CF against profile injection attacks.

Acknowledgements. This work is supported by the Grant 111E218 from TUBITAK.

References

1. Miyahara, K., Pazzani, M.J.: Collaborative filtering with the simple Bayesian classifier. In: The 6th Pacific Rim International Conference on Artificial Intelligence, Melbourne, Australia, pp. 679–689 (2000)
2. O'Mahony, M.P., Hurley, N.J., Silvestre, G.C.M.: Towards robust collaborative filtering. In: O'Neill, M., Sutcliffe, R.F.E., Ryan, C., Eaton, M., Griffith, N.J.L. (eds.) AICS 2002. LNCS (LNAI), vol. 2464, pp. 87–94. Springer, Heidelberg (2002)
3. O'Mahony, M.P., Hurley, N.J., Silvestre, G.C.M.: Promoting recommendations: An attack on collaborative filtering. In: Hameurlain, A., Cicchetti, R., Traunmüller, R. (eds.) DEXA 2002. LNCS, vol. 2453, pp. 494–503. Springer, Heidelberg (2002)
4. Burke, R.D., Mobasher, B., Bhaumik, R.: Limited knowledge shilling attacks in collaborative filtering systems. In: Workshop on Intelligent Techniques for Web Personalization, Edinburgh, UK (2005)
5. Burke, R.D., Mobasher, B., Bhaumik, R., Williams, C.A.: Segment-based injection attacks against collaborative filtering recommender systems. In: The 5th IEEE International Conference on Data Mining, Houston, TX, USA, pp. 577–580 (2005)
6. Dellarocas, C.: Immunizing online reputation reporting systems against unfair ratings and discriminatory behavior. In: The 2nd ACM Conference on Electronic Commerce, Minneapolis, MN, USA, pp. 150–157 (2000)
7. O'Mahony, M.P.: Towards robust and efficient automated collaborative filtering. PhD Dissertation, University College Dublin (2004)
8. Lam, S.K., Riedl, J.T.: Shilling recommender systems for fun and profit. In: The 13th International Conference on WWW, New York, NY, USA, pp. 393–402 (2004)
9. Lam, S.K., Riedl, J.T.: Privacy, shilling, and the value of information in recommender systems. In: User Modeling Workshop on Privacy-Enhanced Personalization, Edinburgh, UK, pp. 85–92 (2005)
10. Mobasher, B., Burke, R.D., Bhaumik, R., Sandvig, J.J.: Attacks and remedies in collaborative recommendation. IEEE Intelligent Systems 22(3), 56–63 (2007)
11. Mobasher, B., Burke, R.D., Bhaumik, R., Williams, C.A.: Towards trustworthy recommender systems: An analysis of attack models and algorithm robustness. ACM Transactions on Internet Technology 7(4), 23–60 (2007)
12. Cheng, Z., Hurley, N.J.: Effective diverse and obfuscated attacks on model-based recommender systems. In: The 3rd ACM International Conference on Recommender Systems, New York, NY, USA, pp. 141–148 (2009)
13. Oostendorp, N., Sami, R.: The copied-item injection attack. In: Workshop on Recommender Systems and the Social Web, New York, NY, USA, pp. 63–70 (2009)
14. Gunes, I., Kaleli, C., Bilge, A., Polat, H.: Shilling attacks against recommender systems: A comprehensive survey. Artificial Intelligence Review (2012), doi: `http://dx.doi.org/10.1007/s10462-012-9364-9`

Author Index